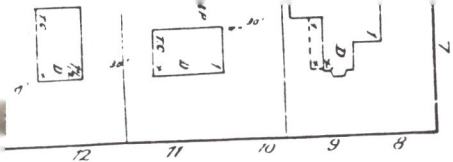

SCHOOL

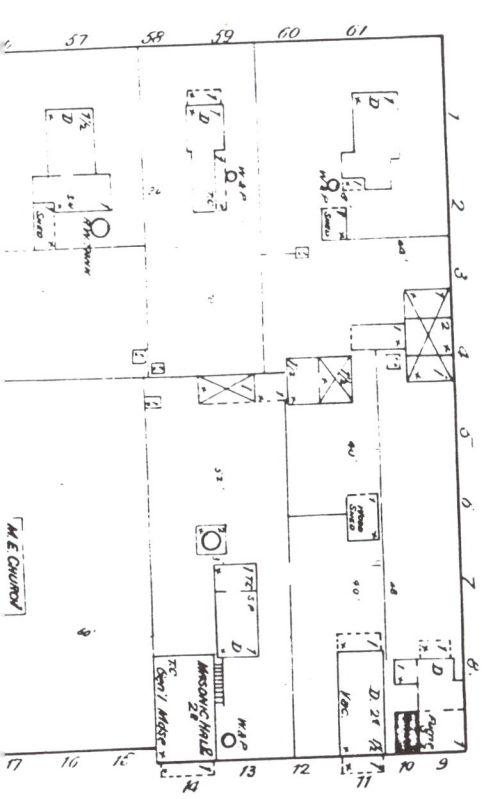

MAIN

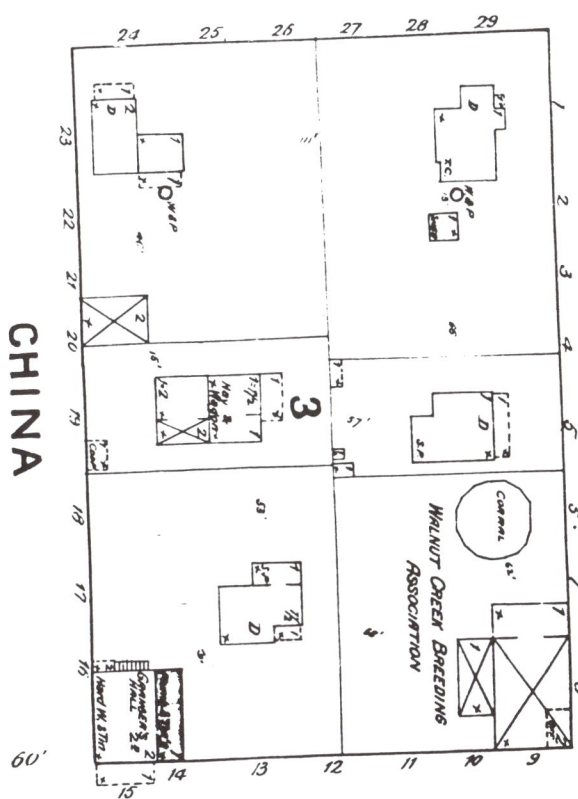

CHINA

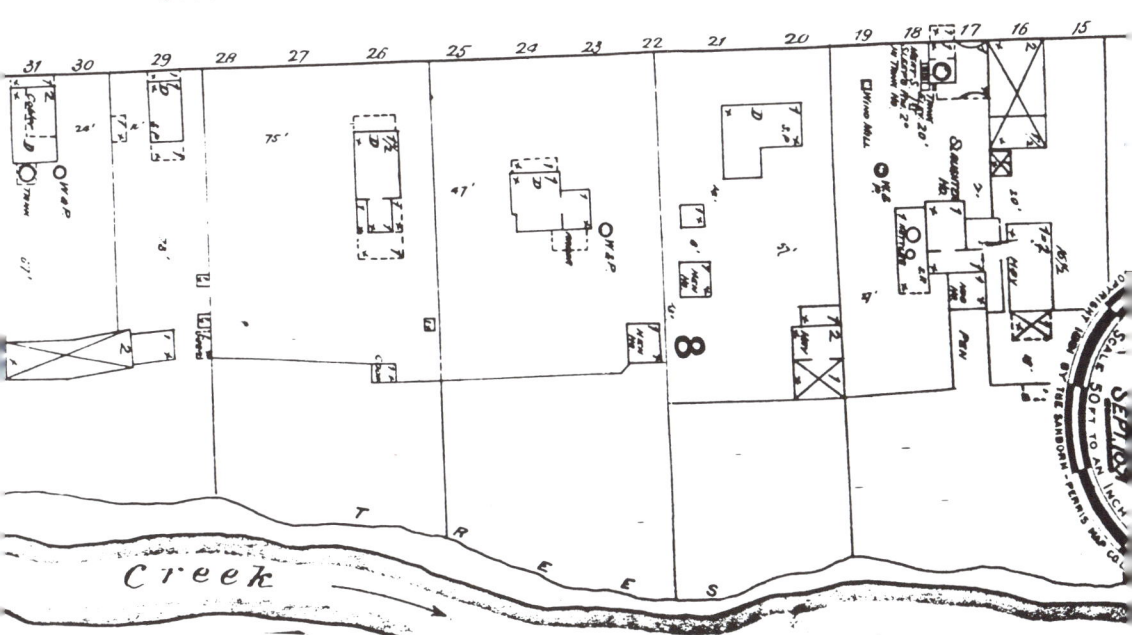

Creek

K, CALIFORNIA—1892

WALNUT CREEK

ARROYO DE LAS NUECES

This view of Pacheco Road (now North Main Street) is the oldest known Walnut Creek picture. It was taken in the early 1870s. The photographer made his glass plate negative standing at the intersection of Lafayette Road (now Mt. Diablo Boulevard).

WALNUT CREEK

ARROYO DE LAS NUECES

By

GEORGE EMANUELS

WALNUT CREEK, CALIFORNIA-1991

ISBN 0-9607520-2-1
Library of Congress Catologue Number 84-70073

Art by Luke Design Associates, Walnut Creek, California

Published and Distributed by
George Emanuels dba DIABLO BOOKS
1317 Canyonwood Court, #1
Walnut Creek, California, 94595
Telephone (415) 939-8644

Printed in the United States of America

*To all the citizens whose efforts have
helped make Walnut Creek the exceptional
community it is
and to those contributors who have shared
their abundance*

ACKNOWLEDGMENTS

An author who is so fortunate as to have a wife and children who are capable of improving his work and are willing to see it through to completion is indeed very fortunate. I acknowledge my debt to my wife, Helen, and our daughter, Joan Pickering, daughter-in-law Claire Emanuels and sons, Roger and Stephen.

Friends who have helped me range from those most knowledgeable of local history and those who allowed me to interview them to others who proofread for me. Each contributed something I needed.

One who suggested specific areas to search is the director for the last ten years of the Walnut Creek Historical Society's Shadelands Ranch Historical Museum. Beverley Clemson read the manuscript with an exacting eye and corrected some historical detail to make the work reliable in every aspect possible. The hours she spent improving my copy are more than I have any right to expect.

Two ladies whose special talents and knowledge gave me important help in the Rossmoor chapter are first, Dulce Blume who generously allowed me to quote from her manuscript, "From the Beginning—Rossmoor, Walnut Creek," and Eunice Mignolo whose twenty years in the office at that retirement community earns her the title I gave her, "The most knowledgeable person, man or woman, in Rossmoor."

Another person whose editorial talent and his willingness to spend hours improving the text I can never give adequate credit to, is Tom Holland. I am fortunate indeed to have Tom for a friend. With his contribution the story flows freely.

Considerable information came from numerous departments at City Hall. I thank City Manager Thomas Dunne for preparing the way to his staff for me. Every employee I approached gave freely and fully of his or her knowledge.

Jack Chapman, the first administrator of Kaiser's Walnut Creek hospital, permitted me full use of a history he recorded for the Kaiser-Permanente Foundation.

I have made many friends since starting the research for *Walnut Creek—Arroyo de las Nueces* and I'm rewarded. Thank each of you for your generous assistance. I hope I have remembered all of you; if I've missed someone I apologize. I've tried to be perfect but . . . Oh! I almost forgot. To you who have bought this book, you have helped me too, for what is a book without its readers? If this one succeeds *you* have made it successful. Thank you too.

The friends who have helped me include the following:

Mark Alexander
Quentin Alexander
Earl Allen
Joyce Anderson
Chet Arthur
Lou Bain
Joan Berryman
Anthony Bliss
Dulcie Blume
Isabel Brubaker
Robert N. Burgess, Jr.
Grant Burton
Gail Bowlby
Barbara Boyle
Doris Brubaker
Lt. John Cashman
Jack Chapman
Glennys Christie
Jeanne Christy
George C. Collier
Bill Connelly
Vivian Cooper
Bob Cowden
Brother Dennis
Thomas Dunne
Grete Egan
Elvyn Evers
Lester Foley
Helen Ford
Elberta Glass
Barbara George

Linn Hakala
Claudia Halderman
Tom Holland
Bill Hotzel
Harmon Howard
Joan Howard
Peter Howard
Margaret Jensen
Virginia Johnston
Helen Jory
Henry Kalman
Myrtle Kitchen
Adele Laine
Lois Lambert
James Lawrence
Steve Lawrence
Dick Lommel
Tony Lupoi
Marshall Maguire
Gus Malmquist
Robert Martens
Karen Matson
Jessie Mauzy
Elliott Mauzy
Alice McBride
Mrs. Delbert McCombs
Terry McLeod
Georgana McNamara
Adrian Mendes
Eunice Mignola
Congressman George Miller

Darrell Mortensen
John Nejedly
Alice Nilsen
Lu Palmer
Joan Pickering
Robert M. Pond
Beth Pruden
Bradlee Pruden
Phyllis Redemann
Charles Reed
Mary Reed
June Reeder
Barbara Rivara
Walter A. Rogers
Mrs. Theodore Russi
Jane Sanford
Mrs. Manuel Santos
Gary Schaub
Sylvia Schloegel
Robert A. Sederholm
Sam Smoker
Ralph Snyder
Grace Sommers
Louis L. Stein
Bob Stone
Martin Stow
Susanne Sundholm
Marlys Tash
Susann Todoroff
Ann Watrous
Genevra Shuey Willey

CONTENTS

ILLUSTRATIONS

INTRODUCTION

*O*n centuries long past streams ran their courses the Creator planned for them and mortals lived along the creeks, gathering from the bushes, the vines, and the trees their sustenance.

Now we are here, where the two watercourses meet and form a larger one, and we call the place Walnut Creek. Before us were the Mexicans and before them the Spanish, and both called the streams the same: the one from the south "Arroyo del Injerto" and the one from the west "Arroyo Las Trampas" which, after joining, they called "Arroyo de las Nueces," literally "The Stream of the Walnuts."

But back before the Spaniards named the creeks, when the natives we call Indians roamed the hills and valleys, they found food plentiful. The women gathered acorns, ground the nuts in stone mortars, leeched the bitterness in their woven baskets and made a mush. They ate the meat of the black walnut which lined the banks of the streams. They pulled fish from the creeks and snared rabbits and small game for meat and for fur.

The females wore girdles or rough skirts of reeds. The males went about entirely naked. They cultivated no grains or vegetables but possessed skills sufficient to make nets, bows and arrows, and their huts of boughs and reeds.

These natives lived along our creeks in bands of relatives or families. The men who headed each group often gained their positions by age, experience, or demonstrable skills or wisdom. Sometimes their bands included as many as a dozen families held together through the father's line. These people went through their daily lives peacefully though they were ever alert to the importance of control of the groves of oaks from which they harvested acorns. A common sound heard on approaching their collection of huts was of women pounding acorns between stone pestles and mortars. They worked only to survive. They did build sweathouses in which they cleansed themselves, and sometimes when refuse accumulated too deeply near their huts they burned down the entire village only to rebuild in a cleaner place.

When they settled disagreements with their neighbors they celebrated by singing and dancing. They made merry over births, marriages or the visit of another family group.

These natives drank no alcohol before the Spaniards came nor did they use firearms before the Anglos arrived. They can be considered civilized if that means living in harmony with one's neighbors.

At least half a dozen groups of fifty to eighty persons made their villages within the boundary of today's City of Walnut Creek. The Mexicans called these settlements "rancheriás."

Archeologists have recorded seventeen Indian habitation sites in the Walnut Creek city limits and only a portion of the area has actually been searched, so it is highly likely that more such sites exist.

Most residential sites are found at the edge of the streams: Pine Creek, Walnut Creek, San Ramon Creek, Las Trampas Creek and Tice Creek, and some adjacent to springs.

David A. Fredrickson, professor of anthropology at Sonoma State University, sheds more light on earlier habitation sites in this area. "It is unlikely that the time range represented by the sites in the Walnut Creek area extends back for 4,000 years. While earlier sites are certainly possible, none has yet been discovered in the vicinity. This may be due to the heavy alluviation (silting) that has taken place over the past couple of thousand years—up to twenty feet of soils have been deposited on the flood plain during this time."

Fredrickson speaks of the hill country surrounding us: "I have verbal reports that special purpose sites (e.g. for hunting and or milling purposes) do occur in the uplands although I have not seen any myself . . ."

As long as Indians lived in the area the land belonged to all of them. No one group owned any specific parcel. After the Spaniards came in 1769 they declared Spain owned all the land. After the

Mexican revolution of 1821 the Mexican government started giving away large grants to its citizens.

This is the order in which occupants built their houses on the east side of Arroyo de las Nueces. When the grantee, Doña Juana Sanchez de Pacheco, received her 17,734-acre grant in 1834, she took two years to make the best use of it. Then, she asked her son-in-law, Francisco García, who had married her daughter, María Antonia, to move to the property from Pueblo San José and to stock the land with cattle. At the time not a single fence existed between Yerba Buena and Sutter's Fort, and Francisco had no duties on the grant most of the year. When hide collecting time came he rode at the head of a band of cousins and brothers-in-law to slaughter and skin the animals Doña Juana wanted harvested. Ultimately Francisco built a small adobe for a headquarters. As the herd multiplied in size the animals ate down the grasses where theretofore deer used to graze. As the deer retreated up into the hills where they could find more luxuriant feed, the Indians found it more trying to hunt the animals whose meat and hides they had hunted for centuries. They focused their resentment on Francisco since he represented the cause of their inconvenience. One night they set fire to the roof of his adobe, which drove him away. California's governor told Doña Juana to keep her family at Pueblo San José and to go to her grant only when necessary.

And so for many years Francisco, often bringing relatives, only came to the rancho to round up the cattle for slaughtering.

Two of Doña Juana's grandsons built themselves houses on her land while she was yet alive. Ysidro Sibrian located his house near the east bank of Walnut Creek, a bit north of where today's Ygnacio Valley Road and Walnut Boulevard cross. His brother, Ygnacio Sibrian, built his house near the sulphur spring for which he named his property. After his grandmother died his mother, María Rosa Pacheco de Sibrian, bequeathed the land to him.

Lumbering ox carts and shod horses came through San Ramon Valley and on to Martinez beating a trail along the creeks. They hugged the west side of Arroyo del Injerto (San Ramon Creek) as they approached the junction with Arroyo Las Trampas. In the vicinity of today's Rudgear Road the trail crossed to the east of the stream. As if to visit the Sibrians along the way the trail followed Ygnacio Valley Road as far as their Sulphur Springs Ranch (Heather Farm) before it turned north heading for Martinez, then but a place to cross the Sacramento River.

Except for the families who owned the grants only a few persons traveled the trail from Martinez through the San Ramon Valley until 1849. The rainy season commenced in October that year and didn't end until next March 22. During that time thirty-six inches of rain fell, making the trail a muddy, slippery quagmire. In summer the evidence of winter travel remained, with deep ruts and wide holes, making the trip a rough one. Riders rode the shoulders lest their horses stumble. Wagon and coach drivers guided their horses uselessly, jolting virtually every yard of the way.

In anticipation of statehood a convention was held in Sacramento in October 1849 to consider delegates to the upcoming constitutional convention. They elected them at another meeting, five days later in Monterey. In January the politicians met again, this time in San José. In September of 1850 San José became the state capitol.

It is not surprising that traffic between Martinez and San José all through the spring of 1850 grew heavier and heavier. Legislators coming from the northern counties came by boat to Benicia, ferried over to Martinez and went on by stage. The stage line which opened that year charged a passenger *two ounces of dust* for the nine-hour trip. By summer competition sprang up and during the ensuing price war the fare dropped to ten dollars.

San Francisco offered an alternate route to San José, but in San Francisco the traveler faced spending the night sleeping in the flea-infested bedding of overcrowded tent houses. Riding the stage coach on to San José he usually rode with eleven other passengers. He paid thirty-five to forty dollars for the one-way passage, about the same fare as charged from Martinez.

On the way south from Martinez the stage may have stopped at Ygnacio Sibrian's Sulphur Spring Ranch to wind the horses. Over the hill and nearer Arroyo de las Nueces they passed by Ygnacio Sibrian's brother, Ysidro's house. Only a mile farther along and across the creek they saw the cabin inhabited by a forty-year-old widower, William Slusher, and his six children. These would be all the dwellings they would pass until they neared Alamo. Across the creek from Ysidro Sibrian's home, off to the west, the travelers may have caught sight of Widow Welch's house, but the activity around William Slusher's cabin would interest them more, his large family a subject for conversation.

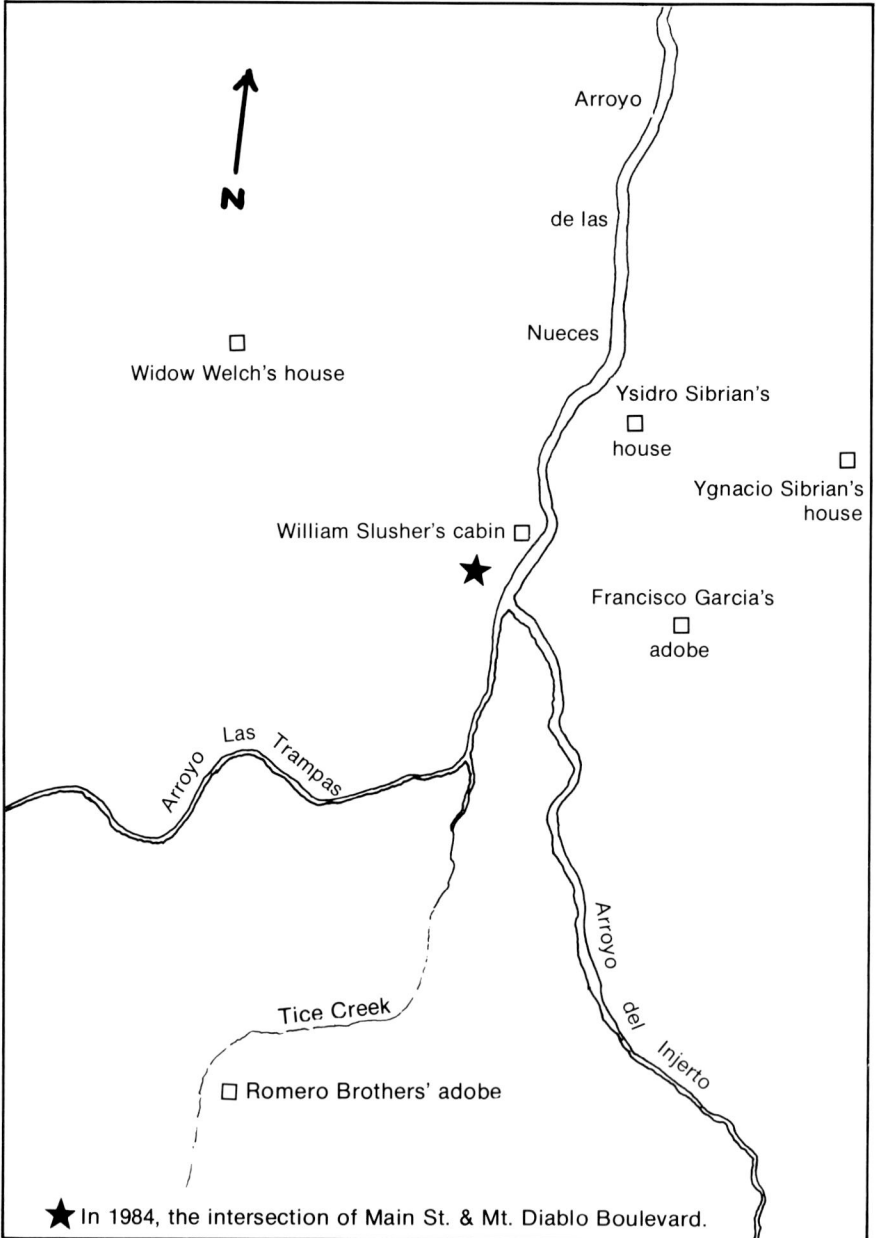

N

Arroyo

de las

Nueces

Widow Welch's house

Ysidro Sibrian's
house

Ygnacio Sibrian's
house

William Slusher's cabin

Francisco Garcia's
adobe

Arroyo Las Trampas

Arroyo del Injerto

Tice Creek

Romero Brothers' adobe

In 1984, the intersection of Main St. & Mt. Diablo Boulevard.

Creeks and dwellings in early 1850.

WALNUT CREEK'S FIRST SETTLERS

Slusher's children were: Maryanne, fourteen, Clayborn, fourteen, John, eleven, Eli, nine, Jane, six, and Mary Ann, three. Undoubtedly Maryanne ran the "household," keeping the cabin as tidy as possible. Her twin would be busy hauling water from the creek, cutting and splitting wood and maybe helping his father hunt game. They undoubtedly grew vegetables and probably kept chickens. They may have traded some of what they raised for staples at the closest trading store, at Alamo or even Brown's at Lafayette.

In 1850 Slusher and his family lived alone—in what is today the central business district of Walnut Creek—but in late fall that year two men arrived who wanted to farm. In October Alexander Boss moved onto land on the east side of the creek, the Homestead District. In November David Glass took up a piece bordering Boss' south boundary, 153 acres stretching as far south as today's Rudgear Road. Credit goes to Glass for opening the first store in the area; he opened a "store" in his shanty. Although he squatted on that parcel, he did eventually pay Ygnacio Sibrian for it in December of 1856.

For the following year and a half, less than half a dozen people came to live between Slusher's cabin and Mrs. Welch's house. Then, in the summer of 1852, civilization did come to The Corners.

Travel had created a road out of the trail but had not improved its surfaces. Conditions were so bad that in July the Court of Sessions created road districts. At the time Contra Costa County included two-thirds of Alameda County, so the problem of maintaining long roads was a formidable one. District One stretched from Martinez to Pueblo San Jose, at least fifty miles, and N. B. Smith received the appointment as overseer," . . . from Martinez as far as the Francisco García farm."

1

Walnut Creek's First Settler

Below is the record of William Slusher's land purchase of 1853 from Innocencio and Incarnación Romero for $650.

"... beginning at a stake a short distance below where the house of William Slusher now stands, thence running 48½ two-pole chains or 99 rods to the foot of the hills, then following along the foot of the hills in a westerly direction following the said Slusher's present fence at a distance of 121 rods due west from last named corner to a stake standing by said fence near the foot of the hills, thence 22 chains or 62 rods to Walnut Creek, thence following down said creek to the place of beginning ... containing by survey made by Warren Brown, County Surveyor, one hundred acres to have and to hold ... and the said Slusher being advised of the sale [of] a pretended sale [sic] from the said Romero to one Cook for the aforesaid land in connection with other lands, hereby ... takes only such title as the said Romero has."

About eighteen months after buying the property Slusher and his *wife*, Caroline, sold the west half, on December 27, 1854, to John Tucker, for $1,500. Four months later, on April 17, 1855, the Slushers sold the other half to John P. McKisick, also for $1,500.

Caroline Slusher did not appear in the records at the same time his six children were named and their ages given. There is no record of their marriage in this county and whether or not Caroline was the children's mother is in doubt. In each of the documents requiring her signature, Caroline Slusher was unable to sign but simply made her mark, "X."

After selling their Walnut Creek acreage William and Caroline moved to Martinez. They bought a two-story house but lived in it contentedly for only six months. Then, in an unusual move, Caroline Slusher (without William) rented the downstairs of their home on the northwest corner of Main and Castro streets.

The agreement speaks eloquently: "I, Caroline Slusher lease to Adolph Canaillas all the first floor of my house in Martinez together with the bar in the front room of the said house and the yard with all improvements for $20 a month."

She also mentions a sign over the front door which reads, "Louisiana." Her lease is dated March 1, 1856.

Walnut Creek's first settler and his wife each made their mark, "X," on the deed eight months later when they sold the Martinez house for $1,100 to Eliza Wilkinson on February 26, 1869.

District Five was "... that road leading from the Moraga Redwoods to that leading from Martinez to [Pueblo] San Jose." E. Miller was named overseer of it. For years this junction would be known as The Corners. The court authorized its overseers to impress all males between the ages of eighteen and forty-five "... to be called to work on these thoroughfares for five days each year, or cause such amounts of work to be done when required by the overseer..."

No school existed along the banks of Arroyo de las Nueces in 1852, the year that Slusher gave up his little place and George Thorn moved in. Thorn is the one who stayed and accumulated several parcels of land in the neighborhood.

Not wanting to wait for the United States census taker's tabulation in 1860, California took its own count in 1852. The names of those listed in the area of The Corners are:

Isaac Dennis, 54, laborer
his wife, 52
Dennis, Jr., 26
Teote Read, 25, laborer
William R. Bishop, 26, schoolmaster
A. K. Comstock
William Comstock

Growth came slowly to this area called The Corners. The few residents looked both west and north to centers of business activity and social life.

By 1852 Lafayette's Nathaniel Jones and Elam Brown had lived in their substantial homes for five years. Brown was operating his horse-powered grist mill, and Benjamin Shreve taught school.

At Alamo a number of Mexican families with inheritable interests in the grant, and at least a half dozen squatters, made their homes there. Two shopkeepers competed for the business.

Captain Orris Fales, who had recently sailed around Cape Horn and then gone on to the Sandwich Islands and Hong Kong, arrived in California in the winter of 1851-1852. Fales was born in Maine and went to sea at age thirteen. He came to The Corners at age thirty-seven after a twenty-four year seafaring career. Fales started out

3

buying a fifty-eight acre parcel along the east side of San Ramon Creek from Ygnacio Sibrian for $500. He built a small cabin there and started farming. He harvested heavy crops of hay and grain and acquired another piece of land, 111 acres on the west side of South Main Street just south of the junction of Las Trampas and Tice Creek. Eventually he bought other parcels and increased his holdings to 300 acres. His farming made him comfortably well-off so that later he built a two-story home, thirty by thirty-six feet, to replace the cabin. Years later he added a one-story addition, fourteen by twenty-six feet, to the new house.

At the end of 1852 a half dozen farmers lived on land they had bought or agreed to buy once the owners received verification of their titles. Ygnacio Sibrian received his on April 18, 1866. Claims and counter claims delayed the Widow Welch's confirmation until July 22, 1870. Those farmers who built their homes on either of the grants did so trusting their hunches their government would eventually verify their judgment.

Across San Francisco Bay the population was estimated at 42,000 persons. The city had burned down three times in its embryonic history, being rebuilt each time with more fire-resistant material. Ygnacio Valley cement went by barge down the Sacramento River to San Francisco, to be used in constructing buildings of brick and stone. In 1852, 44,000 more immigrants came in through the Golden Gate than departed; nevertheless, only a few came to settle anywhere near The Corners.

George Thorn and his family lived without neighbors where one day a city center would rise. In 1853 the road from Martinez to San Ramon Valley still hugged the banks of the creeks except where it wandered out to Ygnacio Sibrian's Sulphur Springs Ranch. John Baker came to farm and though he didn't pay Ygnacio Sibrian for the 120 acres until two years later, he did remain.

Meanwhile the Widow Welch with her lands, everything west of the creek and north of Lacassie, lived about one mile north of Thorn. She was having her grant surveyed and divided into parcels. These lots, as they appear on the maps of the times, were twenty-five acres

4

each. George Thorn bought one in September 1854 and another in January of 1855 for $87.50 each.

The first building other than Slusher's cabin was one built by a Lafayette resident. A nephew of Elam Brown, Milo Hough, came to The Corners in the fall of 1855 and built a hotel at an elevated site, now the intersection of Ygnacio Valley Road and Civic Drive, to escape the floods common to the area. His unpainted, two-story 24′ × 40′ structure contained a bar and a store.

In those days, every western hotel had a bar and a billiard table. Spittoons sat in the corners of each public room, and candles stood in holders on the few tables. No kitchen or dining room is noted in the records but Hough must have included them in his plan. A well with a hand pump, outhouses, and horse-trough adjoined the "hotel." "The Walnut Creek House" gained immediate stature and appeared that way on official county documents well into the next decade. The use of "Walnut Creek" in the title of the hostelry is the first time the translation of "Arroyo de las Nueces" appears.

From 1852 on, prospectors filled San Francisco's lodging houses. Many who were farmers back home went looking for farming prospects north and south of the bay and some came to Contra Costa County. In the five years between 1855 and 1860 immigrants came to Ygnacio Valley and San Ramon Valley and laid claim to and farmed the best land available. Asa Brown bought the 350 acres he had been leasing for $100 a year from Juan and Petra Soto (she was a granddaughter of Doña Juana Sanchez de Pacheco). William Rice paid Ygnacio Sibrian $15,000 for almost two thousand acres for which Sibrian received a clear title six years later.

All through this first decade Ygnacio Sibrian and his wife, Antonia, with their two children, Ygnacio, Jr. and Feliciana, lived on their 255-acre Sulphur Springs Ranch, land now occupied by Muir Hospital and Heather Farm Park. Sibrian kept a small herd of cattle and grew wine grapes on two acres adjoining his house.

5

EARLY SCHOOLS AND POST OFFICES

*A*s in many communities in the west, when the village still answered to the name The Corners, schooling in no way started formally. Customarily, before the residents built a schoolhouse, parents who could read and write sat their offspring down and taught them as much as they knew. Times for tilling, planting, cultivating, hoeing, pruning and slaughtering made tutoring an occasional exercise. Supplying one's family with food, shelter and clothing came first. Education waited.

At The Corners in 1853 the few villagers did not concern themselves with teaching, even though a former schoolmaster lived among them. Twenty-six-year-old William R. Bishop, Illinois-born, was available and known by his profession. But not until 1857 did the first class assemble.

Due to the absence of any school district to the north, between Alamo and Martinez, the Alamo District included The Corners. In 1857 that district provided a schoolhouse where today's South Main Street and Castle Hill Road intersect. Mrs. Hargreaves was the first to instruct Walnut Creek's few village children in that school.

The Alamo District had been organized three years earlier. The population in that village was growing and business opportunities abounded. Two general merchandise stores competed for business, and a post office had been doing business in Alamo since 1853. In the first decade of statehood the number of children increased each year, and soon their school district was the largest in the area and fifth in size in all of Contra Costa County.

Walnut Creek residents finally banded together and formed their own school district on September 29, 1860. They divorced themselves from the Alamo District and named theirs the Central School District. The trustees appointed Captain Orris Fales their school marshal.

The school marshal canvassed the district and counted sixty-eight *white* children, thirty-six girls and thirty-two boys, between the ages of four and eighteen. The district comprised an area approximately 3 by 4½ miles.

There is no record of the new district paying for the building or the Alamo District having bought it in 1853. No picture survives but the structure could have been little more than a shack, or maybe even an abandoned cabin.

Likely, two or three fathers made a door and hung it in a rough frame, patched the roof as needed and built several tables and benches from what rough lumber came to hand. It is certain there were no desks. This was the "school."

The building served the village for thirteen years. Even a few months before it was abandoned a large plurality voted against spending money for a new building closer to the village. Very likely nothing more than a pittance was ever spent on it. It was kept open only a few months at a time. The school could not have been taken very seriously by more than the few families whose children attended it.

The Reverend William Isaac swung open the door for the first group of students on November 19, 1860. Undoubtedly the date was set for the end of the harvest season. By the plan of the trustees, the school term that first year ended on February 1. While twenty-eight students attended classes at one time or another during the 2½-month term, the average daily attendance came to fourteen.

The Rev. Isaac was to receive a salary of fifty dollars a month for the term, the trustees having satisfied themselves he was competent to teach. However, the reverend had a confession to make. He asked the parents to come to the school on the last day of the term and hear him out. He informed them he had never received a certificate to teach as he was required to do and therefore he could not accept the school's money. At a meeting held *six weeks later* the parents decided "... after due deliberation ... to instruct the trustees to [pay and] employ him again for $50 a month."

The Corners grew steadily if not speedily. Central School records show the average daily attendance reached a stable number of twenty-six children by the late 1860s. In the 1867-68 school year one Negro boy attended school regularly but sixteen eligible white boys failed to come to school at all. A great many parents considered age eleven or twelve the age for their sons to give up school as they had had to do, and help their fathers earn the family livelihood. So, irregular or no attendance was a common occurrence in both urban and rural schools well into the twentieth century.

The first significant change at The Corners occurred in 1860. George Thorn sold one of his twenty-five-acre lots on the west side of the creek to Hiram Penniman. Penniman had squatted with his brother-in-law in Ygnacio Valley in 1852 and each built a home there. His purchase from Thorn was a speculation. He rerouted the north-south road away from the creek, straightened it almost, and today's Main Street follows the path he chose. He subdivided the acreage and sold lots. With a partner by the name of Searles, Penniman opened a store at The Corners, but within two years they sold out to McDonald and Wetmore, who turned it into a mercantile establishment where they stocked hardware and fabrics. They located it next door to the Walnut Creek House.

The timing of Penniman's subdivision at The Corners coincided with the one which plotted the town of Pacheco. From 1860 until well after the turn of the century, the road north appears on maps as "Pacheco Road," not Main Street. South of the village it is called "Alamo Road" first, and later "Danville Highway." The road leading to the west appears as "Lafayette Road."

So few people lived near The Corners between 1850 and 1855 that no one gave heed to the need of a post office. What little mail was addressed to residents here before 1859 came to Martinez. That postmaster gave the *Contra Costa Gazette* the names of everyone who had mail awaiting him there. Since the newspaper reached its readers haphazardly, not being delivered by mail, letters destined for The Corners often lay unclaimed until a friend or acquaintance told the addressees they had mail awaiting them at the county seat.

When the Pacheco office opened on August 16, 1859, Harris H. Fassett, postmaster, Walnut Creek mail came addressed to Pacheco. In the short span of about eighteen months that town became so important a trading center that the *Gazette* moved its plant there. Nevertheless, the method of distributing mail along Walnut Creek remained the same as before.

Finally, in 1862, "enough" mail was coming and going out of Walnut Creek that the postmaster-general established a post office here, in McDonald and Wetmore's general merchandise store. On December 1 he appointed James R. McDonald the first postmaster.

For thirteen years the original school south of the village served the area, until 1871.

During the intervening years a few parents made four attempts to vote money enough to build a better school house. Votes cast at an election on August 28, 1869 just to buy a lot for the school, tallied Yes three, No fifteen.

On September 25, one month later, a vote to tax the district residents to build a school came to Yes one, No twenty-six. At the election in 1871, an aroused citizenry of thirty-five voted by a margin of twenty-three to twelve to spend $1,500 and buy a lot and build a school with a belfry. For years they regretted one oversight—they forgot to include the cost of a bell.

The one-room school was built about 450 feet south of the corner of Lafayette Road and School Street. Today that would be the corner of Mt. Diablo Boulevard and Locust Street.

From the front door of the building one looked north, up School Street. At first a lone outhouse stood about thirty feet to the west and a woodshed abutted the school at its southwest corner. By the time the school year 1871-72 rolled around the library had grown to a value of $200. The only schools with more books were the ones at Martinez and Pacheco. The average daily attendance at Central this year reached thirty-three, up from twenty-six four years earlier. Obviously Walnut Creek grew slowly in the 1865-75 decade.

9

Overcrowding of elementary schools was just as common in the 1870s as in the 1970s. By the mid-1870s the single room was too small. Voters finally approved the plan to add a second room in 1878. Now the belfry was in the center of the schoolhouse directly above the partition dividing the two rooms. But the belfry still lacked a bell, and parents held "Strawberry and Ice Cream Festivals" to raise money to buy one as late as June 23, 1882.

Stories of fifteen- to eighteen-year-old boys intimidating their grammar school teachers in the days of one-room school houses are not fables. Such tactics were all too common. Young lady teachers, sometimes no more than three or four years older than their oldest students, very often kept a weapon such as a wagon wheel spoke or similar stick within reach of their desks for defensive purposes.

A singular case of a student usurping the power of his teacher occurred in the Central School in 1887. When E. B. Anderson, a thirty-six-year-old six-foot-tall man, applied for the position of teacher, the trustees frankly told him, " . . . it is a tough school and has had a good many teachers over the last several years, who have been unable to handle the discipline. The rough kids have literally chased the teachers out of school. Consequently great damage has been done to our scholastic standing." Anderson admitted he had never seen the inside of a normal school (teachers' college), but the trustees saw a solid toughness and a firm stance in the slightly built young man. They hired him, but not before they declared, "If you only want the job temporarily we don't want you. We're tired of hiring new teachers all the time."

The two trustees, James Stow and the hotelman William Rogers, sat out in front of Rogers' hotel talking with their freshly hired schoolteacher on the Sunday before the opening of school. A group of tough-looking boys loitered on the other side of the street, giving the new teacher the "once-over." Rogers pointed them out as the young gangsters who had made life unbearable for all the preceding teachers. Some of them were nearly grown men. Putting his fears behind him, Anderson walked over to the boys and began talking. "I'm here to help you boys get an education. If necessary I'll work with you nights, weekends, and holidays in order to help you get it. In return I'll expect cooperation from you. If you are in earnest and want to get an education, we'll get along fine. If not, look out."

Anderson didn't sleep too well that night in January 1888. Years later he wrote, "Morale was very low when I took charge." Anderson's light hair and blue eyes belied the grit and determination he possessed. Teaching positions were not easy to find after the depression year of 1887, and he vowed this was one he wanted to keep.

An observer wrote about what happened the first day of school. "We lined up as usual out on the dirt yard facing the flag beside the school's front door as we did each morning. We saluted the flag, and then climbed the dozen steps to go inside. Mr. Anderson stood just inside the doorway; I was behind but saw a big husky boy trip a much smaller one in front of him, who pitched forward at Mr. Anderson's feet. Without any hesitation Mr. Anderson grabbed the big fellow by his collar at the same time tripping and sending him to the floor. The teacher pounced squarely on top of him, with a strangle hold around his neck.

"After he had choked all the breath out of him and the bully could no longer beg for mercy, Anderson let him up when he nodded his assent to taking a thrashing which the teacher gave him without any mercy before the rest of the students. When he had finished he invited anyone else who wanted to run the school to step forward. No none did and needless to say he had no more trouble." The boy who got the beating was the son of the Methodist preacher, from whom no objection was ever heard.

At the time of Anderson's hiring there were no high schools in the county and only a few in the state. He personally extended Central School's curriculum to include the ninth and tenth grades. He taught the five upper grades while Mrs. Anderson taught the five lower.

E. B. Anderson retired from teaching 11½ years later. Mrs. Anderson became principal for four or five years while he joined the county board of education, serving for five years, president for two. Later the educator served Walnut Creek as its mayor.

Boys and girls found little to do outside their home and farm. Each did his or her chores, and except at school had little opportunity to stay busy. Unfortunately, two brothers, ages ten and thirteen, searching for something to do, found an old pistol in their father's things. I. T. Sherman's sons, Lincoln and Colonel, were having fun firing at a mark near a bridge a few yards from the village. The younger boy had the turn to fire when the gun misfired. He held it by the butt end, holding the hammer back with his finger, while his brother held it by the barrel and placed a fresh cap on the nipple. Suddenly the hammer slipped from Lincoln's finger and the pistol fired. The ball hit Colonel in the stomach and he died the same day (September 17, 1873).

STAGE COACHES

*G*etting around in Walnut Creek's first three or four decades meant either walking, riding a horse, or riding in a buggy, carriage or stage coach. Horses were dangerous, though, and in cities and rural communities alike people died or suffered permanent injury when horses panicked at sudden noises, plunged across fences and crashed a buggy against a tree, loosening it from its load, and then running away headlong, traces and harness dragging, until exhausted. Nevertheless, that was all the transportation there was.

The first line to serve the town collected its passengers at the Martinez ferry about 1850. The first route went to San Jose, but the second, operated by John W. Morris, started running two-horse stages "every day but Sunday, Martinez to Pachecoville, the Walnut Creek House, Lafayette and Oakland." As increasing numbers of passengers used the line, Morris changed over to four-horse teams. The climb over the Fish Ranch Road was just too steep a climb for only two horses. Climbing this hill, horses stopped every one to two hundred yards. The driver, not trusting the brakes before he started up the hill, unchained a pair of chocks which dragged behind the rear wheels, ready to block them whenever the coach rolled back a foot or so. Going on, the chocks dragged behind, in place when needed at the next rest. The driver rested his horses again at the top.

Then, inching his way over the summit heading down the long steep grade, the driver stood on his brake pedal, at the same time hauling back on the reins. The horses almost sat on their hindquarters, the taut reins pulling them back against the rump brake, as the coach crept slowly down the hill.

Agitation for a tunnel through the Oakland hills to lessen the climb over the Fish Ranch Road first took place in Alamo in 1860. Alamo, a busy village, then overshadowed the Walnut Creek House and the handful of dwellings nearby. The San Antonio (Oakland Estuary) and Alamo Turnpike Company called public meetings where prospects for a road and tunnel between those points was discussed. Nothing materialized from these meetings.

Another stage line to Oakland started coming through Walnut Creek three years after the line through "Pachecoville" went into service. Again John Morris was involved. The Morris Brothers established service from Clayton, through Ygnacio Valley and Walnut Creek, to Oakland in 1862.

By 1862 stage coach lines served the village from four sides. One line which had run from Martinez to Oakland via Walnut Creek in the 1850s changed its route when coal was discovered at what became Nortonville and Somersville in 1859. This route went from Martinez to Nortonville and Somersville via Pacheco and Clayton. With this

OAKLAND and PACHECO.

STAGE LINE.

General Agent, L. M. BEAUDRY, Fashion Stable, Oakland.

Stage leaves Oakland daily on arrival of 11.30 boat from San Francisco.

Stage leaves Pacheco daily at 7 A. M.

From Oakland to Pacheco.			TOWNS.	See Page.	From Pacheco to Oakland.		
Fare.	Hours	Miles.			Miles.	Hours	Fare.
$0.00	0	0	*Depart*..........Oakland..........*Arrive.*	109	23	5.30	$2.00
1.50	2.30	14	....................Berkeley....................				
2.00	3	17	....................Lafayette....................		9	1.30	1.50
2.00	4	23	....................Walnut Creek....................		6	.30	1.00
			Arrive..........Pacheco..........*Depart.*	110	0	0	50

Within a year of the founding of Concord in 1869, Winfield S. Burpee established a stage line to Oakland via Ygnacio Valley. He competed with the Pacheco-Oakland stage for only two years then closed down. BANCROFT'S GUIDE carried this timetable for the Pacheco line in 1870.

14

change another line started carrying passengers from Pacheco going through Walnut Creek to Oakland. Another stage operated by Brown and Company of Lafayette, ran from Limerick to Danville, Walnut Creek, Lafayette and Oakland. Limerick was a village on Crow Canyon Road a half mile west of the Danville to Livermore Road (I-680). Passengers made connections between these lines, enabling them to get good service out of Oakland to most parts of eastern Contra Costa County.

On the July Fourth holiday in 1868, so many people rode conveyances into Oakland destined for San Francisco that travelers filled the platform at the Oakland ferry dock. People kept arriving. Minutes before the boat arrived, without any warning and with the cracking of heavy timbers, the platform gave way, throwing over one hundred persons into the bay. In the confusion, each person tried to save himself. Ten persons drowned, although early reports stated a number more were missing.

At about the same time, another tragedy occurred at Lafayette, the earliest to touch the central area. Robert Linville, with his hired man, was milking his cows a short distance from his house. He heard a crackling sound and whirled around to see flames pouring from his windows. He ran toward the house and found his wife outside, her feet in a spring of water and her clothes entirely burned off. In agony she cried the word "lamp," while Linville rushed on to save his two children, one a babe of two months and the other two years old. Flames drove him back and the children perished, the mother dying an hour later.

Neighbors speculated Mrs. Linville's cry sprang from her having upset a lighted lamp which somehow ignited her garment, then rolled around the floor setting fire to other articles nearby. Bedding and the house's dry wood quickly kindled the blaze.

One by one villages and towns in the Diablo and San Ramon valleys succeeded in obtaining post offices; Walnut Creek was the last. At that time the postage for a first class letter cost one cent. The rate stayed the same for twenty-three years, then doubled to two cents.

15

The Post Office Department called for bids for a new contract when Walnut Creek was added to the Star Route. The carrier was to bring the mail from Oakland to Lafayette, Alamo, Danville, Pacheco and Martinez. He was to leave Oakland at 9:00 A.M. and arrive in Martinez, forty miles away, at 7:00 P.M. The requests to bid asked for four quotations: for deliveries six days a week, three times, twice or once a week.

The contract went to B. F. Mann, who underbid his three competitors, J. W. Avard, William Hillegas, and the stage line operator, J. W. Morris. Mann agreed to deliver the mail once a week for $450. Morris' bid of $1,800 for six deliveries a week was the highest.

Hiram R. Penniman was named postmaster four years after the first postmaster, James McDonald. He too was a storekeeper, a partner in the firm of Sears and Penniman. The office changed hands on an average of every 4½ years until 1927, when Laurence Bornholtz headed the Walnut Creek office. He kept the office for twenty years. (A list of all the postmasters is in the appendix.)

For almost eighty years the office was close to the corner of Main and Cypress. In 1947 it was established on East Street, but only for four years. The office was moved in 1951 to 1524 Locust Street. As late as 1951 Roy Bunker was Walnut Creek's sole carrier, serving all of the town and a part of what is now Lafayette.

In 1931 the average daily stamp sales were twenty-eight dollars. In 1983 the local spokesman refuses to reveal the figure. In 1931 the Walnut Creek post office employed four persons, and today 270 persons handle the mail here. The present main post office opened in 1973.

First Class Postage Rates

1885	2¢		1974	10¢
1915	3¢		1976	13¢
1963	5¢		1978	15¢
1968	6¢		1980	18¢
1971	8¢		1981	20¢

1862

The coal field traffic and the freight business from San Francisco in 1870 brought into service the steamer *Pilot*. This shallow draft craft under W. S. Fassett, master, came up Walnut Creek to Pacheco where it connected with stages from Somersville, Nortonville, Clayton, Danville, Alamo and Walnut Creek.

While this service reduced the travel over dusty or muddy, rough rutted roads to Walnut Creek from Oakland, the *Pilot* often met quartering winds, spraying the craft with salt water and sometimes violently pitching or rolling, depending on the wind's direction.

Shortly after the founding of Concord in 1869, Winfield S. Burpee, a Walnut Creek saloon keeper, in 1870 started running stage coaches from Concord to Oakland via Ygnacio Valley and Walnut Creek. His route cost him money and he dropped it in 1872.

Nevertheless, stage coaches continued to be the backbone of passenger travel throughout the area until the coming of the Southern Pacific Railroad in 1891. Even then lines still ran from the railroad to Clayton and Lafayette.

Eighteen-sixty-two dawned as a year to remember. The rains fell from the previous October until mid-March with only a few letups. Some county roads disappeared under water. Carriages and wagons ventured out only for the direst necessities. It was a wonder someone in town didn't drown, even though Walnut Creek was still a village of no more than eight cottages, a blacksmith shop, one store and the Walnut Creek House. Inside the cottages candles ran low and the householders hoarded their dwindling supply of firewood for cooking stoves and fireplaces.

More frequent use of chamber pots replaced muddy trips to

outhouses. Whether bucketed from dug wells or hand pumped from driven wells, water turned murky and had to be boiled. The family cow, fed mildewed hay, went off her feed. In mid-March the sun came out and started drying fields, roads and animals.

The Morris Brothers stage from Clayton to Oakland ran on time once again.

Men and women walked the dirt roads which did for streets in 1862, with care. Droppings from horses and dogs fell everywhere. Herders drove cattle, and shepherds guided their flocks down the village's main roads. Hogs also went through on foot, and all of them left their share of waste. The sun dried it (when it didn't rain), and animals and vehicles pulverized it and mixed it with the road surface. Flies flew everywhere. Fences surrounded most cottages, not to keep pets in, but to keep animals out.

Most families kept a cow and made their own butter. There was no butcher shop in Walnut Creek, but farmers who did their own slaughtering received credit from the local store when they brought in their excess meat. Villagers needed to buy it without delay since refrigeration didn't exist.

Wives made most of the family's clothes, those lucky enough to have a treadle sewing machine spending less time at it than those without.

Even in 1862 no church existed in the village of Walnut Creek. Fire and police protection didn't come for many years. Of course electricity and telephones were not in use anywhere. Coal oil (kerosene) lighted lamps a continent away. Three years earlier petroleum had been discovered seeping from the ground in Pennsylvania valleys, and shipment to California in appreciable quantity would have to wait for a transcontinental railway.

Real estate changed hands once again when Ygnacio Sibrian received the highest price yet for the 13.4 acres he sold William Rice. The parcel ran south along the creek from Ygnacio Valley Road, containing the heart of today's Homestead District. Rice paid $268, or twenty dollars an acre, for it. Eventually Rice's holdings included all of the Lakewood District and some of Ygnacio Valley's flat land, south of

Ygnacio Valley Road. He admitted later to the 1870 census taker he valued his property at $50,000 (in 1879 dollars) and his personal property at $11,835.

As if rain and flood were not enough, tragedy struck too in 1862. Most villagers knew James Tice and his son, James W. Tice, as good neighbors. The son had a quarrel with nearby farmer James Magee. He claimed Magee had stolen his mare, and Magee just as definitely asserted the mare to be his and, more to the point, he would keep her in his corral as long as he liked.

Seeming to have a change of heart, young Tice went over to Magee's farm to apologize and shake hands. Magee wouldn't shake and ordered Tice off his property. He had a shotgun in his hands, prepared for trouble. He made the mistake of turning away as if to end the conversation. Tice drew his pistol and shot Magee in the left side. Magee exclaimed, "Oh, I'm a dead man, sure!" As he fell, clutching his side, he sank to his knees, groaning, then dropped to the ground, dead.

Tice got on his horse and rode to Martinez, giving himself up to the sheriff. The trial lasted almost six months. On May 30, 1863, the district judge handed down his verdict, "Not guilty."

HOMER STOW SHUEY

One young man who did much to develop the village of Walnut Creek was Homer Stow Shuey. His venturesome father deserves a mention, too. John Shuey rode to California with one companion in 1847. He stayed only a month and then returned to his wife and two children at Adams County, Illinois. He must have liked what he saw here because he came back again on horseback with pack animals in 1850, trading in stock. This time he returned home via Cape Horn and New York. In 1856 he came again, this time by way of Panama, bringing his wife and eight children, and a nephew, James Stow, who would also leave his mark on Walnut Creek.

Their welcome to San Francisco was unforgettable. They arrived on May 22, the day the vigilantes hung James Casey and Charles Cora for the shooting death of the newspaper editor, James King of William. The Shuey children and their parents walked from the steamer *Golden Age* with its 1,400 passengers up Sacramento Street past Fort Gunny-bags, eyes glued on the bodies still slowly turning on their ropes.

John Shuey almost immediately went to farming in Moraga Valley and worked there three years before selling out and moving to Fruitvale.

Between the time his father left Moraga and he went off peddling from a wagon, sixteen-year-old Homer attended State College, then at Fruitvale, now a section of Oakland. From his days at Moraga he became well acquainted at Lafayette and often spent weeks at a time at that village. One morning in October 1859 after several neighbors found their horses missing, Homer and a friend, David Carrick, had their saddles stolen. A posse of six or eight friends chased after the thieves, easily following their fresh tracks in the damp soil. The pursuit took them across San Ramon Creek between Walnut Creek and Alamo, toward Mount Diablo. The posse surprised the thieves who had stopped and picketed their horses. They were three Mexicans. The pursuers called out, "Surrender!" but one thief broke for the brush and took a fusilade, falling mortally wounded, hit in the head. His two companions gave themselves up. The wounded man, about twenty-five years old, was carried to the Walnut Creek House, where he died that night.

Young Shuey, tired of farming, took off to the mines. Two years later he left gold hunting to others and returned to Contra Costa. A merchant at heart, Homer went to peddling from a wagon as he traveled through the country. He returned to Lafayette in 1868 long enough to woo and wed eighteen-year-old Genevra Dougherty. The couple had eight children: Virgil, Jenette, Florence, Ednah, William, Maurice, George, Robert, and Charles. In 1871 Shuey settled down and opened a mercantile store in Walnut Creek with his brother, Marcus Martin Shuey, as partner.

One year after his marriage Homer bought fifty-seven acres of central Walnut Creek, a rectangular shaped hay field beginning at Mt. Diablo Boulevard and running 1,100 feet along North Main, and west 2,100 feet on Mt. Diablo Boulevard. Shuey also acquired an adjoining twenty-five parcel which George Thorn had bought from the Widow Welch. Neither place had roads or streets.

When Homer Shuey filed his subdivision map and started selling lots in 1871, street names were different than they are now. Cypress was called "China" and Locust was named "School." Main was designated "Pacheco" and California appeared as "Granger." Well into the 1930s Mt. Diablo Boulevard was called "Lafayette Road."

On Shuey's map his lots are fifty feet wide and 140 feet deep. Yet one of the early buyers, Ah Lo, the village laundryman, bought a twenty-five-foot piece fronting on Main Street and he paid thirty-five dollars. Hang Kee operated the same laundry in the 1890s. (For a list of Shuey's buyers in the 1870s see page 263 of the appendix.)

Even though he sold dozens of lots in the center of the village, selling real estate was only a sideline with Shuey. He kept adding variety to his stock and became the dominant merchant of the '70s and '80s. He dissolved the partnership with his brother in 1878 and operated the business alone from then on. When he advertised in 1882 in the *Walnut Creek Independent* he featured dry goods, men's and boys' clothing, ladies' hosiery, shoes, stationery, garden and flower seeds, crockery, hardware, tinware, wood and willow ware, candies, nuts, canned goods, as agents for farm machinery, and "We buy farm produce." He listed his address as Main and Bonanza. The town's population at this time totaled at most three hundred.

As peaceful a place as the village usually was in the 1870s, an occasional tragedy did startle the townspeople. A bloody affray occurred on March 2, 1877, about three-quarters of a mile from town. Ramon Romero stabbed José Arrayo. Men held Romero until a sheriff's deputy came from Martinez and arrested him. Arrayo died a week later, and Romero was charged with murder. On November 23 he was convicted and sent to San Quentin for life.

Genevra Dougherty Shuey.

Homer Stow Shuey.

22

Walnut Creek merchants gained a degree of affluence during the balance of the decade starting in 1864 that they theretofore had not known. True, they couldn't yet afford a church, but they did enough business to have to pay the federal tax imposed to pay for the Civil War. While not complete (many pages of IRS collections are illegible from water stains), the records indicate the postmaster, J. R. McDonald, earned the largest income in the community: $2,487 in 1864 on which he paid a $74.61 tax. Milo Hough did next best. He paid a tax of $51 involving his operation of the hotel, billiard table and bar. L. G. Peel operated a retail store and bar for which he paid a tax of $29.16. Ygnacio Sibrian had no income to tax but he paid three dollars for the three carriages he owned.

Walnut Creek was prosperous enough in 1865 to attract a second physician, Dr. W. F. Bradbury, in addition to Dr. Smith.

One Barnabas Webb, a forty-three-year-old farmer, not to be confused with Frank Webb, another farmer, had the most elaborate carriage, if not the most expensive in the village. He also owned a piano, the only one noted in the records. Each of Sibrian's carriages was assessed at $100, but Webb's fetched a value of $250 for which he paid a three-dollar tax. Webb's piano was assessed at $200 and the tax bill for it came to six dollars.

The Lawrence G. Peel store sat on the property at the corner of Main and Mt. Diablo, at 1315 North Main Street. Peel came from Ireland when he was forty-three years old. He operated the store for fifteen years, until 1878. When he died his store was sold to Albert Sherburne, "capitalist," as he had identified himself to the census taker, and his ranch was bought by Antonio Botelho.

Fire came to the unprotected village on April 3, 1867. Milo Hough's Walnut Creek House burned to the ground. Hough, only forty-three years old at the time, did not rebuild. Instead, a competitor built the Walnut Creek & Mt. Diablo Central Hotel on the east side of the creek on what is today the site of Capwell's store.

St. Paul's Mission on Locust Street, ca. 1925.

THE FIRST FOUR CHURCHES

During the fifteen years, 1864-1879, Walnut Creek can be accused of being a sleepy little village. No sidewalks lined the streets. Each person had his own well. Bell hadn't invented the telephone and Edison hadn't originated the electric light. In 1870 the village still had no church and neither a police nor a fire department. The most important businesses in the settlement were the livery stables, the horses they housed, and the tons of hay they required. Every person rode a horse or hitched one or more to his wagon or farm implements.

Aside from the half dozen commercial lots near Walnut Creek, property in every direction raised grain or hay. Captain Fales' farm, which included today's Kaiser property and the Newell tract, grew hay and grain. William Rice's acreage, now Lakewood and the Homestead District, grew similar crops. In the area of today's BART station, George Thorn's farm turned off bales of hay and many sacks of grain. In every direction men worked at tilling, sowing and harvesting with horses. Slow work meant a slow pace of living. Day and evening men and women stayed busy just keeping pace with their needs.

With large families to feed, even though their needs were simple, it took many working hours to supply the necessities.

After they grew, traded or bought their food, clothing and shelter, there still existed another human requirement: social contact. Whether working in the long days of summer or by the dark of early morning and early evening in winter, at day's end the farmer and his wife were more inclined to rest than to hitch up the horse and carriage. But the seventh day was another matter. Even then animals must have their feed and water, and food must be cooked, so Sunday was not a day of much leisure. Yet the need to visit one's neighbor persisted. Religious observances brought many neighbors together.

A group of citizens espousing the Methodist faith organized on February 12, 1869. Among them was a saloon keeper, an ex-hotel owner, several farmers, two merchants and a lumber dealer. In 1872 they built a church on land donated by Homer S. Shuey, a sixty- by ninety-foot lot at about 1361 Main Street. Captain Fales and William Rice each contributed $500 and the balance came from such citizens as W. S. Burpee, E. A. Shumway, James S. Stow, Milo Hough, M. E. Shuey, John Baker, John W. Jones, Frank Webb, and Arthur S. Williams. At first the Reverend A. Kernick, a circuit preacher for the San Ramon Valley-Lafayette area, conducted services twice a month. Oil lamps supplied illumination in the church, and wood and coal stoves the heat.

In 1911 movers turned the church around and moved it 200 feet closer to Locust Street. James Stow gave the Locust Street frontage and accepted the Main Street lot in return for paying the moving costs. Later he built the two-story Stow Building on it.

The next group to form a congregation took several more years to accomplish the task. Presbyterians started their Sunday School several years before they held church services. One of their number, Mrs. Frank Webb, taught Sunday School in the Central School house in the early 1870s. The congregation held its initial Sunday service in the same building on June 1, 1878.

The Presbyterians met in Central School for almost six years and then built their own edifice at what is now about 1321 Locust Street. Only four other structures stood on the block between Mt. Diablo and Cypress at the time. The building was completed with the latest in heating and lighting: a hot-air furnace and gas lamps. The belfry on this church stood above the front left corner, as one faced it, whereas that of the Methodist Church rose from the center. The Presbyterian Church stood for sixty-six years. In 1951 the congregation built a larger one at 1720 Oakland Boulevard.

The Catholic faithful met in private homes for nearly nine years, from 1875. Antonio Botelho, who came in 1872 and bought fifty-three acres lying between Fales on the south and Homer Shuey on the north, gave the land for St. Mary's Church at what is today about 1325 South Main Street (Hendrick's Pianos). The church opened its doors for its first service on October 12, 1884. From the beginning its 100 seats filled early. Yet, the building served the parish adequately until 1940. That year a new 300-seat church at 3029 Mt. Diablo Boulevard replaced the South Main Street building. But as large as the new church was, eleven years later more room had to be added. When the addition was completed it made St. Mary's a 520-seat church.

The history of the oldest church building still in use in Walnut Creek starts with the man who built it.

An Episcopalian and building contractor, Cornelius Waite moved here from Oakland in the spring of 1887. He found no place of worship for his faith in the Walnut Creek-Danville area. He met a fellow Episcopalian, a Captain Harrison of Danville, who sold him a lot in Walnut Creek.

The two men discussed the need for a church on several occasions. In short time they visited their bishop, who responded by sending Mr. Merlyn Jones, rector, from Oakland to appraise the need represented by Harrison and Waite.

Jones drove his buggy to Walnut Creek on a scheduled Sunday and met a congregation of eight persons in Waite's parlor. He gave them communion and after the service, according to Waite, "the group gathered outside, under a tree, where we promised ourselves we would build a church."

The ladies in the small group commenced a fund drive immediately, selling jams and homemade preserves from their buggies as they drove around the countryside. Before long they bought a lot for their prospective building at 1548 Locust Street for $175.

Meanwhile the Rev. James Abercrombie came to Walnut Creek and held the second service in the Central School. After this, Episcopal church services were held once a month in the town hall.

Partly influenced by the ownership of the lot, and partly by the enthusiasm of the parishioners, when Harrison and Waite next called on the bishop he established Walnut Creek in a new diocese and acceded to their request for financial assistance, committing such funds as would be needed. Between Harrison and Waite, Waite agreed to be the contractor and build the church.

The bishop also appointed the Rev. Hamilton, in 1888, to be in charge of Walnut Creek and vicinity, and established the mission, St. Paul's.

Waite built the church, completely out of redwood, for a total cost of about $1,600, and the initial service was held on April 28, 1889. Three clergymen officiated: the Rev. Abercrombie, the Rev. Hamlect and the Rev. Hobart Chetwood. In two years the parishioners paid back the commitment to the bishop.

For thirty years various ministers served St. Paul's and occasionally one of them was the Rev. G. E. Davis of Martinez. Another was a lay reader from Berkeley, Mr. Andruss. He walked out from Berkeley on Saturday, conducted the Sunday service and then went on a fourteen-mile hike to the top of Mount Diablo. He stayed in Walnut Creek Sunday night and walked back to Berkeley on Monday.

In 1931 the parishioners built a parish hall at a cost of $2,818. In 1940 the Rev. James P. Trotter became vicar, and in 1946, when St. Paul's became a parish, he was appointed the first rector.

In 1947 the parishioners, having outgrown the little redwood church, bought land for a new building on Trinity Avenue. When they moved in 1958 they brought along the original structure and it still serves them in 1984 as a chapel.

THE STOW FAMILY

*A*few men who came to the village in the early days lived out their lives from youth to their dying days in Walnut Creek. They were ordinary people but something set them a notch apart from their contemporaries. One such has left a rich trail of history behind him.

In company with his mother, nine-year-old James A. Stow came to California with his uncle, John S. Shuey, arriving in San Francisco on the day in 1856 when Cora and Casey were hung at Fort Gunnybags.

James and his mother went to Oroville, were reunited with Mr. Stow, and lived successively in Butte, Nevada and Sacramento counties before moving back to San Francisco in 1858. Mr. Stow died there the next year. The boy and his mother moved to Danville where James went to grammar school. At age sixteen he went to work for his cousins, Homer S. Shuey and M. M. Shuey, in their store in Walnut Creek. After thirteen years with them, he opened his own mercantile business in 1877. He received the appointment as postmaster the following year, and then won the election for county assessor in 1879.

In 1873, James Stow, twenty-five, had married Miss Alice Glass, daughter of the pioneer, David Glass. James built their home on Lilac Drive facing South Main on land he bought from Captain Fales. The couple had eleven children, and from the 1890s on, the Stows became one of the town's most prominent families. For many years a saying was repeated around town: "At any time of day you may see a Stow on some corner of Main Street."

The couple's children were:

Russell, who served as Walnut Creek's constable for many years. With Todd Nottingham he operated a bar on Main Street.

James Orville (Ike), who conducted an ice business and soda works in town. He had a sheep ranch in Alhambra Valley but built his home here on Granger Way (California Drive).

Harry, best known for the terms he served as county supervisor.

Garfield, a real estate broker, who made his home in Oakland.

Rufus, who made his home in his father's house on Lilac Drive. For many years Rufus worked at Mare Island Naval Shipyard.

Chadwick, who lived in Martinez and operated a bar.

Eleanor, who became a medical doctor and married Frank Bancroft, the son of Albert Little Bancroft.

Pearl, who married Joseph Lawrence of the Walnut Creek Meat Market.

Carey, who married livery stable owner Lew Palmer.

Armand, a banker in Pittsburg, California.

After Mrs. Stow's death, James married Lillie Gardner, and they had one son, Bering. Lillie Stow never received the acknowledgement she expected from her husband's children. All their lives they referred to her as "Auntie."

At one time, with his brother John, James held the mail contracts: Oakland to Clayton and the Star Route, Walnut Creek to Danville.

James Stow's children relate their recollections of the pioneer's religious views. "Father was very anti-Catholic, was constantly inviting traveling ministers of other faiths to Sunday dinner and we hated it. He wouldn't even let us swing from the school gate on Sunday. At one time he fought with the Methodist minister so bitterly that he and two friends, Cameron the blacksmith and Ruby Burpee, the saloonkeeper's daughter, founded the Presbyterian Church.

In the late 1870s, when Stow became postmaster, all the roads in town were lined with wide-spreading shade trees. In spring, summer and early fall, leaves almost hid many of the houses along Main as well as on Locust Street. The dirt roads met the fences around the homes without sidewalks between them. An occasional building arose on a vacant lot and a wooden sidewalk might be built in front of it. In the 1870s and 1880s a number of buildings went up which served the village well until after the turn of the century.

The first town hall, northwest corner of Main and Bonanza, ca. 1885.

James Stow built one of the new commercial structures of the period. He erected a two-story frame building on the west side of Main Street, at 1375 North Main. He established his mercantile business on the ground floor and leased the upstairs to the Masonic Lodge.

Alamo Lodge Number 122, F & AM, first convened in 1858 in Alamo. After ten years, an earthquake on October 21, 1868 destroyed their hall. They went to Danville for several years and then relocated in Walnut Creek over Stow's store.

In 1916 the Masons paid $700 for their present site on Mt. Diablo Boulevard and Locust Street.

Another addition to the village was the 1878 construction at Central School. This was the year that the second room was added to the overcrowded grammar school.

In 1893, Stow subdivided "Stow's Addition to the Town of Walnut Creek." His thirty-three lots covered both sides of Trinity Avenue from a block west of California Drive down to Locust.

James Stow was a county supervisor in 1900 when the officials of Contra Costa and Alameda counties voted to build a tunnel through the Berkeley hills. In spite of all the agitation for a route to avoid the steep climb over the Fish Ranch Road or over the Moraga-Canyon Colorado grade, the plan had failed to get enough support for forty years.

THE 1880s AND THE ROGERS HOTEL

uring the years 1880 to 1883 more changes may have taken place in Walnut Creek than occurred in any similar period during the next forty years, until the city paved Main Street in 1921.

The village population in 1880 totaled about three hundred persons. Most residents tethered a milk cow on one of the many vacant lots in the village. They made their own butter, kept chickens and put up extra eggs in the heavy laying season in an open crock half full of water glass (potassium silicate). In dry weather a tank wagon sprayed water on Main Street to keep clouds of dust from flying into every house and shop.

Stage coaches from the four points of the compass clattered into the village, stopping, after 1880, at the Rogers Hotel. The horses slaked their thirst in the trough in front of the hotel. Drivers dropped off mail sacks and rolls of newspapers. The stop also served thirsty passengers at Rogers' Bar or Burpee's Saloon across the street.

With the exception of those local residents having their own corrals, all others unharnessed or unsaddled their horses at the stable. With many horses coming and going A. E. Hodges and his stable boys stayed busy harnessing or unharnessing, wiping down sweaty animals, currying and combing, forking hay into mangers or hanging feed bags of grain around the horses' necks.

In the early days, Hodges' barns, harness room, wagon shed and corrals filled the entire block of what is today bounded by Main Street, back to the creek (under Broadway), by Duncan and Mt. Diablo Boulevard. The harness room, fronting on Main, had a sleeping room on one side of it. A windmill and tank twenty-five feet high stood on

33

the center of the block. A hay shed sat against the fence on the south boundary which today would be the Mt. Diablo Boulevard planter strip. The town's "lockup," a small, square, whitewashed frame structure, faced the hay shed from the south side of today's Broadway Plaza and Mt. Diablo Boulevard's intersection. Between the lockup and the creek was a well, powered by a horse going round and round the shaft pumping water into a tank twenty-five feet high.

A grove of tall trees bordered the creek. A strip of dry ground ran between the trees and the creek. Villagers knew this place as "The Barbecue Grounds" where Fourth of July and other celebrations took place.

Across Main Street from the front of the stable, a row of small buildings next to Sherburne's on the corner housed the fire house, the undertaker, the barber and a dentist. Elliott Mauzy, son of the town's plumber, recalls his early grammar school days with a chuckle. "Often when we kids walked home from school we passed the stables. A pile of coffins inside a dark corner of that building excited our morbid curiosity. We'd sneak in and have a look, knowing full well one of the stable-hands would see us. He'd shout a curse at us to get out and we'd scamper away, afraid he'd throw something at us."

Subsequent operators of the livery business included Farmer Sanford, who for a time was a partner of A. E. Hodges. By 1890 Hodges ran the stable alone. Five or six years later Lew Palmer, a five-foot seven-inch, fifty-nine-year-old native of New York State, took over.

By 1905 Joel Harlan operated the business. When he died, his wife, Ruby, a partner in the town's funeral parlor across the street from the stable and a county deputy coroner, took over active operation of the livery stable.

William B. Rogers first arrived in California at Empire City, Stanislaus County, in 1852, at the age of twenty-five. He operated the Iowa Hotel there for one year and then moved to the San Ramon Valley. He farmed there for fourteen years and then joined the police department in San Francisco. On subsequent visits back to Contra

Oak Saloon, ca. 1880. Left to right, unknown, Mike Young, Nathaniel Jones, E. C. Palmer, Frazer Ridgeway, Mike Kirsch, Joe Thurston.

Costa County, he became aware that Walnut Creek needed a new hostelry. Finally, in 1880 he went ahead and built the Rogers Hotel on the northeast corner of Main and Duncan streets.

Rogers' two-story frame structure fronted thirty feet on Main Street and ran back seventy feet on Duncan. At first a wooden awning shaded the frontage. To the left of the front door a wide window looked out from the parlor, and to the right another window let light into the office and the bar. The central doorway led down a hall to the dining room, and on the right, behind the bar, was the dining room with kitchen just beyond. Behind the parlor, on the left side of the hall, a stairway led to the sleeping rooms above. At the back of the hotel stood a windmill with a twenty-five-foot-high water tank. Farther back a series of small sheds formed a fence along Duncan Street. Coal oil lamps swung from the ceilings of the public rooms, and glass bowl lamps adorned the private rooms. Even though cuspidors stood in the corners of all the public rooms, dark stains spotted the wooden floors. A sixty-five-foot-wide vacant lot adjoined the hotel to the north. At the back of both lots fenced corrals and covered stalls housed roomers' horses.

Residents of the area needing to cross Walnut Creek went from Main Street down Duncan, to the only bridge crossing the creek south of Ygnacio Valley Road. The wooden bridge, wide enough for one carriage, also had a pedestrian walkway and crossed the stream a few feet from the corrals.

Stage coaches made the Rogers Hotel their Walnut Creek stop. A wooden horse trough sat in the road directly in front of the hotel's front door. A hand pump on the well at one end of the trough supplied the water. Mr. Rogers employed a Chinese cook to buy the food and prepare it for his guests. One source of trade for the hostelry was the prospective buyers for farms and town lots. Another source of business came from "drummers," traveling salesmen out drumming up business. These men came to town with their sample cases, rented rooms in which to display their merchandise, then called on owners of the three general merchandise stores in town to invite them to inspect

Rogers Hotel in the 1880s, looking south. Oak Saloon in right center. Note hotel horse trough at corner of Main and Duncan.

their goods. Traveling men often dined with their customers and also patronized Rogers' bar.

By 1890 the hotel filled regularly and Rogers enlarged it by more than doubling the size. He widened it to a 100-foot frontage, with a canopied porch, a parlor sixty feet long, and a dining room twice its original size. He even provided an inner courtyard which made a spacious hostelry of the property. The remodeling created a U-shaped building. Windows and glass doors from the dining room and parlor gave the guests a view of a garden complete with a garden swing.

The infant son Mr. and Mrs. Rogers carried across the plains in 1852 was named Walter A. Rogers. He'd been born in Iowa only a few months before his parents started on their trek to the Golden State. By the time of the remodeling of his father's establishment in the 1890s, Walter stood five feet six inches, had a light complexion, blue eyes and dark hair. He took over the management of the hotel at the time of the additions. He bought one of the new gas generators and installed gas lamps throughout. He fitted each room with its own stove. He had the horse trough moved away from the front to the Duncan Street side. He commenced advertising when the Southern Pacific Railroad started passenger service in 1891: "Special Accommodations to Travelling Men—Free Bus to all Trains."

Walter A. Rogers, Jr. was born at the hotel in 1909. One of his schoolmates of grammar school days relates her memories of the hotel about 1920. She is Hazel Worgg Sellick, now living in Oregon. The daughter of the sole bakery owner in those days writes, "... Walt Rogers must have memories of our childhood playing at his father's hotel. Walt and I used to play hide-and-seek or chase each other through the halls and we gave Sam, the Chinaman, a very bad time. The halls and verandas were great places to run."

After Sam went to work for Rogers in the 1880s he became so attached to the family that he gave up his own name, which sounded to Rogers like "Lockee," and let it be known that from then on his name was Sam Rogers. Although Sam didn't wait on tables he did virtually everything else connected with the food. When the Volstead Act closed the saloon in 1920, Sam was an old man. Rogers also closed the

The original bar in the Rogers Hotel, ca. 1882.

Louis L. Stein collection

577

dining room and Sam had nothing to do until George Grimes and Ernest Nottingham gave him a job at their pool hall. Here he handled the cash register, collecting for time on the billiard tables and selling tobacco.

Sam's fondest wish was to go home to China before he died. When he finally decided he would go, Ike Stow, the ice merchant, drove Sam over to San Francisco a few weeks ahead of time so he could buy a steamer ticket.

When people in town heard of Sam's intention they took up a collection, intending to buy him a present. On the appointed evening Sam came to work and couldn't understand why people came to the pool hall in such great numbers. Only when the crowd gathered around a pool table and Ike Stow called him over did Sam learn that the gathering was in his honor. Stow first told him about his friends wanting to give him something to remember them by. Then he put the sack of coins on the table in front of him. As the full understanding came to him, Sam raised his hands in protest, "No, every coin is a friend. Me no spend."

Days later, ahead of sailing day, Sam went to San Francisco. No one ever heard from him again. A story, unsubstantiated, went around town that "Sam was killed in San Francisco. He never got to China."

The Rogers Hotel Chronology, 1880-1954
1880 William Bolton Rogers built the hotel
1892 Son, Walter Austin Rogers assumed management
1905 William B. Rogers died December 29
1909 Walter A. Rogers, Jr. born November 9
1918 Renamed "Las Palmas Hotel"
1930 Renamed "Ala Costa Hotel," Tony Antomlis, owner
1936 Renamed "Colonial Inn," Mr. and Mrs. Dean, owners
1943 Renamed "El Curtola Restaurant," Laurence Curtola, owner
1954 Torn down

Rogers Hotel, ca. 1890. Northeast corner of Main and Duncan streets. Note horse trough at corner. Stage coach Oakland to Lafayette, Walnut Creek, Danville, and San Ramon.

In a conversation with Beverly Clemson, the Shadelands Ranch Historical Museum director, Carroll Walker, who was born in Walnut Creek in 1893, told of one of his recollections of the Rogers Hotel.

"I want to tell you a story on myself," began Carroll Walker. "This was before World War I, maybe 1914, when Coy Sharp and Pete and I used to pal around together. We were around fourteen or fifteen years old. This city kid used to come to Walnut Creek and stay at the Rogers Hotel with his grandmother for the summer. He had a fishing rod, reel, and creel. We fished with bent pins and worms. He used flies. I don't think he ever caught any of the Walnut Creek fish; they were worm eaters. He was snooty and thought us kids were backward and we thought he was too fancy. We didn't talk to each other much.

"But one day we asked him if he wanted to rope and brand a calf. Sharps had a calf around eight months old that they were going to butcher soon and the older folks were away. So we went over to Sharps, near Bonanza and Mt. Diablo, and we wet down the barnyard real good. Then we built a fire and got the branding iron hot, not red hot, but hot enough to sear a little. We tied the rope on the calf and then around the waist of the city kid. We told him to hold it. Then we branded the calf up under the shoulder where the folks wouldn't see it. Of course, the calf was anxious to get away and when it was done, it leaped up and started dragging the city kid with it, he being tied to the calf. It dragged him all over the barnyard until it was tired. The city kid was pretty sore. He went down to the Rogers Hotel and the next day, he and his grandmother were gone and never came back."

DOCTORS AND DRUGGISTS

Back in 1877 a new medical doctor came to town, Dr. C. C. Kelley. In 1880 Dr. W. E. Hook and Dr. E. E. Brown also practiced here. The custom of the day had been that doctors filled whatever prescriptions they prescribed, but Walnut Creek's first druggist arrived in 1869—fifty-three-year-old, short and stocky Samuel F. Johnson. The second pharmacy on record is one opened by Dr. J. E. Pearson and his wife in April 1878.

Dr. Pearson, born in New York in 1827, suffered a loss common to many men in the days when they repaired machinery themselves, around the farm or in a shop. The voter's registration list of 1896 describes him, besides having gray eyes and gray hair, as having lost the first two fingers of his left hand. Pearson opened his drug store on what is today the Firestone Tire Store's parking lot on Mt. Diablo Boulevard. Mrs. Pearson, Sara on her druggist's license, was the third female issued the permit in California.

In April 1888, S. P. Johnson, according to his newspaper ad, established "a first class drug store, selling drugs, paint, hardware, window glass, toiletries, perfumes, school supplies, lamps, dolls, tobaccos, etc." He located his store on the east side of Main Street about one hundred feet north of the intersection with Bonanza.

Both Johnson and Pearson were licensed physicians as well as druggists. The medical doctors who came after them are:

Dr. W. F. Lynch, who began his practice in 1885.

Dr. Joseph T. Breneman, born in Ohio in 1849, five feet eight inches tall, dark eyes and gray hair. The doctor's index finger on his left hand had stiffened.

Dr. Claude R. Leech took Breneman's place in 1897. He stood

Tom Owens, Rogers Hotel handyman, with his pet coyote cubs.

five feet five inches. Leech was born in Pennsylvania in 1869. He too had lost part of his left index finger in an accident.

Dr. Fred Watt practiced here from 1902 to 1904.

Dr. Carolyn Cole, the first woman doctor in Walnut Creek, came in 1910 but practiced here only part-time.

Dr. Louise A. Oldenbourg, anesthesiologist, started her practice here in 1915.

One day several years after Dr. Leech's death in 1934, Mrs. Leech reminisced about the days when she and the doctor came to town in 1897. "When Dr. Leech and I came here this town was so tiny there wasn't another young couple in town, nor a single baby! . . . I loved the informality and warmth of small town life.

"This was a funny little town in '98. Our streets were not paved. We had no sidewalks, no street lights. If you ventured out after dark without a lantern your progress was punctuated by bumping first into one hitching rack and then into another . . . We had any amount of adobe mud in winter and any amount of dust in summer . . . Walnut Creek had no lighting system, no water system [and] no sewage system."

She recalled the excitement people felt about the arrival of the evening train. "We would hitch up the horse, and when we heard the whistle, get over to the station at top speed to see the train come up 'around the bend,' the engine puffing . . . "

She remembers the pace of living in Walnut Creek. "We had some leisure in those days, and time to take life sanely and enjoy our families and friends." Remember she wrote those lines in 1940; what would be her reaction in 1984?

Many sanitary practices of those times, or rather the lack thereof, would not be tolerated today. Yet, before a water and sewer system served Walnut Creek, the medical reports indicate a lack of epidemics. Even the close proximity of private wells to cesspools failed to cause serious illness. But other kinds of accidents occurred frequently.

Broken bones resulted from falls from horses or wagons. Startled by a barking dog, a patiently waiting horse might bolt, upsetting those climbing into or seated in a carriage. A runaway team could create havoc, overturning a loaded wagon. A kicking cow or a butting goat sometimes broke its owner's bones. Reports include injuries to men and women buggy drivers caused by an eager young horse "feeling his oats." Sometimes the driver failed to pull back hard enough on the reins to slow his horse to a safe speed as he approached a turn. Many are the deaths caused when a driver or passenger, thrown from an overturned buggy, landed head first on the road or against a fence or tree.

Farm related accidents came frequently. One day a Walnut Creek farmer, William Holman, driving a hay rake, was thrown from his implement when his frightened horses bolted. He fell forward but hung onto the pole (tongue) to avoid being caught in the rake's teeth. One wheel fell off and the axle broke as the team dragged him across two ditches, tearing through gates for a quarter of a mile before stopping. Dr. Leech reported Holman suffered only two broken ribs and numerous cuts and bruises.

Isabelle Brubaker collection

The Rogers Hotel after the expansion. Note the horse trough moved from in front to the Duncan Street side.

46

VOLUNTEER FIRE DEPARTMENT

*I*n 1883 volunteers took an important step when they formed the fire department. Before protection was organized, fire was everyone's problem. Grass fires frequently consumed hay and grain but seldom did fires of any consequence threaten homes in the village.

Two memorable conflagrations are part of the pre-1900 history. When the Walnut Creek House burned to the ground on April 3, 1867, the next to the oldest landmark in Walnut Creek disappeared forever. William Slusher's cabin was older.

Another blaze which totally destroyed an important early building was the one on December 20, 1879. That night Albert Sherburne's mercantile establishment burned down. He conducted his business at what is now 1315 Main Street (Arthur's Deli). Sherburne opened the store in 1870 and although he rebuilt the store after the fire, he didn't go back into business. He rented space to John Gambs for another store and to his son-in-law, Winifred S. Burpee, for a saloon.

Though sentiment had been in favor of organizing a fire company, it took the loss of Sherburne's store to stir the villagers into action. It also took time to raise enough money to buy equipment. In 1883 the volunteers elected hotelman Rogers as foreman of their fire company. The organization bought a single-axle cart which carried a reel of hose loose on the axle. The 100 feet of hose was 2½ inches in diameter and was rubber-lined canvas hose sporting a four-foot-long brass nozzle at one end. A bell and red lantern hung atop the frame.

Ten years later the volunteers bought a more important piece of rolling stock, a hook and ladder truck. Both pieces were moved by manpower. The hook and ladder truck contained a pump operated by

47

men on both sides rocking an eight-foot oak bar up and down. No water hydrants existed in Walnut Creek until well after 1900, so until then the pumper stopped alongside someone's well and firemen dropped a suction hose into it while others rocked the pump bars. The hook and ladder truck came with 200 feet of 2-inch rubber hose and 400 feet of 1½-inch canvas hose.

In case an open well was too far away, firemen reached for the twenty-four leather buckets hanging on the truck, filling them from a tank (windmills and tanks stood all over town) and, forming a chain gang, doused the fire with water.

The fire house, with a bell in a cupola atop the roof, was located in the center of the business district, between Burpee's Saloon and the barber shop, at about 1327 North Main Street.

One afternoon in 1894 a cry rang out, "Fire! Fire! In the Chinaman's wash house. Fire! Fire!" Volunteers pulled the hook and ladder truck down the street to the Chinese laundry on the west side of Main Street (at about 1355 North Main) and, according to a newspaper report, "before the boys could hook up the hose a few well-aimed buckets put out the blaze."

Not until after 1900 did firemen have a dependable source of water. Then the water which filled the 15,000-gallon tank on Farmer Lacassie's 310 acres, one-and-a-half miles northwest of town, ran into a two-inch pipe to a line which stretched the length of Main Street. Eight hydrants spaced along the east side of Main supplied the volunteers with the water they needed.

Walnut Creek Volunteer Fire Department, ca. 1890, with the first piece of equipment, a hose truck.

THE TELEPHONE

The earliest telephone came to Walnut Creek in the 1880-1883 period. Telephones had gone into service for the first time in 1878, between New Haven, Connecticut and New York City. Long distance lines didn't go into operation until 1892, when New York and Chicago were connected.

In 1881 the Contra Costa County Telephone and Telegraph Company applied to the county supervisors for a franchise "to install poles along the county road, Martinez to Danville." Approval came on August 3, 1881, and by autumn the company advertised bonds for sale to finance the enterprise. The first line came from Martinez to Walnut Creek in the winter of 1881. James A. Borland, Southern Pacific agent at Martinez, served as secretary of the new company. It was he who relayed the first message to Walnut Creek on January 11, 1882.

A son of the Philip Lamp family of Orinda broke an arm so badly his parents wouldn't move him. But Mr. Lamp rode into his village where a new telephone line connected Orinda to Berkeley. The operator there relayed Lamp's call to Borland in Martinez. He in turn called the only number in Walnut Creek, the Leitch and Sanford Mortuary, with the first message, "Dr. Hook, come to my farm in Moraga Valley. I have a son with a multiple-fractured arm. Philip Lamp."

For a long time very few Walnut Creek residents showed any interest in having a telephone. They'd gotten along without them all their lives and so had their parents, so why should they burden themselves with the extra expense? For virtually twenty years the Contra Costa County Company struggled along. Ultimately, about 1899, their system went into the hands of the Sunset Telephone and

Telegraph Company. G. W. Geary served as their first agent but in 1903 A. Lebrecht, clothing store owner, took his place. He was a Bavarian, born in 1851. Henry T. Jones was the first farmer to order a telephone, but in 1903 two other rural subscribers signed up, Mrs. Fannie Bancroft, Aloha Farm, Suburban 31, and F. Gavin, manager, Bancroft Ranch, Suburban 33.

In 1904, twenty years after the first hookup, the Walnut Creek circuit served six subscribers:

Henry T. Jones, farmer	Main 11
J. M. Stow, residence	Main 24
W. A. Rogers, hotel	Main 23
Palmer and Harlan, livery	Main 21
Foskett, Ellworthy, and Keller, butchers	Main 25
Dr. S. W. Watt, residence	Main 26

Still people didn't take to the instrument, except reluctantly. In 1909, five years after the listings above, only thirteen Walnut Creek residences received telephone service. With sixteen business instruments in use, the total for that year was just twenty-nine telephones. In all of Contra Costa County 1,148 numbers were listed in the directory.

All the instruments in those days hung from the wall: a blond oak box with a crank on the right to generate a signal and a lever on the left to hang the ear piece.

As late as 1913 Walnut Creek did not have its own exchange; all the calls came through Concord's with the prefix Walnut, replacing Main.

Bradley Brothers, confectioners, opened the first Walnut Creek exchange in a rear corner of their store in the 1300 block of Main Street in 1916. They built a small glass enclosure for the switchboard. Forty cords and sockets dotted the board. The operator sat in front of the board waiting for a light to flash indicating a subscriber wanted service. She would plug a cord into a socket under the light and answer, "Number, please?" Then she plugged the caller's cord into the appropriate socket. By 1919 the women handled seventy-eight customers.

In 1940 Walnut Creek connections totaled 1,056 and when World War II started the telephone company banned all new connections for the duration. At one time, in 1947, the telephone company had a waiting list of 777 would-be customers.

The complete change to automatic dial service in Walnut Creek came in 1955.

THE FIRST TWO NEWSPAPERS

Pioneers climbed mountains and pioneers forded rushing streams, but few of them worked harder, with less hope of reaching their El Dorado, than the weekly newspaper publishers in frontier towns.

Those men set their own type, ran their own press, solicited advertising themselves, and tried to sell subscriptions to everyone they met. Most found themselves in debt after working seventy or eighty hours a week. Even running a job printing shop as well couldn't insure their survival. A great many proved the adage of the day: "Those with printer's ink in their blood will never get rich."

Back in 1882 a venturesome printer, G. B. Leavitt, came to Walnut Creek and set himself up as the village's first newspaper man. Nothing is known of his previous ventures, but on March 24 of 1882 he printed the town's first newspaper. He called it *The Walnut Creek Independent.* On the masthead of his four-page weekly his motto read, "Hew to the Line. Let the Chips Fall Where They May." The village population at the time barely topped 300, including children. He advertised subscriptions at three dollars a year. Some of his advertisers included the newly-arrived jeweler and watchmaker, George Gardner; the Oak Saloon, C. W. Rogers, proprietor, corner of Main and Oakland Road; J. R. Young, contractor and builder; H. S. Shuey, who took a full column to list all his merchandise; Mrs. Vicker, Main Street, who advertised "Meals—25¢"; A. W. Hammitt, who advertised opening his "one-price cash store at 'Main and Lafayette,'" replacing F. Gambs. Gambs had gone into business only two years before. Hammitt's "one-price" referred to the two-price practice of many merchants—those who charged had to pay a higher price than those who paid cash.

Not enough advertisers bought space and not nearly enough subscribers put down their three dollars for Leavitt to survive. His final issue, number seventeen, came out on July 14, 1882.

Twelve years later the partnership of E. R. Vanlandingham and W. C. Lewis published the *Walnut Creek Sentinel*. Issue number one came out on March 9, 1894. Its masthead read, "Eternal Vigilance is the Price of Liberty." In spite of the increase in population to about 475, including children, the *Sentinel* published only one more issue than its predecessor and died in July 1894.

Four churches advertised in the *Sentinel*:

    St. Paul's Episcopal—Rev. Lee—School Street
    Presbyterian Church—Rev. Breck—School Street
    Methodist Church—Rev. McFaul—Main Street
    Catholic Church—Rev. Father Damien O'Brien—
       Main Street

A partial list of advertisers on June 22, 1894 includes:

Huntington and Graber, Main Street, blacksmithing, shoeing, wagon making

Stone Bros., stoves, pumps, ranges, drove wells a specialty
H. Voslander, Main Street, shoemaker
A. E. Hodges, corner Main and Bonanza, livery stable
R. H. Latimer, drug store and post office
F. Gambs, general merchandise
A. G. Cameron, blacksmith and carriage maker
T. J. Young, general merchandise
A. Lebrecht, clothing
H. S. Shuey, Main Street, lumber
J. T. Breneman, M.D., physician
Dr. Noble, Rogers Hotel, residence, physician and surgeon
Drs. S. J. Symons and J. M. Dunn, D.D.S., dental parlor
F. E. Weston, real estate and insurance and notary
J. Reading, watchmaker
G. F. Dunningan, candy, fruit and notions
E. Kimball, pumps and windmills

Blacksmith Elmer Cameron pausing while shaping a shoe.

Professor Louis Proll, instructor in the violin

E. C. Palmer, succeeded F. Sanford, stables and feed

J. A. Shuey, dry goods, furnishings and groceries, Danville

Nathaniel Jones, "stud, Marquis, mahogany bay, 15½ hands high, weighing 1,350 lbs., 4 years old, best for breeding, terms $15—if not successful no pay."

Mrs. Vickers, Walnut Creek Restaurant, Main Street, "meals 25¢"

Vicente Martinez, barber

Johnson's Drug Store

Hang Kee, laundry ("Chinese help of all kinds furnished")

W. A. Rogers, "1st class bar and billiard room—Special Accommodations for Traveling Men—Free bus to all trains"

Walnut Creek Market, Arthur Williams, proprietor. "Meat wagons to Pacheco, Lafayette, Danville, San Ramon."

N. W. Leitch and F. Sanford, undertakers and embalmers, telephone 240

James Hammond, "Crane Steel Windmills," carpenter and builder, located at McCaws Blacksmith Shop

Back in the days when Rogers built his hotel the town's residents longed for diversions—ones they knew San Franciscans could enjoy and they were denied. Working men were accustomed to a six-day week, and Sunday was a special day. Across the bay a popular Sunday attraction in the 1880s was watching balloonists and their paying passengers float up from Woodward's Gardens or Central Park and disappear over the San Bruno hills.

On a Sunday in July 1885 loungers in front of Rogers Hotel set up a cry which brought virtually every able-bodied person in Walnut Creek to his feet. They pointed to the west where one passenger in a descending balloon waved from the swinging basket.

Boys racing on their bicycles and men on their horses vied to be the first to reach the daring aeronaut. The next issue of the *Contra Costa Gazette* told the story.

"Prof. Van Tassel made an ascension Sunday afternoon from Central Park, San Francisco, in a gas balloon, 'City of London,' which

577

Looking north on Main Street from Duncan Street, ca. 1883.

has a capacity of 70,000 cubic feet. The balloon drifted upward shortly after 3:30 P.M. and soon disappeared above the fog. Above the bay the aeronaut caught a glimpse of a steamer and for the next two hours he saw nothing below him but fog. The balloon descended at 5:34 in Cox's field near Walnut Creek. Van Tassel watched for his opportunity and sprang to the ground at the same time pulling the knife cord, slashing the huge balloon from bottom to top. The balloon rose a short distance and came down in a cornfield at the edge of town. An altitude of 7000 feet was reached during the trip. All Walnut Creek turned out to see the balloon and interview the bold occupant." (*Contra Costa Gazette*, Saturday, August 1, 1885)

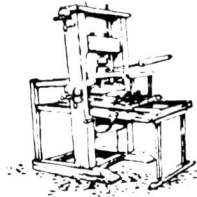

BUTCHERS

*I*n the earliest days of the village the people who sold fresh meat were the farmers. Having neither ice nor any means of keeping meat fresh, the mercantile and grocery stores could not stock it. Farmers who butchered a beef, hog or lamb traded or sold meat while it was fresh. After thirty years the practice ended.

One butcher shop in Walnut Creek has a long history at virtually one location. The Walnut Creek Meat Market, with three owners, goes back to 1890 on property on the east side of North Main Street.

Twenty-two-year-old Arthur Williams came to Walnut Creek about 1870. He was born in New York, worked as a butcher there, and some time before he came west he lost part of a digit, as so many butchers did. He lost the first joint of the third finger on his right hand. He stood five feet eleven and a half inches and had brown hair and blue eyes. His florid complexion would have better suited a bartender than a butcher. The first record of him in Walnut Creek is a $100 contribution he made for the construction of the Methodist Church in 1872.

In September 1877 Williams paid Homer Shuey $100 for the northwest corner of Locust and Cypress streets. His was a deep lot—it went all the way west to California Drive. He built a home on the corner facing Locust and erected a slaughter house at the corner of California. Williams bought and butchered livestock there; he also rendered fat in two kettles set up outdoors.

To the north of his house, along Locust Street, he set out a croquet court for his and his friends' amusement. Williams took his water supply from his well, his pump powered by a horse plodding around the well. This one-horse power pump sent water up into a tank some twenty feet high.

577

Main Street looking south, ca. 1883.

Lucy Williams objected to the odor of the slaughter house and the swarms of flies always near her back door. It took her just about ten years to make her husband move his business up to Main Street.

On a lot on the east side of Main Street, about 150 feet south of Bonanza, Williams built another slaughter house. This time he built his tank house flush with the front line of Main Street, using the ground level for his shop and the level above for a sleeping room. A wooden cornice on the store front shaded the sidewalk. About sixty feet behind the wooden sidewalk he added a pen for livestock, the slaughter house with the kettles alongside and an outhouse.

Williams ran a profitable business. He sold almost all of his meat from the three meat wagons he sent regularly to Pacheco, Lafayette, Danville and San Ramon.

At age fifty Williams retired, selling out to the Concord butchers, Foskett, Ellworthy and Keller.

In retirement Williams served the village as constable, a position he held as late as 1915, forty-five years after he arrived in Walnut Creek.

Vivian Cooper remembers how popular Williams became as the town constable. "When Mr. Williams died in 1915, I remember the entire student body of Central School went to the church. Even though he had reported some of the kids many times for playing hookey, they all respectfully paraded single file around his coffin."

Foskett, Ellworthy and Keller ran the butcher shop until they sold out to the Lawrences in 1910. A 1908 map of the town shows the two slaughter houses with the kettles and appurtenances still standing.

The Lawrence family is to Walnut Creek what Babe Ruth is to baseball. Although they didn't found the town, they made their own tradition in it. Their tradition began when José Lorenço, a country butcher in the Azore Islands, left St. George (São Jorge) Island for California. He went to Half Moon Bay, anglicized his name to Jesse Lawrence and took a bride, Pauline Bartholomew. The couple's first son, Joseph, was born in Half Moon Bay in 1896. Their other children were Fred, Harry, Lester, Rosie and Addie.

Lawrence left Half Moon Bay and went to Hayward where he worked as a butcher for a short time. Soon he opened his own shop in Danville. When Foskett and his partners wished to close out their Walnut Creek branch in 1910, they found a willing buyer in Jesse Lawrence, who maintained his Danville branch at the same time.

A little girl then, Vivian Cooper remembers the kindly soft-spoken gentleman who was Lawrence in his late years. Somehow he knew the little girl hankered after a pony. Each time Vivian's mother took her into the shop Mr. Lawrence would ask her, "Has your father bought you that pony yet?" Never could she answer, "Yes."

Another recollection of early days involved the Walnut Creek Meat Market supplying a special order for the town's barber.

Vicente Martinez was the only barber in Walnut Creek for years, before 1910. Phil Journal, another barber, came just after 1910. Vicente had a large grape arbor in the back of his barber shop on Main Street, where every year he held a barbecue for his select friends. Residents felt it an honor to be invited to this affair.

The barber would order a bull's head from the Walnut Creek Meat Company and he prepared it in the Spanish style and baked it in a pit. It was claimed a great delicacy by some, much like luau pig to the Hawaiians.

Why Martinez never held his party at his home, on Main almost directly opposite Lacassie Street, is something of a mystery.

Mr. and Mrs. Jesse Lawrence both died during the influenza epidemic of 1918, only a day apart. The ownership of the business went to the eldest son, Joe, and his sister Lou's husband, Al Stephans. Later Joe's brothers Fred and Harry bought full partnerships in the Walnut Creek Meat Company.

Harry Lawrence looked after the routes their butcher wagons covered. Harry or one of his butchers went to most of the rural areas twice a week. Few homes had even an ice box, since ice delivery in the rural areas was infrequent. So to serve fresh meat frequent calls by the butcher were necessary. Each wagon had a step in back on which the butcher stood while he reached in, uncovered a cut of meat and sliced off what his customer asked for.

In 1932 the Lawrences built a new slaughter house a mile and a half out Ygnacio Valley Road on what is now the San Marcos development.

Joe married Pearl Stow, daughter of James Stow, and the couple had seven children. Their daughter-in-law, Marion Lawrence, widow of Paul, remembers him as a public-spirited man. "He was always doing things for the community. He served as a board member of the Mt. Diablo High School District, and as president of the Acalanes Union High School District, he contributed land on the north side of that school to the district. He served Walnut Creek as mayor and fire commissioner and the Bank of America as a director."

She also recalls, "Even before the Great Depression farmers knew if it was all they had they could trade Joe their produce for his meat."

Mrs. Lawrence remembers the difficult times Joe and Pearl had during the 1930s. "My father-in-law worked from sunup until sunset many times. He would come home so tired Pearl would go out with him to put up the horses and feed them. She was afraid he would fall asleep, his day tired him so."

In the late 1930s, Steve Lawrence, the present owner, worked in the market part-time. But before then, when he was only five years old, his Grandfather Joe would take him along on stock buying trips. "I always looked forward to the return trip when my grandfather would never fail to stop in Danville and buy me a milkshake. We went to Tassajara and beyond, buying cattle, sheep and hogs. In years past we raised some of our own stock. July was always the worst month of our year. That was when we'd have to buy feed, our own hills being dry and bare of grass. People seemed to buy less meat that month too.

"My family didn't make much money out of the market. There were five families to share in the profits and I can remember my father saying there were some years when the total profit ran between $3,000 and $5,000 for the entire year."

In 1940 the Lawrences sold their Danville market, concentrating on the Walnut Creek trade, always offering such high quality that even now, almost fifty years later, the Walnut Creek Meat Market still earns the reputation for selling only the highest quality meat.

A rancher and his wife watch the butcher cut them meat in the Walnut Creek Meat Market's Model T Ford truck, ca. 1923.

Arthur Williams' Walnut Creek Meat Market with three butcher wagons, ca. 1900. Left to right: Frank Donner, Charles Moisen, Lucy and Arthur Williams, "Blackberry Joe."

THE STEAM TRAIN

gitation for a level route to Oakland came to life in 1871. Publicity at the time read, "The main purpose of the road and tunnel is to bring the trade of a large and productive portion of Contra Costa County to Oakland . . . instead of going to Martinez or climbing the mountains between the Bay and the center of Contra Costa County."

Captain Card made the initial proposal in 1871 and sold some of his wealthy friends on it, including J. B. Mason and Socrates Huff. Nothing came from this idea.

As if to keep as much trade as possible in Martinez, a more practical suggestion reached the surveying stage in 1873. That year George K. Peterson surveyed the route for a narrow gauge railway from Martinez to Limerick, a village at the east end of Crow Canyon Road. The promoters estimated the cost of building at $240,000 with an annual operating cost of $60,000.

The same month the report on the narrow gauge was published in Walnut Creek, Mr. Boardman presented his survey of the route through the Oakland Hills. This included a tunnel he estimated would cost $40,000. More meetings were held but nothing came of this proposal either.

In 1875 the *Oakland News* claimed articles of incorporation had been filed for building a "standard gauge railway from Oakland to Alamo, 15 miles." Again nothing materialized.

By 1885 Walnut Creek had 300 residents in the one-mile-square town; traffic to Pacheco had faded away. Walnut Creek offered all the services available in Pacheco and Martinez, so the principal stage line to Oakland commenced its run in front of the Rogers Hotel. Theodore Moore owned the line.

Meanwhile the promoters of a narrow gauge railroad, the California and Nevada, succeeded in building a railroad from Emeryville to Orinda. The initail passenger run left Emeryville at 8:00 A.M. on the first Sunday of April 1888. The train returned from Orinda at noon. So many sightseers were waiting at the 40th and San Pablo Avenue terminal that first day, the train immediately made another round trip.

The California and Nevada Railroad Company claimed it had surveyed the route from Orinda to Walnut Creek and Clayton and would likely be running trains on it before the end of the year. The officers claimed the railroad would be extended through San Joaquin, Stanislaus and Tuolomne counties, thence across the Sierra to the Nevada line.

No part of the railroad was ever completed east of Orinda, but Walnut Creek did receive service. Beginning in April 1888, Farmer Sanford, local livery stable owner, ran a stage coach from Main and Duncan streets to Orinda, meeting the train on its arrival.

Efforts to build a railroad through Walnut Creek kept surfacing. Through the winter of 1887-88 local people formed the San Ramon Valley Railroad, Inc. to construct a line from Avon to Pleasanton. Although only valley residents appeared on the board of directors of this company, word went around that the Southern Pacific Company was behind the plan. Directors of the San Ramon Vally Railroad went to the Southern Pacific and offered to step aside if the Southern Pacific would build the line. But the Southern Pacific refused their offer, saying, "Buying [all that] land for a right-of-way and stations makes the idea uneconomical."

The locals got the message and, by successfully asking farmers to donate land along the right-of-way, the board members were able to offer the Southern Pacific Company a free route from Avon to Limerick. They went ahead and built the line, and the first train ran on June 7, 1891. The Walnut Creek station wasn't built until 1901, when Antonio Botelho donated the land for it. South of the station the company had built corrals and installed water troughs, both necessary for holding livestock for shipment. Freshly baked bread came to Walnut Creek on the first train every morning. Grocers drove their wagons to the station to pick up wooden crates shipped by the Langendorf Baking Company in Oakland. Back at their stores they retailed it for five cents a loaf.

Acknowledging the importance of the railroad to them, the Rogers Hotel advertised, "Our surreys meet each train."

While the San Ramon branch of the Southern Pacific ran only from Avon to Limerick for the first ten years, a time of no-growth in the Walnut Creek population, freight traffic along the line did increase due to additional acreage planted to fruit for drying and grapes for making wine.

The Southern Pacific extended the railroad from Limerick to Pleasanton in 1904. Sunday "Picnic Specials" involved longer trains than ran weekdays. The specials ran a circuit from Oakland out through Hayward and Niles Canyon to Pleasanton. Then they traveled the San Ramon Valley Branch to Walnut Creek, Avon, Martinez and back to Oakland. Even with the regular railroad service, a new stage line started running in 1907. That year Basil A. Perry began serving valley residents by driving a four-horse stage from Piedmont to Walnut Creek and Danville. Perry kept his line going until sometime in 1909.

A very important development in 1911 emphasized the San Ramon line's value to the Southern Pacific Company. In June they started re-laying track, replacing the original with heavier ninety-pound rail. They then routed their main line freight trains, after the cars crossed Carquinez Straits on the train ferry, to San Francisco via Walnut Creek, Niles Canyon and the new Dunbarton Bridge. This route saved the wear and tear on locomotives and the fuel necessary to pull trains over the 1,000-foot Altamont Pass route from Stockton. Heavier passenger service resulted along the branch and just before the electric line started running in 1911, four passenger coaches, with two baggage cars, made up each weekday train.

Southern Pacific passenger train schedule between Walnut Creek and San Francisco, 1910:

Daily

Lv.	San Francisco	7:30 A.M.	4:00 P.M.
Arr.	Walnut Creek	11:04 A.M.	6:12 P.M.
Lv.	Walnut Creek	6:55 A.M.	4:00 P.M.
Arr.	San Francisco	9:15 A.M.	6:15 P.M.

Sunday

Lv.	San Francisco	7:30 A.M.
Arr.	Walnut Creek	10:13 A.M.
Lv.	Walnut Creek	4:00 P.M.
Arr.	San Francisco	6:15 P.M.

Southern Pacific station, 1902.

PORTUGUESE

*I*n the larger cities early in this century those who spoke English poorly (and many of those with a dark skin) found it very difficult to become a part of the Anglo-Protestant society. For the most part only menial jobs were available to them. Often they worked only irregularly. However, in Walnut Creek many of them fared better because earlier emigrants from their homelands had succeeded by working harder and longer hours (milkers) than their English speaking contemporaries.

All through the early growing years in Walnut Creek, Portuguese immigrants or their descendants made a mark on the town. Their industry, foresight, thrift and business acumen made their heritage a valuable adjunct to the community.

Sailing ship captains, short-handed, often put in to the Azore Islands where they knew they would find work-hungry, capable seafaring men, willing to sign on to go to any port in America. Some jumped ship in New England and many deserted in San Francisco. More often than not, after working in California for a year or two, they would send enough money home so that their relatives could come to California.

Many of Portuguese heritage raised livestock and there were so many families east of Alamo that at one time the area was called "Portuguese Gulch." Among their number is the town's first banker, two early automobile dealers, many successful farmers, a city mayor, and Walnut Creek's pioneer real estate broker. One farmer became so successful he gave the Southern Pacific land for a right-of-way and a station, enough to help influence the railroad to build a line through the valley.

One of the first Portuguese immigrants in the area was Manuel J. Machado, about whom very little is known—only that he leased land from Antonio Sibrian on March 5, 1877.

Antonio S. Botelho, age thirty-eight in 1868, came to California that year and received his naturalization papers in Alameda on November 16, 1871. A native of the Azore Island of São Jorge, he had typical Portuguese features, olive skin with black hair and brown eyes.

Botelho first bought the L. G. Peel farm which ran south of Las Trampas Creek and west of San Ramon Creek. He built his corrals and barn west of the county road to Alamo (today between Simon's parking lot and Las Trampas Creek). By common usage the county road to Alamo ran through his field. In 1879 the county supervisors asked Botelho and his neighbors for a sixty-foot right-of-way for the county road. They complied and granted the easement on February 1, 1879.

In 1882 he bought a run-down hotel on a one-acre site which gave his name to a part of downtown Walnut Creek. The hotel he bought had been built to supply the need for a hostelry after the Walnut Creek House burned to the ground in 1867.

All through the 1870s John J. Noone and his wife Hannah ran the Walnut Creek & Mt. Diablo Central Hotel. It was constructed on one acre of land, described in a document in the county recorder's office, " . . . bounded on the north by lands of Downing and Forester, on the east by Walnut Creek [sic] and on the south and west by the county roads [Newell and South Main Street]." At the same time he and his wife operated the Walnut Creek hostelry, they also owned and ran the Danville Hotel. Their home was a 217-acre farm between Alamo and Danville.

The Noones gave most of their attention to the Danville Hotel and gradually their Walnut Creek hostelry showed signs of lack of care. They advertised the property for sale in 1882 and Antonio Botelho bought it. He refurbished the hotel, making a spacious home of it.

Botelho's Island was more than just his one acre. It is all of that property which rests against the crotch formed by the junction of Las Trampas and San Ramon creeks, today under the Bank of America

Walnut Creek & Mt. Diablo Central Hotel. Sold to Antonio Botelho in 1882 for his residence.

parking lot. This so-called island ran south between the two creeks past Newell Avenue. Today virtually all of the Broadway Shopping Center is on Botelho's Island.

In 1885, fourteen years after receiving his citizenship papers, Botelho arranged to buy 290 acres of downtown Walnut Creek from Orris Fales' widow, Esther Fales, for $2,000. This parcel bordered Las Trampas Creek to the south but ran east across San Ramon Creek to San Miguel Drive.

Antonio Botelho farmed his property economically; he was the first in the area to harvest grain with a fourteen-horse team pulling on his big combine. He became well-enough-off so that when the Southern Pacific denied the 1890 request of San Ramon-Concord business and farm leaders to build a branch line through from Avon to Limerick (at the east end of the Crow Canyon Road) on the basis that the cost of the land for a right-of-way would make the proposal uneconomical, he was one of the first to offer free to the railroad the land they would need. Others followed suit and the Southern Pacific built the branch in 1891.

It is reported by those who remember him that he gave land for St. Mary's Catholic Church (where Hendrick's piano store is) and for Central School. At any rate, he never tired of writing his friends and relatives in the Azores, telling them about the church, the school and the railroad built on his farm.

Mr. and Mrs. Botelho raised a family of two daughters and four sons. Mrs. Botelho is remembered as a tiny, wiry person. One son, Frank, when he was nineteen years old, paid John Pierson $100 for the fifty-foot-wide lot on the southwest corner of Main and Bonanza. He first built a blacksmith shop there but gradually turned it into an automobile repair shop. By 1911 he was a dealer, selling E.M.F. autos and later, Studebakers. Before long Frank rented his garage to Lester Lawrence, a brother and brother-in-law of the owners of the Walnut Creek Meat Company. Lester remained a tenant of Frank Botelho until July 4, 1937. Lester's son, James, remembers the moving day. "All of the work benches were on casters. We'd tied them together single file and drove down Main Street with our tow truck. We pulled them down to the new show room and shop that Father's brother, Harry, had built next to the El Rey Theater." (To make room for a new building on the southwest corner of North Main and Civic Drive, wreckers tore down the show room, shop, and the El Rey Theater in December 1983.)

Another family of Portuguese ancestry who made lasting impressions on Walnut Creek were the Silveiras. Joseph C. Silveira was born in Folsom, California in 1876 of parents who came from the Azore Island of Flores before 1870. His parents moved to Fairfield about 1882, where Joe went to high school during 1894-98. The family was poor enough that he did janitorial work at the school to pay for his books. After high school he went to the University of California at Berkeley for several semesters. Tiring of the regimentation of the classroom and facing too many years of study, he went back to Solano County, passed a teachers' examination and taught in a small school. He soon recognized he had too little patience with children, particularly slow learners, and left the school after one year.

On May 20, 1900 Silveira married Constance Freitas and took her to San Francisco, where he went to work as a bookkeeper for the Pacific Pump and Windmill Company.

In 1903 the young man bought a faltering general merchandise and grocery store in Walnut Creek and named it the Valley Mercantile Company. The building stood at 1403 North Main Street. In 1910 he moved it to a corner location he bought from Fred Geary: the southwest corner of Main and Cypress. His store fronted on Main, and along the Cypress Street side he built a dock where customers could load their wagons. Alongside the dock he installed a horse trough.

Silveira had a very good well at his house and a poor one at his store. His house occupied the northeast quarter of the block bounded by Mt. Diablo Boulevard, Locust, Olympic and California streets. He had a plumber install pipe from his house down to the store, almost three blocks away.

Mr. and Mrs. Silveira's friendly and accommodating ways increased their trade. Both worked in the store. Mrs. Silveira was the first merchant in town to offer the Delineator Magazine and Butterick patterns in a day when women made most of their clothes. She stocked yardage goods and would give whatever time a lady wished to choose her material. She helped those cutting out fabrics for the first time, making herself unusually valuable to many of her customers. In the days before self-service (1940), a counter separated the customer from the merchandise. Mrs. Silveira, hard of hearing and unable to understand many of her Japanese customers, gave them the freedom of coming behind the counter to help themselves.

Vivian, youngest of the Silveira's children, remembers one of her duties as a young girl. "We kept a milk cow where we lived. There was plenty of pasturage on our neighbors' lots. My brother Ed would milk her and I would deliver the milk [ca. 1920]. I remember two of our customers were the Mauzys and the Nougarys."

The Valley Mercantile prospered by filling another need. There was no bank in those days and as a convenience to the townspeople, Silveira offered a banking service. No one questioned his integrity. Customers deposited sums which he entered in a separate ledger, and he paid out withdrawals whenever asked. When he had accumulated more cash than he wished to keep in the store's safe, he would go by train to Martinez and deposit the surplus there.

Daughter Vivian has a vivid recollection of a fatal incident occurring in their store. "A Portuguese family in Moraga Valley, the Domingos, instead of rushing for medical help in Berkeley, through the old tunnel, drove their buggy with their critically ill son to our store. Dr. Leech was out on a call and before he returned, the boy died. I remember them carrying the body down Main Street to the mortuary next to where Arthur's Deli is now."

Joe Silveira's banking service served the town so well that he and some of his business friends formed the San Ramon Valley Bank in June 1907, with $25,000 capital. He remained active in its day-to-day affairs, serving for a long time as cashier.

The first building to house the bank stood on the south side of Duncan Street midway between Main Street and the creek. It measured eighteen feet wide and twenty-five feet long. Within a year Silveira established the fledgling bank in a modern building on the

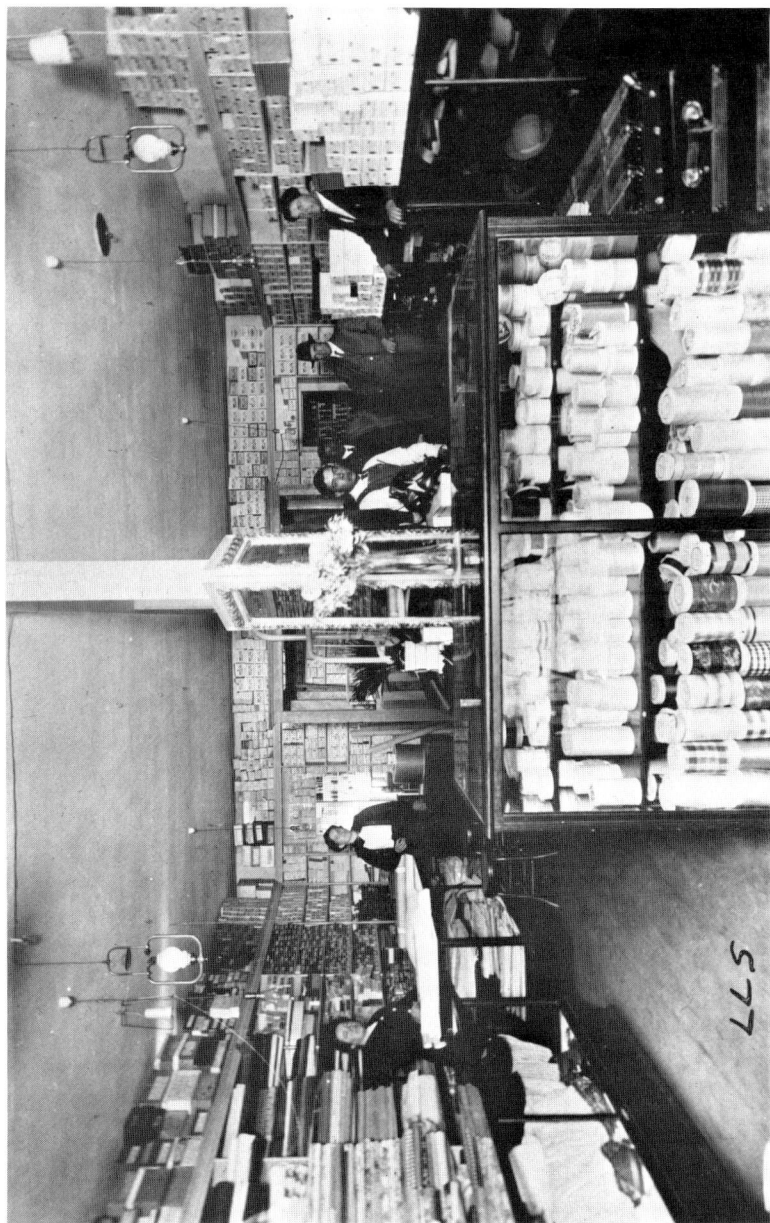

Valley Mercantile Company, Jos. Silveira, proprietor. Fancy wear department, 1907.

southeast corner of Main and Duncan streets. Next door to the south Judge Duncan presided over the justice court, and Harlan's Livery Stable was the next structure south. In 1907 the bank established a Danville branch and in 1912 opened another in Concord. That same year R. N. Burgess of Walnut Creek established the First National Bank of Walnut Creek. In 1925 Silveira's bank took it over in a merger. In 1927 the San Ramon Valley Bank sold out to the Liberty Bank, which in turn became the Bank of Italy in 1930. Within a few years a new name appeared on all Bank of Italy branches: Bank of America.

Joe Machado's son, Frank Marshall, Walnut Creek's leading real estate broker both before and after incorporation in 1914, also served as the town's treasurer. As such he retained a desk in the tiny town office next to Judge Duncan's court. He frequently transacted business there until a competitor complained of unfair influence by a city official, one doing private business from a public office. Marshall acquiesced and promptly opened his own office elsewhere.

The Perreira family grazed several hundred acres of poor crop land, fine for grazing, at the head of San Luis Road. Today multiple dwellings cover their hillsides.

Joseph Oliveira came from Pico Island in the Azores about 1898. He worked for a time at the Sulphur Spring Ranch and also for the orchardist, Eli Hutchinson. He married in 1901. About 1915 Oliveira had accumulated enough money to buy fifty acres of what is today the heart of Lafayette's Glenside District.

Frank Borges came in 1890 and in 1899 bought a 700-acre spread, now known as the Borges Ranch, in Ygnacio Valley, operated today by the City of Walnut Creek as part of the park system.

John Bello, another Portuguese rancher, raised stock on land he owned at the end of Springbrook Road.

Raul Machado, a blacksmith from the Azores, first went to work for Joseph Oliveira. Next, Oliveira got him a job working in Joe Botelho's blacksmith shop. In his early and late hours he milked cows for O. Holmes. Finally Machado opened his own blacksmith shop on Mt. Diablo Boulevard and operated it until recent years, behind the Union Oil service station at Mt. Diablo and California Drive. He

San Ramon Valley Bank, 1908, at southwest corner Main and Duncan.

retired to his Newell Avenue home, where he still tends his extensive rose garden.

Joe Souza grazed cattle on several hundred acres of land bounded on the west by Pleasant Hill Road.

Joe Gomes built a home on Locust near Cypress after a flood at Pacheco washed him out.

Joe Dias, another cattleman, also moved into town and built his house on the same block as Gomes.

Frank Rose, a saloon keeper from early days, maintained his bar on the southwest corner of Main and Mt. Diablo Boulevard. On the Main Street side he had a horse trough which was filled by a hand pump on the well.

Frank Macedo, another Azorian, successfully operated a dairy here. He came from Pico Island and, when he first arrived, went to work for Eli Hutchinson, the Ygnacio Valley orchardist. He and his wife, Isabel, saved their money and bought acreage, part of Captain Fales' farm. Today Lilac Drive and the freeway cross the eastern end of the property. His dairy was west of the freeway. When Fales owned the land he dedicated a small plot to the county for a cemetery, even allowing space for a potter's field for the friendless poor. In recent years a story about the cemetery has gone around, involving a ditch digger machine operator and two laborers, one black and one white. The operator tore open a lead-lined coffin, and the white man gasped, paled and dropped his shovel in the rush to leave the scene. He ran down the grade while his black counterpart stood there shaking with laughter.

Macedo was very successful, so much so that when the fraternal benefit society, Iramandade do Divino Espirito Santo, needed money in 1973 to improve its hall next to the Catholic Church, he loaned this Portuguese society $117,500.

There were many examples of Portuguese youths who established themselves with dignity and financial success alongside their Anglo counterparts. One who succeeded in spite of a handicap was John Serpa.

When John Serpa was a young man, barely out of his teens, he was known around town as an accomplished mechanic on gasoline engines. H. H. Bancroft employed him off and on during the year to service and keep the engines on his equipment in working order.

One morning in about 1918, John set out to work on a spray rig engine. The engine was running and the Japanese foreman, Yasuhe Sakamoto, shouted above the exhaust, "Turn it off first, Johnny!" But Johnny didn't turn it off. Instead he put his left hand down in the machinery. With a scream he pulled back, tugging against something which gripped his hand. Sakamoto shut off the engine and turned to steady the reeling Johnny. The boy screamed, "Oh! Oh! My God!" Sakamoto picked him up and threw him down on a flatbed Model T truck. Johnny fought to rise, thrashing and twisting in pain. Blood was spurting from the stump at the end of his arm. Japanese field hands nearby ran over and at a nod from their foreman they tied the screaming victim as best they could to the truck bed. "Kill me! Kill me! I can't . . ." Mrs. Sakamoto rushed up with a bottle of sake and poured it over the gaping stump. Her husband started the truck and with two men holding Johnny as firmly as they could, started for Walnut Creek and Dr. Leech's office. Fortunately Dr. Leech was in and he administered opiates and a tourniquet. When Mr. Sakamoto, shaken as he was by the ordeal, returned to the Bancroft farm, his first act was to find a shovel and bury Johnny's hand in a spot he reported later as "beside a eucalyptus tree."

John Serpa made a full recovery and did very well. He and his brother Manuel opened an automobile repair shop and operated it profitably for a number of years. Their garage was on the east side of Main Street next to the south corner of Mt. Diablo Boulevard. They took on an automobile agency, but after a disagreement decided to go their own ways. John Serpa opened a Buick agency in Walnut Creek, selling cars for more than eighteen years. He then moved to Martinez, opened a new dealership and became a leading citizen of that town.

The spiritual life for the families of Portuguese heritage centered around St. Mary's Catholic Church. The focal point of their social life was the building next door, on the south side of the church. It

81

housed the Holy Ghost Society, Iramandade do Divino Espirito Santo (I.D.E.S.). The Walnut Creek branch of this society was formed on October 16, 1898. Its founding officers included President Antonio M. Oliveira, Vice-President Antonio Mendonca, Secretary M. F. Coelho and Treasurer Joaquin de Mello.

While the I.D.E.S. is a fraternal and beneficial society still in existence, its annual celebration is a religious one: the Holy Ghost Festival. It is usually held on Pentecost Sunday, forty days after Easter.

The religious basis goes back to a famine in Portugal in the eighteenth century. At one time hunger and starvation were so widespread that Queen Isabella, a deeply religious sovereign, prayed to God for succor for her people. In her prayers she promised to deliver her crown jewels if He would somehow send food to her people. Simultaneously a storm came up which blew food-laden ships, which had been becalmed for weeks, into port. The queen had the food distributed free to all the suffering people.

Farmers from a wide area around Walnut Creek gave cattle, lambs, hogs and goats. Farmers barbecued and served thousands who came to the celebration, but much of the meat was auctioned off to benefit the society. As many as 4,000 persons sat down to eat the food prepared by the generous hardworking men and women of the I.D.E.S. Society. Carnival operators set up rides, games of chance and a merry-go-round.

On both days of the celebration, a parade with many horse entries would pass through town. The parades included several marching bands: the Pittsburg Band, the Concord Drum Corps, and the Moose Drill Team. Saturday night and Sunday afternoon featured a band concert and the free barbecue. A dance capped both schedules.

I.D.E.S. members regularly chose a queen to be crowned at the festival. The crowning of the queen and the procession of her court and rod bearers always highlighted the final evening, climaxed by a special mass at the church.

Festivals were held in Walnut Creek from 1898 until 1973 except for the four years of World War II, 1942 to 1945.

As the years went on, fewer and fewer sons farmed as their fathers had, and the number of donated animals dropped lower and lower. Unfortunately, the number of people who came to celebrate increased. The expenses grew higher and higher and the number who defrayed them dwindled. As a consequence, the last Holy Ghost Celebration in Walnut Creek was held on March 1, 1973.

The festival continues to be held in some communities where tradition is still upheld. The contemporary festival, in part, supplies generous helpings of barbecued meat free to every attendee. A large wreath of sweet bread, ruska, is auctioned off for the Holy Ghost. Mint and cinnamon are sprinkled on bread soaked in beef broth.

(For a list of ninety-five Walnut Creek residents of Portuguese ancestry, see page 266 of the appendix.)

Old (Inter-city) Tunnel, the first to connect Alameda and Contra Costa counties, ca. 1909.

THE OLD TUNNEL

The plan to build a tunnel through the Oakland hills was re-
vived once every ten years after the initial public meeting of
1860. Nevertheless nothing came of the periodic agitation
until the loss of business in Oakland stores to San Francisco merchants
spurred the plan in 1900.

Ever since the Southern Pacific Railroad inaugurated passenger
service to San Francisco in 1891, the comfortable two-hour ride from
Walnut Creek to San Francisco took trade away from Oakland.
Shoppers could leave Walnut Creek on the early train, arrive in San
Francisco about 9:00 A.M. and spend the entire day shopping and
dining, then leave at 4:00 P.M. and arrive back home at 6:30 P.M.

Oakland merchants goaded their supervisors to shorten the buggy
ride to Walnut Creek by building a tunnel. Both counties agreed to the
plan, but the Contra Costa County treasury didn't have its share of the
money for the project. The county offered what it could and an eager
group of Oakland merchants under the banner "Merchants Exchange"
donated the rest, about one-fifth of the total. When the bore opened in
1903, Supervisor James Stow shared the spotlight with his colleagues.

Engineers located the western entrance of the bore on the road
they named Tunnel Road, today called Old Tunnel Road. The
concrete monument which was unveiled at the opening ceremony in
1903 still stands near the entrance in 1984. It is inscribed with the names
of the supervisors of both counties.

The eastern opening is about 150 feet higher and almost directly
above the Contra Costa end of the Caldecott Tunnel.

The new tunnel allowed loaded wagons, rather than driving over
the Moraga Road through Canyon, to shorten the trip by three miles

and save 320 feet of climbing. It was wide enough to barely allow two buggies to pass if the drivers were careful. Wagons had to wait for another to clear before entering the tunnel.

There was no illumination in the tunnel for the first ten years and only when the Canary Cottage at the east end of the bore opened, selling soft drinks and sandwiches, was electricity available. Then, when wires with bare globes were hung from the ceiling, the owner of the Cottage was given free electricity on the condition he would replace burned out light globes as needed. This he did without the use of a ladder. When a wagon loaded high with hay approached the tunnel, he would climb to the top of the load and call out for the driver to pull ahead. When he reached the burned out globe he would call out for the driver to stop and replace the bulb.

A Rossmoor resident, Mrs. Alice Russi, in 1983 recalls how Supervisor Stow aided her father. "My father farmed in Happy Valley (Lafayette) just prior to 1900. Formerly he had a store in the village and was fairly well known. Apparently he needed a job to help my mother raise us four children. I know he asked Supervisor Stow for a job when work on the tunnel started about 1901. The work involved scraping dirt and mud out, with horses dragging scrapers.

"That summer [1901] my mother packed us all up and with our wagon loaded down with cots, bedding, two tents, a kitchen stove and supplies, we drove our team through Orinda up to near the Buckley Ranch near where the work was to start. Buckley's farm house sat just above where the east entrance of the Caldecott Tunnel is now. Father set up camp near a strawberry patch I can still see. Mr. Buckley posted a 'Poisoned Berries' sign on his patch. He wore a long beard and looked severe to us kids. Mother would drive our team into Berkeley for supplies. Father, who was born in Lafayette, stood just under six feet, weighed maybe 185 pounds and wore a mustache.

"A creek ran downhill nearby and I can remember how one young man would end his day. After loosening his horses from the scraper he would bring them down to the creek where a shallow dam held back a pool of water. After a day of dragging the muck out of the tunnel his horses would be smeared up to their bellies in it. He would have them stand in the pool while he washed them clean. He did it every evening. We children lived a wonderful life all summer. Father came and ate lunch with us and did no chores after dinner as he would have done at home. I've always felt grateful to Mr. Stow for getting Father the job back then."

Holdups of slow moving drivers was not uncommon. Wagon drivers, usually wearing overalls, seldom had much money on them. Automobile owners obviously were better off. A report of one such armed robbery appeared in the Martinez paper.

At 2 o'clock on Thursday, June 22, 1911 a masked gunman forced Frank McClane out of his automobile as he approached the intercity tunnel. The highwayman forced him to stand at the side of the road while he searched McClane's pockets and took his watch and small change. The man told his victim to drive on and not look back as he disappeared in the brush.

This is the second affair of the kind in this area.

Contra Costa Gazette, June 23, 1911

EARLY FESTIVALS

Before the Grape Festival in 1911 and the first Walnut Festival in 1936, the 450 Walnut Creek residents enthusiastically staged a fair they named the Moonlight Circus in China Alley. Cypress Street was China Alley in 1894.

The site they chose was at the corner of Cypress and Locust, between the homes of Mr. Williams and Mr. Burpee, on opposite corners.

Ladies of the Presbyterian Church who organized the circus allocated space for a score of booths. A speaker's platform was decorated with colored Chinese lanterns, their candles flickering in the breeze of June 22. Coal oil lanterns lit each booth.

According to the *Walnut Creek Sentinel*, the rope at the entrance dropped at 8:00 P.M. With Louise Johnson giving the welcoming address, the show started. The crowd surged forward, swelled with curious visitors from San Ramon, Alhambra, Moraga and Diablo valleys. Chilled by an unseasonably cold wind, the people spent their money slowly. "Icy wind blew through the whiskers of such as had them [yet] the ice cream and lemonade stands did a flourishing business while chills and ague played leap frog down his [*sic*] back."

May Ford and Hattie Geary sold lemonade, and if the customer wanted pineapple syrup they poured it without charge. "Mesdames Burpee and Williams doled out liberal dishes of ice cream with the invitation to 'help yourself to cake.' Mesdames Webb and Shuey headed the coffee booth, but the soap bubble booth was a failure. The brisk wind was too much of a discouragement. Misses Johnson and Palmer sold plenty of popcorn. Weird notes of celestial music filled the air as did the aroma of Mr. Williams nearby slaughter house."

The "Freak Booth" did a steady business all evening. It presented a "Bearded Lady," the original "Babes in Wood," "Chang the Chinese Giant" and two *imported* "German Song and Dance Artists." Over in Mrs. Williams' parlor, Paul Bancroft explained his picture exhibition of views he took at the World's Columbian Exposition held in Chicago the year before. Bancroft also gave two solo performances, the first a recitation and the other a violin obligato.

After the town's violin teacher, Professor Louis Proll, and his orchestra entertained from the stage, Griffing Bancroft gave a long address, introducing a paper model of a Mexican ship hanging from a beam over his head. At the end of his speech he invited spectators to bid for a chance, after being blindfolded, to come up and knock the ship down. Lively bidding ended at seventy-five cents to W. S. Burpee who, blindfolded, failed. The town's popular barber, Vicente Martinez, cracked open the hull, scattering candy around the tent. Professor Proll scored an artistic representation of the hula-hula dance. Colonel Dunnings as the bearded lady was perfect.

A report of the event concludes with the comment, "Ladies of the Presbyterian Church deserve great appreciation for their untiring efforts. Total receipts $64."

Walnut Creek has had a love affair with parades and festivals at least as far back as The Circus in China Alley.

Nowadays volunteers still give their time and, with more experience now, put on an annual festival which sometimes clears more than $50,000 to benefit community concerns.

The second celebration in Walnut Creek was the Grape Festival of 1911. Grapes brought in more earnings to local farmers than any other single harvest at the time. There were other things to celebrate. Electricity came to Walnut Creek. It brought lights to see by and motors to pump the well water—only two of the benefits of the arrival of power through the wires. Too, the Oakland and Antioch electric trains, fast and frequent, came to town in 1911. No matter that there were no more than 500 people living in Walnut Creek—a Grape

Festival would attract more. And so it did. Another thing made people aware of Walnut Creek that year. *The Contra Costa Courier-Journal,* the new weekly newspaper, commenced publication and succeeded where two others had failed.

Everyone around town knew that big changes and growth were only a year or two away—cause for celebration. They decorated Main Street from Mt. Diablo to Civic. On October 5, at the entrance to town, on Main after making the turn from Mt. Diablo, two grape arbors stretched across the street, anchored at the four corners by towering stacks of baled hay. No ordinary bales were these, but five wire bales, each weighing 100 pounds. The four stacks were made of forty-eight bales. Every twenty-five feet down Main, on both sides of the street, stood stacks six bales high.

The day of the big parade it was as though everyone owning an automobile showed it off. Men and children with horses decorated their bridles, curried and combed their mounts and paraded the length of Main Street. Grape vines hung from porches, eaves and store fronts. The parade was led by an open automobile (there were no others then) driven by the assistant district attorney and local lawyer, Alfred S. Ormsby. Sitting high on the folded down top was the queen of the festival, Mary Ridgeway, a young and attractive bookkeeper. Her princesses sat on either side of her: Misses Sybil Brown of Lafayette and Gertrude A. Walker of Walnut Creek.

Architect Woolletta drew up the plans for the festival and Director-General Fred S. Brooks carried them out. F. H. Snively got together one of the finest poultry exhibits ever seen in California. "Constable Arthur Williams deserves especial commendation as regards policing the Carnival," reported the *Courier.* "Only one case of pickpocket was found and the man [was] caught.

"R. N. Burgess Co. subscribed largely and did everything they could to make the Carnival a success."

Prizes for the best wines at the Grape Festival went to: first, Italian Swiss Colony; second, Naphtaly; third, John Swett and Company. The prizes for walnuts: first, Ygnacio Valley; second, Concord and

Clayton Valley; and third, Alamo. The first prize for olive oil and nursery stock was picked off by Thomas Duane. The prize for grape juice went Martinez way to John Swett and Company.

In spite of all the parade entries, the baseball game between the married men from Concord and Walnut Creek was the most popular event. The second was a tilting contest on horseback in which two horsemen tried to knock each other off their mounts with brooms. *The* feature of the Grape Festival of 1911 was the "aeroplane." The plane was a pusher biplane made in Pittsburg, California, and flown by Weldon Cook of Oakland. It was the first flying machine most of the festival goers had ever seen. After all, only three years earlier, Wilbur Wright set the altitude record of 361 feet. Cook took up one passenger at a time and on the ground S. G. Whittelsey, Walnut Creek surveyor, handled the daring, eager crowd. The Grape Festival allowed everyone who had anything to display, clothing or means of transportation or anything else, to show it off. The event was a great success.

The next three years there were not enough new things to celebrate. Then Europe fell under the shadow of war and no one cared about another festival. After World War I times were hard; wine grapes as a crop were doomed when Congress passed the Volstead Act which prohibited the manufacture of all alcoholic beverages. Farmers pulled out their vines and started planting walnuts. Money was just too scarce to spend on a celebration—"celebrate what?"

LASTING MEMORIES

To say you were going to Walnut Creek for a drive anytime between 1920 and 1945 was almost to confess you would stop at the Bradley Brothers soda fountain and candy store on Main Street. For a time the brothers operated the only ice cream and confectionery in town.

Ed Bradley was born in North Carolina in 1882, went to business school in Los Angeles in 1905, and spent four years in Burlingame before coming to Walnut Creek in 1913. He went into business with George Emery in a small shop next to the Walnut Creek Meat Market, selling ice cream and notions.

In 1915 Ed's brother, Guy, came to town. He bought out Emery. The two brothers got $2,800 together and bought the lot at 1370-74 North Main Street in the center of the business district. They went into debt to build a two-story building and did a profitable business right from the start. Several years later, when the cashier of the San Ramon Valley Bank pointed out how much more business they could do in larger quarters, they assumed the mountainous debt of $6,000 to add on to their store. Their store was soon 100 feet wide, as large as any in town.

The Bradley brothers expanded their merchandise line to include candy, stationery, notions and ice cream. They installed a 2½-gallon electric ice cream machine in their window and prepared many of the flavors they used. They claimed to be the first to offer pumpkin flavored ice cream and introduced it one Thanksgiving season.

Bradley's had a marble-topped counter with revolving stools and glass-topped wire-legged tables with wire-legged chairs installed near the front windows.

93

In 1916 the brothers founded Walnut Creek's first telephone exchange in a back corner of the store.

The Bradley Bothers confectionery was a mecca for Sunday drivers after 1916. With competition from Lommel's Creamery beginning in 1940, the brothers began thinking of retirement. They closed the store in 1945.

Guy Bradley graciously assumed the title of "Mr. Fixit" to all the widows around town, until he died in 1955 at age seventy-nine.

Ed Bradley celebrated his one hundredth birthday in August of 1983. He died three months later.

Early Walnut Creek resident Carroll Walker recalls how children's pranks sometimes created misunderstandings between their parents and neighbors during World War I.

Emotions ran high between the various nationalities and their relative attitudes about the war, and they often colored everyday happenings.

Three boys used to walk up on the ridge behind Lacassie Avenue. At one point, straight down the hill, three little ranches cornered together: Mrs. Lacassie's, Mr. Stein's and Mr. Bello's. Mrs. Lacassie was a French woman, Mr. Stein was German, and Mr. Bello was Portuguese. All three of these farmers had cattle grazing there, milk cows primarily. Mr. Stein had a small herd of Holsteins of which he was very proud and he frequently boasted that this German breed was most superior. There were quite a few rocks on the hill, and these young boys, in the manner of most, were fooling around one day and decided to roll some of the boulders down the hill.

As it happened, the boulders were rather large and one of them tore through a fence. This scared the kids pretty badly so they skedaddled home, being sure that none of them would ever tell who tore down the fence. A day or two later they each began to hear what the results were. Their parents started talking about someone who had torn down the fence, and Mr. Stein was positive it was either Mr. Bello or Mrs. Lacassie since the cattle all mixed together, and he was sure they were trying to get his bull to breed with their cattle because of its exceptional quality. Mrs. Lacassie

94

and Mr. Bello, on the other hand, were just as certain that the German was trying to steal their cows because of the rich milk they gave. Of course the story grew hotter and hotter and the three exchanged some angry words. Accusations were flung and ardently denied, but the fences were repaired and relative peace returned. There was no indication whatever that they ever figured out how the fences really were broken down. The boys thought this was a huge joke, and so after a few weeks they decided to try it again. Sure enough, there was a repetition of the same heated feelings. The rest of that summer the boys pulled the same stunt three or four times until the fun wore off.

Walker has more memories of pre-World War I days.

Before World War I the army sent troops out from the Presidio in San Francisco for maneuvers. You must remember back in those days there were lots of rolling hills and fields and only a handful of people in the area. They set up their operations above the Bello ranch west of downtown in one of the gullies. This was for target practice and they set up cardboard targets about twenty-four by thirty-six inches to represent the size of a man. These were set on stakes on the east slope of the little canyon. The troops hid in the gullies on the west side of the hill across from the targets. However, in addition, there were two or three machine gun nests on top of the hill, hidden in some of the large oak trees.

Again, three or four of the kids decided to climb up on top of the hill and just watch to see what was going on, playing war being a universal attraction to young boys. The boys, of course, did not know about the machine guns hidden on top of the hill. Sure enough, the shooting started and as the targets went down one by one and the advance wasn't stopped, all of a sudden the machine guns started. The kids had never even heard of a machine gun then, but typical farm boys knew that no gun could shoot like that. They were scared to death and turned around and took off for home like bats out of hell, so to speak. The soldiers of course knew they were there and were watching them, and as the kids ran they could hear the soldiers laughing.

Even then the gossip ran high about the boys who didn't go to war. One well-to-do man from San Francisco came over to Walnut Creek and bought a ranch. He had a son just the right age to enlist.

However, the father put his son on the ranch and the boy was classified as a rancher and not required to serve in the military.

The father bought a pickup truck, a small one, and they put two or three sacks of grain in the back of it. The son did all his driving in the little truck with the grain in back. The townspeople were prone to say the grain sacks were never changed, never moved, and eventually they wore out and the grain began to spill. Then the boy would put in a new sack. This went on until the war ended.

Charles Reed, now retired, but still living in Walnut Creek, remembers some highlights of his boyhood in the early 1920s. "Mr. Silver, who had the *Courier-Journal*, also printed the advertising posters for the Ramona Theater. He'd have several of us kids ride the running boards of his car, and whenever the driver stopped alongside a pole we'd hop off and tack a poster on it."

He remembers the baseball field where Gemco's gas station is now. "Out at the end of left field a high water tank was the best place to watch the action. The kids climbed up there, filling the platform, every game." At that time the Walnut Creek Cannery covered the area where Gemco is now. At harvest time, from 1921 well into the 1950s, odors blew downtown when they canned tomato and cocktail sauce. The bleach used at the Walnut Association processing plant, along with the tomato smell, made an objectionable stench all through town.

Reed chuckled at his recollection of the town barber in the '20s. "His shop was on the east side of Main just south of the Ramona. It was a real tonsorial parlor. It was in a little fifteen-foot by fifteen-foot whitewashed building. John Bednary, a Hungarian by birth, was a polished gentleman, who, away from his work, dressed as we imagined a count would. The ladies knew him for his tango. But John cut hair slowly, as though he was an artist when he shaved someone. Mr. Osborne, the Coast Counties Gas Company boss, pulled pranks on John every once in a while. Once Mr. Osborne ordered a haircut, shave and facial massage. He gave John a postdated check, on purpose, to pay the bill. We all heard how high John blew when the bank refused to accept the check."

Reed recalls another prank Osborne played: "John was so slow,

Osborne once brought his lunch with him and the others who came in congratulated him on his foresight. But John thought him rude. Everyone really liked Bednary—he was a great favorite."

Reed adds several more recollections of the 1920s. "In my early days Locust and Main streets were called 'Back and Front streets.' I can still see the blacksmith at Main and Bonanza in his leather apron looking up with his tongs in one hand as we kids taunted him. He'd make out to chase us though he never actually did."

Regarding the unpaved streets in town, Reed says, "In 1916 the county paved the road from Concord to our city limits to about where Civic crosses Main. Main Street remained unpaved for another five years."

Helen Emanuels also remembers those dusty streets. "Back when I was about thirteen a group of six of us rode into town from Ygnacio Valley, one summer day. It was the day before they started paving Main Street.

"My friends were Lucy and Anne Bancroft, their cousin Martin Bancroft, 'Dinks' Dillon and Paul Lawrence. We rode our horses in just to have a soda.

"Once we reached Main Street we raced each other down the street. Our hair flew and we whooped and hollered all the way. We reined up short in front of Bradley's, kicking up clouds of dust. I can still see one of the Bradley brothers, in his white apron, coming out of the store to see what all the commotion was about."

Another person who remembers unpaved Main Street in 1920 is Ming Danno of Pebble Beach. Then a teenage cowboy, born and raised at Port Chicago, Ming rode for the cattleman Frank Dutra.

"Frank regularly sold herds of cattle to a Hayward butcher. He always hired a bunch of us to drive them there from the hills east of Ygnacio Valley. We'd ride Ygnacio Valley Road, through Walnut Creek on Main Street, and then by way of Crow Canyon Road to the Hayward slaughter house. We'd have the cattle penned up the night before, and by starting at daybreak, at least in the summer time, if we kept them moving we could have them penned up before dark.

"But going through Walnut Creek always slowed us up. It seemed like whatever we did to prevent it, some of them would break away down by the old Catholic Church on South Main Street [Hendrick's Piano Company now]. Just before we crossed the bridge over Las Trampas Creek, between there and the church, the sight of green grass and the smell of water in the creek was too much for cattle just off dry range. You can imagine the hollering and cussing that went on before we got them going again. Of course the cattle made a mess of Main Street.

"I remember one time we had a herd of bulls to drive through town. We came in on Ygnacio Valley Road as usual [Civic Drive now], and as we hit Main Street, one big bull tried to escape us and ran into the Chevrolet garage. As I started in after him an old-fashioned square monkey wrench came flying out the door. It missed the bull and nearly hit me. I went in after him on my little Nevada mustang and roped him around the horns. What with cars everywhere, and a light horse, I can tell you I had one whale of a time getting that bull back out to the street. Then, how was I supposed to get my rope off him?

"Well, one of the other cowboys got a rope on a hind leg and we stretched him out—me in front pulling on his horns and my buddy in back stretching a leg out.

"Finally, a third one of us got off his horse and slowly approached the bull from the front. When he got close enough I slacked off my line maybe six inches or so, just enough for him to tear the rope off the horns. Then my friend backed away immediately, you can be sure of that. We tore up Main Street pretty bad that morning."

WALNUT FESTIVALS

*I*n the days after the 1911 Grape Festival and before the 1936 Walnut Festival, the men around town were hard put for entertainment. The Ramona Theater, Grimes and Nottingham's Pool Hall, and in season, the Willow Athletic Club's weekly baseball game were their usual diversions. Occasionally they came up with something original.

The first and only Frog Derby in Walnut Creek, one such "original diversion," was staged on May 12, 1932. Elliot Mauzy tells of his father's entry. "Dad made a trip up to Angel's Camp where he bought himself what was supposed to be a jumping frog. The only trouble was I don't think anyone ever told the frog. The contest was a big event for the town—anything was big during the Great Depression. Anyway, Dad's frog wasn't much of a jumper and he didn't win anything."

Finally, early in 1935, a group made plans to hold another festival, but along in July they called it off; no one was willing to put up money for it.

In 1936, fully twenty-five years after the Grape Festival of 1911, people felt the old urge once again. Work on the Caldecott Tunnel was well along and Walnut Creek would fill with more daytime visitors than it would ever know. Thousands would sell their homes in Berkeley and Oakland and move out once the tunnel opened. Such was the feeling around town.

On Friday, October 2, 1936, the first Walnut Festival opened. Hazel Avise, chairwoman, welcomed the participants in front of the old Walnut House on Locust Street.

Elmer Cameron led the parade and, atop his palomino, Johnny Walker led the 200 equestrian entries.

Walker, son of the pioneer James T. Walker, had lived on his father's stock ranch on North Gate Road with his mother until she sold the place in 1908. His mare foaled every year up there but every year mountain lions came down to his corrals and killed the foal. One year, his last on the ranch, Johnny virtually slept with the young horse, protecting it. The palomino he rode in this parade was that same one he had slept with.

The parade entry of the Mt. Diablo Men's Garden Club was an automobile completely covered with flowers. However, the winning float was another automobile, "decorated with fresh flowers and containing the beautiful little daughters of its members," reported the *Courier-Journal*. Flags flew from every post, eave and telephone pole in town. Veterans and fraternal organizations either had floats or a marching entry. A group of black veterans from Oakland and even a group of kilted bagpipers marched in the parade. The judges awarded the prize for the best out-of-town float to Antioch, and Concord received the second place ribbon for its entry, "Wisteria Pergola."

Saturday was Children's Day, with a pet parade, a pie-eating contest and several kinds of races.

The feature of the Saturday night schedule was the eruption of red fire from the peak of Mt. Diablo, a wooden billboard replica of the real mountain. All through the evening the Mt. Diablo Band played from the American Legion's compound, "Days of '49."

Mayor Bradley crowned the queen that last night in what a newspaper reporter of the day described as "the huge exhibition tent." Dancing went on until midnight.

After the last sound died away Sunday night, and the exhibition tent came down, the Walnut Festival Association totaled its accounts. Gross income $1,000, expenses $600, net $400. The Festival Association's goal had been to raise enough to buy the city a municipal park. That would have to wait for another day.

Elliott Mauzy recalls some changes in the Walnut Festival format in later years.

"When Marshall Maguire was president, in 1948, I think, we held it in the city park. That year the PTA wanted a booth, but first we had to

1911 Grape Festival. Looking north on Main Street from Mt. Diablo Boulevard. Mary Ridgeway, queen. Alfred Ormsby, driver.

have a talk with the city fathers. They objected to giving permission because it would open up booths to others. 'We may not be able to handle the crowds.'

"As you know, that's what makes it such a success—the more booths the merrier. That year my wife, Lucille, was PTA president. She had over 400 cakes donated and we couldn't begin to handle the requests for coffee. I went down to our plumbing shop and brought up the biggest gas burner [for lead melting] we had and turned it into a water heater. The PTA booth was the only food booth that year."

No one could have predicted how successful the association would ultimately be from those early Walnut Festivals. In the intervening years the income of the non-profit private association has built the building which houses the Clay Arts classes; given seats for the Civic Arts Theater; given funds to the Alexander Lindsay Junior Museum; built restroom facilities and furnished playground equipment at Civic Park; and funded a swimming pool and lights at a local high school.

In the 1960s the Walnut Festival Association donated $105,000 to buy a baseball field of nine acres adjacent to Heather Farm Park and bought bleachers for Civic Park and the Clarke Pool.

In the 1970s they spent $18,000 to move the Senior Citizens Building to Heather Farm, where it now houses the Festival Association's offices.

In the 1980s the association bought permanent fencing for Heather Farm and donated $24,000 to the city for vandal-free bathrooms there.

Eighty-five charities benefit from the food and game concessions at the Walnut Festival. This annual affair is the area's largest single source of funds for these charities and civic projects. In just the past twelve years more than $500,000 has been earned by clubs at the local event.

Surely the volunteers who make the Walnut Festival such a regular success are among Walnut Creek's most important citizens.

A list of presidents of the Walnut Festival Association from 1947 to 1984 appears on page 265 of the appendix.

EDUCATION

The Central School grew from an average daily attendance of twenty-six pupils in 1867-68 to thirty-three ten years later. Even then the need for better facilities existed, so obvious that a report to the county superintendent of schools in 1877 included the declaration, "The District does not have suitable accommodations for all who wanted to attend." After the trustees had the second room added (1885-86) the average daily attendance climbed to seventy-three.

The school never did have classrooms enough. Usually the voters failed to approve the bonds on the first few ballots and sometimes the trustees were timid about asking the electorate for the necessary funds.

On June 6, 1911 the voters, by a sixty-eight to eight count, approved a measure calling for a $20,000 indebtedness for two more classrooms, making four in all. Even with this addition completed, overcrowding resulted soon again. Charles Reed relates his childhood experience. "Because the Walnut Creek Grammar School [the name "Central" was dropped in 1912] was overcrowded in 1911, the third and fourth grades had to go to class in the Masonic Hall, over Dr. Potter's office on Main Street [about 1381 Main Street]. They went to classes there for four or five years. During that time School Street was renamed Locust."

Rented quarters may have been used longer because the old school wasn't turned into a ten-room building until 1928. The ten rooms included a 750-seat auditorium, gymnasium, administration offices and a nurse's room. The improvements cost $45,000.

The teachers for the year 1928 were: Robert E. Gibson, principal, Miss Marion Harris, eighth grade, Mrs. Mabel E. McLaggen, seventh grade, Mrs. Bertha McNeil, sixth grade, Miss Florence Rule, fourth and fifth grades, Miss J. Neilsen, third and fourth grades, Miss Elizabeth Collins, second grade.

Three hundred and forty-five students attended the school in 1930 plus seventy more in a kindergarten.

Fortunately, the Great Depression hit *after* the voters approved the bond issue and the children occupied the building. Teachers' salaries dropped in the following years. In 1930, the superintendent, R. E. Gibson, received $3,180 but in 1936, with the lesser title of supervising principal, he was paid only $2,900. Teachers' salaries averaged $1,695 in 1930 and even less, only $1,360, six years later.

The grammar school was added to in 1939 and again in 1947. After 1948 four new sites were purchased: 16 acres off Newell Avenue, 16 acres on Walnut Boulevard, 11 acres between Orchard and Buena Vista and 13.8 acres on Tice Valley Road.

Walnut Creek Grammar School Enrollment

1860	28
1875	62
1898	44
1911	63
1920	255
1930	345
1939	498
1949	1,490
1959	4,393

Walnut Creek Grammar School Superintendents

Robert E. Gibson	until June 30, 1942
Eleanor Smith	until June 30, 1944
Sheldon Rankin	until June 30, 1959
Richard F. Fickel	until June 30, 1963
Elmo Guilieri	until June 30, 1981
Kenneth Meinecke	at present

Central Grammar School, ca. 1890.

For virtually fifty years graduates of the Central School went no further than the eighth grade. No higher education was taught in area public schools until the Mt. Diablo High School opened in 1901 in Concord. Even then no public transportation was available.

In 1910, San Ramon High School opened in Danville. Mrs. Estelle Campbell, in 1983, recalls the first year she went there. "Someone, I don't remember who, drove a wagon with benches on it, like a bus, and we rode on it to Danville from Walnut Creek."

A year later, in June 1911, the Oakland, Antioch Railway ran a train five days a week from Walnut Creek to Concord to coincide with the Mt. Diablo High Schol class schedule. Beginning in 1913, the train picked up students at Moraga and Lafayette as well. At first the railway ran one car but on a protest from the high school principal they added a second car. Boys were to remain in one car and girls in the other. Tickets cost the students ten cents each way.

Pupils who remained after hours for any reason, team practice, athletic contests or for disciplinary reasons, had a long wait for another train home. If they missed the 4:44 from Concord they had to wait until 6:24 for the next train. Helen Emanuels remembers her long walks.

105

"When I stayed late for basketball practice or for a game I had to walk all the way home, to Ygnacio Valley. We lived five miles from the school. I didn't particularly look forward to that long walk but did it, knowing it was the only way."

Back in the '20s and '30s there was one group of children who never did attend school. They were gypsy youngsters. Gypsies camped anywhere they liked in those days, on their annual trek through town. They pitched their tents on Botelho's Island (where Las Lomas High is now) or on the baseball diamond where Gemco's gas station is today. Matriarchs dominated their camps. They usually dressed in full skirts, multicolored and floral patterns. They wore bandanas, gold hoop earrings, gold bracelets and large rings. Young girls, with their liquid eyes and black hair, looking their best, were made up so as to be recognized as likely brides.

In the fall entire familes of thirty or forty worked harvesting crops, mostly grapes or walnuts. They lived a nomadic life for nine or ten months every year.

In Walnut Creek, attractive, dark-eyed, younger women scattered across town, offering to tell fortunes for a fee. Older women, trying not to attract notice, peddled pins, needles and notions from house to house. Men supplied the camp's needs, trading or buying as needed. The word swiftly passed around town, "The gypsies have come!" Mothers kept their youngsters indoors until their fear of kidnapping disappeared, after the gypsies moved on.

In 1940 Walnut Creek voters helped those from Lafayette and elsewhere to form the Acalanes Union High School District so that Walnut Creek students could go to school on Pleasant Hill Road instead of in Concord.

The Acalanes Union High School District organized the Las Lomas High School for Walnut Creek students in 1951. It opened with Leland Russell, principal, and a staff of eight teachers with 140 to 150 pupils. Ten classrooms, a gymnasium, girls' and boys' locker rooms and incidental expenses brought the total cost to $507,000.

School Street (Locust) looking north.

It can be said much of our country's progress in its first 150 years grew out of the education our young people received in one-room schools. There teachers divided their attention among all eight grades. Still there have always been some parents who wanted and could afford to give their offspring the benefit of individual tutorage. One of the earliest instances of private attention occurred in the San Ramon Valley. In the 1860s, farmer Abner Bryant hired a youth with no previous teaching experience to live on his Sycamore Valley farm and tutor his sons. The young man was Bret Harte and Bryant's job was his first.

In the early 1900s private schools in Berkeley attracted a few students from the Walnut Creek area, but by far the majority of parents, because of their own backgrounds, saw no need for their children to attend any school but Central. Children seldom went beyond the sixth or seventh grades, working beside their parents in field or shop from age twelve on.

Between 1910 and 1930 attitudes toward the extent of education changed. Boys and girls both attended Mt. Diablo High in Concord and an increasing number of graduates went on to a university education.

The first private school in Walnut Creek opened as the result of two aware parents wishing to give their oldest daughter the special attention she was capable of accepting.

Berkeley resident William Palmer, a MacMillan Publishing Company employee, and his wife (both accredited teachers), seeking the rural atmosphere, moved to Walnut Creek in 1936. Palmer had taught in Napa County, and before their marriage, Mrs. Palmer taught in the Monterey-Carmel area.

They bought a large home at 2731 Oak Road and moved there with their three daughters. The oldest, Rosemary, in the eighth grade, was showing unusual ability. In 1939, sensing her daughter's capacity to learn beyond her age level, Mrs. Palmer kept Rosemary home and tutored the girl herself. Before long it was only natural she did the same with her other two daughters.

Central School class, approximately 1910. Left to right, back row: Walter Pierson, Robert Walker, Mattie Welch, Jeannette Nielson, Cranston Walker, Eldred Walker, Louie Garcia. Middle row: Elmer Riley, Sanford Jennings, unknown, Carroll Walker, Violet Martinez, Kate Marshall, Matt Lawrence, Pete Loefler. Front row: Osbourne Young, George Buck, Harry Garcia, Bill Pierson, Glennie Welch, Marjorie Holman, August Sweyers, Coy Sharp, Charles Jennings, Walter Ormsby. Instructors: primary grades one through four, Miss Bickerstaff, on left; upper grades, Miss Clarey, on right.

Having a large home, the Palmers started accepting other girls as boarding students. World War II broke out in the Pacific shortly afterward, and with many Bay Area fathers off to war and mothers working in war-related industries, the Palmers took in more girls and soon reached their capacity of thirty boarders.

In 1950 they discontinued boarding students and opened a coeducational day school. Meantime the Palmers' youngest daughter, Joan, was earning her degree at Humboldt State University. While there she fell in love with a classmate, Adrian Mendes. He too earned his teaching credential and the two married, after graduation, in 1953.

Adrian served with the military in the Far East for two years, returning to find his in-laws wanting to retire.

Mr. and Mrs. Palmer turned over the reins to the young couple that year. At that time about sixty students attended Palmer School, and it has grown steadily ever since. Today approximately three hundred study there. The appeal of the school is so strong that children from Fremont, Oakland and Berkeley commute daily via BART.

Schoolmaster Adrian Mendes is proud of the tenure and continuity of the school's staff. "Joan's and my children are the third generation to teach here. I know of no other private school in California that can claim this. Our sons, Lance and Sam, teach here now as well as Sam's wife, Susan Schroder Mendes."

Students come from throughout the East Bay to another independent day school in Walnut Creek. Established in 1960, the Seven Hills School opened in Alexander Lindsay's home at 975 North San Carlos Drive. It is a non-profit, tax-exempt organization governed by a board of directors.

The Seven Hills School serves preschool through the eighth grade children. It is located on 9½ acres and employs forty-five teachers to instruct 350 students—first through eighth grades.

Lu Pilgrim heads Seven Hills School. She says, "The original builders and owners of the Lindsay home were a Mr. and Mrs. Hale." She describes the school's unusual location, "With the Heather Farm recreation area and wildlife refuge next door, the school's campus provides a congenial environment for learning.

"We constantly see reminders of Alexander Lindsay around our goldfish pool. He'd go off in his pickup truck with his children on trips to interesting places. Once they went to Mexico and came back with a truck load of whale bones. We still have them."

Central Grammar School 1922 graduating class. Left to right, top row: Mrs. Garside, Mathew Shields, John Hughes, Damon Eckley, ? Saunders, Roy Young, John Rushtin, Alfred Heide, Thomas Johnson, Laverne Moore. Second row: Hazel Worrg, Lola Blankert, Doris Reynolds, Mrytle Dumas, Felicia Townsend, Thomas Schnoor, Scott Griffith. Third row: Elsa Haberland, Augusta Frank, Catherine Donahue, Peggy Bennett, Elberta Semans, Ruth Simmons, Beryl Townsend, Alice Near. Fourth row: Randall Humble, unknown, ? Post, Robert Rule.

111

William Lunsman starting out to sprinkle the city streets.

THE TOWN MATURES

The years 1910 to 1914 may not have been the end of the "Age of Innocence" but they did encompass a period of considerable change, of maturing, in Walnut Creek.

The volunteers protected the community with their hand-drawn fire carts. All the streets were still unpaved, muddy in winter and rutted rough and dusty in summer. The clip-clop of horses' feet still outnumbered the blasts of auto horns. But electric lights appeared in house after house in 1910, and kerosene sales dropped. Every fourth or fifth house had a telephone, yet as late as January 1911 only 1,148 telephones, business and residential, served all of Contra Costa County. Electric trains started coming into Walnut Creek and what had been long exhausting trips were now just comfortable rides. One rode to San Francisco in an hour and fifteen minutes or to Sacramento in only two hours.

There were no service stations yet, but a motorist in need of gasoline pulled up in front of a garage and blew his horn, the signal for the garage mechanic to wheel out his square tank and wind a crank which pumped fuel into the car.

Walnut Creek's population declined from 450 in the late 1890s to 400 ten years later. Even as late as 1914 the count was no more than 500. In the surrounding valleys the demand for small farms induced many owners to divide some of their acreage. So in the 1910-14 era, more people moved into the rural Walnut Creek area, and the calls for goods and services increased.

Before the citizens incorporated the town in 1914, two organizations served their needs: The Town Hall Association and the Walnut Creek Improvement Club. The former concentrated on a town meeting place, while the latter sought to upgrade the community as needed.

Originally the northwest corner of Main and Bonanza had a two-story building, the lower occupied by a general merchandise store and the second floor by the A.O.U.W. Society. When that building burned down in 1895, Mrs. Xarissa R. Hill, owner of the lot, gave it to the Town Hall Association.

The association solicited funds to rebuild the building. But it was mainly a loan from the San Ramon Valley Bank in 1907 that enabled them to put up a new two-story, forty feet by seventy feet hall. It had steam radiators for heat and kerosene lamps for light. Outside, a horse trough stood in front of the Main Street entrance.

The Women's Club undertook the responsibility of raising money to service the debt. Club volunteers staged many shows but came to rely on dances followed by dinners for most of their income.

Originally the new building had no basement, but the ladies found it inconvenient to set up the dinner tables while the dances went on, and prepare food in the same room too. So a group of men pitched in. They opened up the front of the building, scraped dirt out, shoveled it into wagons and hauled it off. They poured a wainscot and floor of concrete and installed a kitchen in the northwest corner. The original dance floor wore so quickly they replaced it with a maple floor. Couples felt this floor undulate when dancing, but it served for the life of the building. Children received ten cents each to wax the floors before the first dance of the evening.

The community, woefully short of entertainment in the days before radio and television, took to the monthly dances like ducks to water. Often hundreds attended the events, mostly good-natured couples out for a good time at a price they could afford, at first fifty cents for both dinner and dancing. However, the town marshal had his hands full at many of the monthly affairs. Some young men, emboldened by liquor and jealous of envious looks at their partners, stepped outside to offer or defend a challenge with fists. Liquor was off-limits inside the hall, so bottles were often stashed under bushes and elsewhere while the owner danced. Many is the high school student who successfully searched for liquor and with his friends went over to the banks of the creek for their first experience with Demon Rum.

A citizens' committee came to a trustees' meeting in September 1923, appealing, "Conditions at the Town Hall are so deplorable, we implore you to close down the hall to *all* dances for six months."

Before Ted Berling put on movies in the hall, an occasional medicine show came to town. To attract customers for their potions they brought along sleight-of-hand performers and in some cases showed postcard views on a Magic Lantern.

In the 1920s Theodore Berling rented the Town Hall on Saturday nights. He brought first-run films from the Oakland theater he worked for. He covered the maple floor with canvas before setting up the chairs. Since he had only one projector, he had to rewind each reel before he could show the next. His impatient audience would stamp and whistle between reels.

One Saturday night, Judge Duncan may have saved a disastrous stampede during a movie. Smoke rose from a waste basket, probably started by a discarded cigarette. Several people rose, overturning some chairs in their rush to get out the one small exit. Duncan stood up and in his stentorian voice commanded, "Sit down!" People stopped in their tracks and sheepishly returned to their chairs. Someone carried the smoldering trash from the room.

The mortgage on the Town Hall hung around the necks of the association members like a lead weight on a swimmer. The money-raising activities never met their goals and the city gave up trying to make the hall pay its way. The San Ramon Valley Bank took the property over in June of 1918 and then leased it back. The townspeople kept on using it as though nothing had happened.

A citizens' committee headed by ex-Mayor Frank Mauzy appeared before the trustees in October 1928 demanding, "Tear down the Town Hall. It's a serious fire menace and not a credit to Main Street."

Torn down it was and for several years the Veterans' Building on Locust Street was the scene of the dances.

The year 1911 was a time of progress in yet another direction. The Women's Improvement Club, later the Women's Club of Walnut Creek, decided the community needed a public library and took the initiative by starting one. They rented a vacant cottage on Olympic, across from today's Kentucky Fried Chicken. The women swept it out, washed it down and painted the interior. They hired a carpenter to build shelves and brought a desk, an old stove, and chairs from their homes to furnish it. They raised money among themselves to buy books and subscribe to periodicals, and they opened the library in 1912.

Late in 1914, the club applied for a Carnegie Library Foundation grant. In May of 1915 the Carnegie Foundation granted it a "Carnegie Library grant for a bungalow type building costing $2,500." Club members asked the town trustees if they would like to donate a substantial lot for the building, but the answer came back, "No."

Also in May, 1915, Mr. and Mrs. Dewing, local farmers, offered their 84- by 115-foot lot on the southwest corner of Main and Lincoln streets for a *special* price of $1,008, which the club rejected.

However, Robert N. Burgess, real estate developer, gave a lot on East Street near the corner of Main, where the Women's Improvement Club opened its Carnegie Library in October 1916. The town trustees agreed to pay the utility bills and the club for all the other expenses.

Even as late as 1930 the city's contribution to the library was miniscule. The June 1931 account for the previous *year* lists: "For library salaries, fuel and lights, $147.01."

While the citizens voted to incorporate in May 1914, the citizenry who opposed the plan rose up only a year and a half later, on October 6, 1916, by filing a petition asking for an election on disincorporating. On that day Mrs. A. S. Ormsby filed such a petition with 144 signatures. Subsequently 49 signatures were disqualified and since 95 were insufficient, no election was held.

Two months later, E. B. Anderson filed an affadavit saying he "... had circulated the petition and had seen all but one person sign it ..." Trustees received his affadavit, which they would consider a basis for calling the election, but they buried it and none was held.

116

Looking west along Mt. Diablo Boulevard from Main Street at flag pole dedication on July 4, 1917. Bareheaded American Legion members listening to address. School children, led by boys with drums, have paraded to the intersection.

However, an election was held three years later. The objections to incorporation lingered on and the voters cast their ballots on March 8, 1919. The count: eighty-three for and sixty-nine against. While the vote to disincorporate was higher, it lost by eighteen because the necessary two-thirds vote was not obtained.

The defeated foes of incorporation licked their wounds in silence until the spring of 1921, when they went out again with their petitions. This time they lost by a bigger margin. Two hundred and thirty votes were cast with only 100 favoring disincorporation. Thus ended their efforts.

Excerpts of Minutes of Early Trustees' Meetings

October 22, 1914. First board of trustees' meeting. Harry Spencer, Joseph Lawrence, William F. Robinson, Armand Stow, Winifred Burpee, trustees. Joseph Silveira, treasurer. Mary A. Ridgeway, clerk.

October 26, 1914. James Carr appointed poundmaster and George O. Duncan, recorder. Poundmaster's duties include prohibiting stock to run at large on streets or vacant lots.

February 1915. Trustee reported " . . . the streets are woefully full of chuck holes and advised the ordering of crushed rock for filling the same . . . "

February 15, 1915. A. N. Paterson appointed town marshal.

March 31, 1915. " . . . members of the Women's Club to choose appropriate street names for the streets."

April 7, 1915. Town marshal appeared before the trustees asking that " . . . he be supplied with a reliable gun" and was instructed "to buy a reliable and sufficient gun at the lowest price possible."

June 7, 1916. William Lunsman granted the contract for sprinkling the city (dirt) streets at $3.50 per day upon request. John P. Rose was granted permission to keep his saloon open until 2:00 A.M. upon payment of an additional five-dollar license fee.

August 16, 1916. The Cowell Lime and Cement Company (Clayton) was thanked for installing a cement watering trough in front of the Town Hall.

October 16, 1916. Contracted to gravel Bonanza Street with 199 yards of gravel to cost no more than $1.50 per yard.

November 1915. Trustees approved an expenditure for the construction of a flagpole at the intersection of Main Street and Mt. Diablo Boulevard. Trustee Stow instructed to "attend to the construction." Nothing came of the idea and again, on May 2, 1916, the trustees authorized an expenditure for the pole at the same intersection with three lights on it to be furnished by the Pacific Gas and Electric Company.

August 1917. F. S. Dirion was appointed night watchman at fifty dollars per month.

December 1917. H. M. Stow granted a contract to grade and spread rock on Main Street, 4 inches deep, 20 feet wide, and 2,000 feet long.

April 1918. Appointed W. R. Wood as fire chief.

August 1918. In answer to the national call for a "Conserve Electricity" Drive the trustees dispensed with all street lights but four at Main and Mt. Diablo and one at Bonanza and Mt. Diablo.

November 1918. Trustees ordered all saloons, ice cream parlors, soda water fountains, pool and card rooms closed due to the influenza epidemic raging over the country and further ordered everyone on public streets, stores and businesses to wear face masks.

November 1918. Pacific Gas and Electric ordered to turn on all street lights.

March 1920. The trustees asked the Contra Costa County Supervisors to build the highway through Walnut Creek. The supervisors immediately refused and the trustees started talking of paving Main and Mt. Diablo.

May 1920. Trustees adopted the measure to lay (the first) sewer line along Main, Shuey, Hubbard Place, Almond Avenue and Putnam Place.

August 12, 1920. Trustees approved paving Main Street with 5 inches of concrete and 1½ inches of Warrenite. (Work completed in November 1921)

November 20, 1920. (While the streets were all unpaved) The trustees ordered curbs and cement sidewalks (for the first time) from Main and Mt. Diablo Boulevard to 100 feet north of Main and Bonanza.

1920 election. One hundred forty-three voters cast ballots.

July 6, 1921. Raymond Spencer was named fire chief, filling the "long unfilled post."

December 7, 1921. Mrs. James F. Mauzy appeared before the trustees for the Parent-Teachers Association asking " . . . you must stop the carrying of concealed weapons by children under age." At the same meeting Dr. Leech appeared to complain about the condition of the town's septic tank.

1921. Total tax receipts: $3,751.31 with $298.48 delinquent.

November 1, 1922. The trustees granted the Willow Athletic Club the privilege of using the Town Hall for basketball games for $2.50 per practice and $15 per game.

September 23, 1923. "Conditions at the Town Hall are so deplorable, we implore you to close down the Hall to all dances for six months."

December 1925. Mr. Charles Howard, et al, urged the trustees to provide a recreation park for school children.

1926. Locust Street paved.

1926. $40 a month approved for a children's playground to a maximum of $400.

1926. Mt. Diablo still called Lafayette Street.

October 1928. A "Citizens' Committee" appeared before the trustees asking, "Tear down the Town Hall; it is a serious fire menace." "It is not a credit to Main Street," wrote ex-Mayor Frank Mauzy.

1938. City budget totaled $3,800.

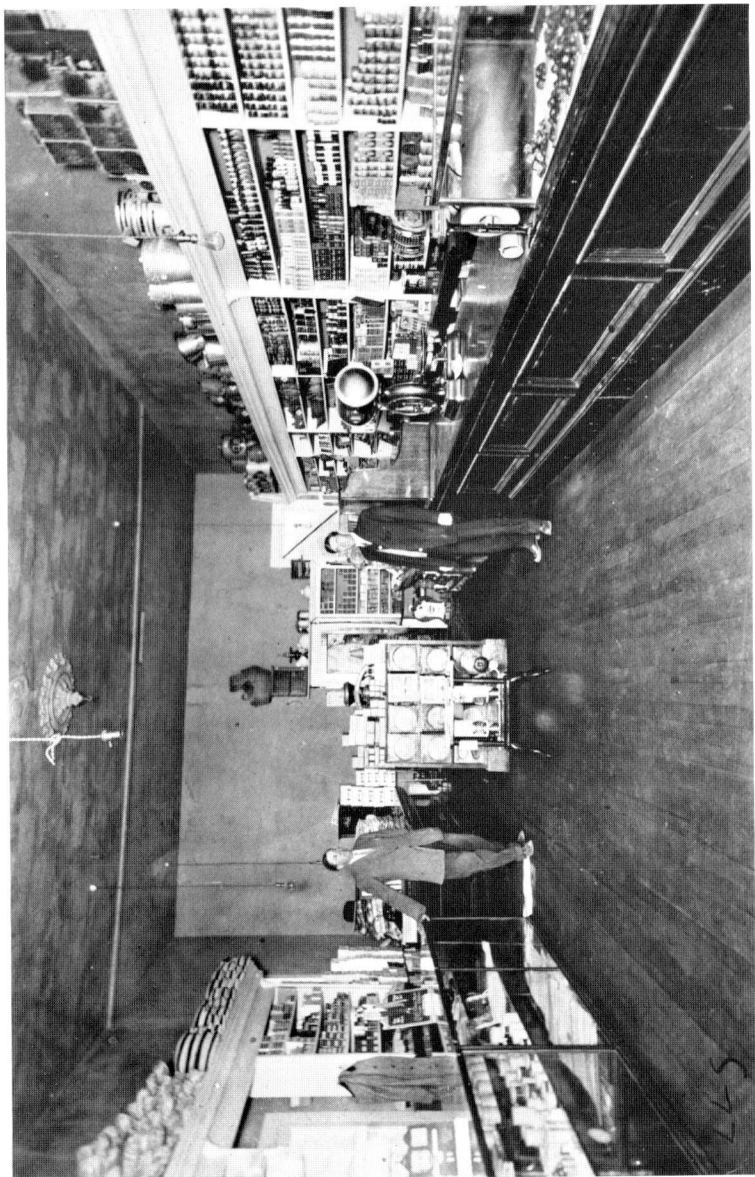

Silver and Acree store on Main Street.

Some 1914-1924 Ordinances Passed by the Walnut Creek Trustees

December 17, 1914 — #3

" . . . this ordinance is required for the *immediate* preservation of the public peace, health and safety [because] certain persons are making a practice . . . of permitting . . . livestock . . . to run at large upon the public streets.

"It shall be unlawful for any person . . . owning or controlling any horse, mule, ass, goat, cow, calf, bull, ox, or hog . . . to graze, feed or run at large upon any public street or unfenced lot . . . nothing shall prohibit the driving of stock through the town when in charge of a competent herder."

December 17, 1914 — #6

"Every person . . . owning . . . real property . . . upon which improvements have been constructed . . . within 200 feet of any existing public sewer shall connect such improvement with such sewer." PLACES OF PUBLIC NOTICE: Town Hall, Post Office, Mr. Burpee's Saloon.

March 31, 1915 — #10

"It shall be unlawful for any person or persons to play baseball, football or any other games involving the throwing or striking of a ball on Main Street . . . "

August 17, 1916 — #14

"It shall be unlawful . . . to drive any horse, jackass, cow, mule, or other large animal over or upon any [wooden] sidewalk."

March 11, 1921 — #23

"It shall be unlawful to give or hold any public dance or ball in the Town of Walnut Creek without first obtaining a permit to do so from the Town Marshal."

August 26, 1921 — #28

Established a volunteer fire department for Walnut Creek.

May 21, 1924 — #32

Curfew—"No one under the age of 18 shall go abroad or wander on the streets of Walnut Creek after 9 PM or before 4 AM."

May 21, 1924 — #33

"It shall be unlawful for any person to roam or loiter about the public streets between midnight and 4 AM without having lawful business . . ."

June 25, 1924 — #34

Town Council authorized the first expenditure for the volunteer fire department—$3,000.

Firsts in Walnut Creek

1877 First public meetings held to consider building a tunnel through the Berkeley hills.

1891 First steam train ran through town, Oakland to San Ramon Valley.

1903 Old high level tunnel opened, the "Inter-City Tunnel."

1912 Walnut Creek Women's Club opened the first library.

1920 First service station built.

1921 City council authorizes a volunteer fire department on August 26.

1925 City limits expanded from one square mile to forty-two square miles.

1927 Council authorized installation of seven "Stop" signs.

1928 Theodore Berling hired as the first chief of police on August 1.

1930 Coast Counties Gas Company commenced serving Walnut Creek.

1937 Caldecott Tunnel opened.

1937 Water and sewer systems modernized.

1946 Central Contra Costa Sanitary District took over the city sewer system.

1947 First parking meters installed with only one-cent and five-cent coins, yet city revenue came to sixty dollars a day—no loss of business as merchants feared.

1951 The East Bay Municipal Utility District took over water service from California Water Service Company.

Though the city population grew slowly and the demand for services remained at a low level, between incorporation and 1956, the

123

five elected trustees ran Walnut Creek. Initially, beginning in 1914, the town trustees elected the mayor from among themselves and he, as president of the board, also assumed the title of commissioner of finance. At that time and for many years after, each of the other trustees became commissioners of one of the following: town planning, streets, health and sanitation, water and light.

At the trustees meeting of August 1, 1927, that body changed their titles from trustees to councilmen by a simple word to that effect to the city clerk. However, they still held the title of commissioner of each of the departments.

Two events occurred in 1928 which created a need to change the duties of the councilmen. The first was the city's purchase of the private water company in March, and the other was the hiring of a chief of police on August 1.

Yet, the old division of responsibility permitted occasional abuse of authority. For example: once in a while a commissioner saw an employee carrying out instructions from his superior which he thought less than desirable. Because of his authority as a commissioner, he countermanded the instructions on the spot. A police commissioner, once at least, changed orders the police chief had given a patrolman.

Since the councilmen appointed both the city clerk and the treasurer, the two were subject to pressure. One new city treasurer, Ed Silveira, son of the town's pioneer banker, refused to pay a personal expense voucher submitted along with the mayor's expense account, a practice which had been a common occurrence earlier. Silveira stood by his principles and made the mayor end the practice.

In 1956 the state legislature enacted a provision to the state code which made it possible for cities to end the practice of making city councilmen de facto department heads.

This measure provided for city councils to hire a city manager who would manage all city employees and departments. The code required the treasurer and city clerk be elected officers whereby they would not be beholden to either council members or a city manager.

124

Since Walnut Creek hired its first city manager, four men have occupied that office.

The former Reno, Nevada city manager, Ira Gunn, came to Walnut Creek in that capacity in the summer of 1956. He remained here until February 1958.

Laverne Kimball came to Walnut Creek as city manager on March 1, 1958. His term is noteworthy for the large number of residential subdivisions established in the late '50s and early '60s. Kimball left on June 24, 1964 to accept the appointment as assistant general manager of the Bay Area Rapid Transit District during its construction years. He left BART after ten years to head a large transit district in the east.

Ralph Snyder came on December 1, 1964, serving as city manager for eight years. His tenure was notable for the development of the downtown area. The $6.75 million bond issue of 1965 set in motion the Little Master Plan which included increasing the flow of water in Walnut Creek, thereby reducing the threat of flooding, and to complete the construction of California Boulevard from Mt. Diablo to North Main, and other street improvements. It further developed Heather Farm and Larkey Park. His period as the city's executive officer was a time of very rapid growth, and homeowners made their numbers felt in city planning. As a result of a no-growth opinion on the part of homeowners on Shell Ridge, the city bought a substantial part of the Ridge area.

Snyder left Walnut Creek on April 30, 1972, and his successor was Thomas Dunne, the current city manager of Walnut Creek.

Dunne's tenure is notable for increased city-owned facilities built without any indebtedness. The community has a new maintenance yard; traffic signals have been modernized; and a new city hall costing over $3 million has been constructed. Street improvements and flood control measures are ongoing projects. At one time property taxes were the largest source of city funds but now, after supporting retail expansion in the core area, the city receives its major funding from the state sales tax.

Dunne thinks of himself as a fiscal conservative and a liberal when it comes to pursuing new ideas. Walnut Creek may have been the first community in the nation to adopt a two-year budget. Obviously this cuts the work of budget preparation in half. This practice has been reviewed in state and national journals and adopted in many communities nationwide.

The city manager admits he could not have accomplished the tasks he set out to achieve without the full support of the elected officials and the management staff. He states, "I would like contemporaries to think of us as an outstanding organization, from individual employees to the council."

The 7,000-member International City Management Association recently elected Walnut Creek's city manager their president, a fitting tribute to him and to his community.

JUSTICES OF THE PEACE

For 110 years following statehood, the justice system as it affected Walnut Creek followed the pattern of most of rural America. In each township (thirty-six square miles) the voters elected a justice of the peace and a constable. Whenever the constable apprehended a violator committing a misdemeanor, he cited that person to appear for a hearing before the justice of the peace. When the constable doubted the violator's intention to appear he would lock him up in the town jail. Walnut Creek's place of confinement was a low, square, whitewashed frame shed on ground that today is in the east-bound lane of Mt. Diablo Boulevard, opposite the Broadway Plaza intersection.

Felony violators were apprehended by deputies from the county sheriff's office and held in Martinez.

No legal training was mandatory for a candidate to either office, justice of the peace or constable. They ran for election every four years, at which time the voters decided to keep them or turn them out.

An army captain in the Spanish-American War in 1898 and an attorney in civilian life, George Duncan served as justice of the peace here from the time he received his army discharge until his death in 1933. Captain and Mrs. Duncan raised three children, all born in Walnut Creek: Georgana, Wallace and Curtis.

The townspeople elected Forrest Bailey following Captain Duncan. Bailey, also a lawyer, was reelected repeatedly and served as justice of the peace for about fifteen years.

Bailey was a practical man, as evidenced by his handling of a holdup perpetrator one night in 1943. As market owner Chet Arthur closed and locked his front door at 1315 North Main Street, someone shoved a steel-like article in his back and yelled, "Give me the sack [money]!"

When he saw the man put both his hands in his jacket pockets, simulating two weapons, Arthur took a wild chance and jumped him. Half turning and tripping in his escape, the would-be robber fell with Arthur grabbing an upraised arm. He twisted it behind the man's back and just as quickly did the same with the other arm.

A cry came from the Bungalow Barbecue across the street. "Need some help?" Ward Schuyler, the owner, called out.

"Yeah, call Johnny!" answered the struggling Arthur.

The night watchman came running and handcuffed the man and then called the sheriff in Martinez to come after his prisoner.

Waiting, the prisoner suddenly bolted, ran down a side street, and outran the winded night watchman.

Later, searchers found him still handcuffed in the Walnut Creek Hotel.

At the justice court hearing a few days later, Arthur testified and identified the accused. Before passing sentence, the practical justice of the peace asked the witness, "Do you think I ought to fine this fellow $200 and give him thirty days or just send him to San Quentin and the city get nothing?"

At hearing the informality between the judge and witness, the accused made some fresh, slighting remarks about the court. Bailey immediately responded, "Ninety days in the county jail and a $300 fine!"

The prisoner turned out to be a Moraga resident with a wife and children, yet the Martinez jail keeper reported not once did a visitor come to see the man during his ninety days there. A week before he was due to be released the family paid the City of Walnut Creek the $300 fine.

Clifford Thompson won the election to replace Bailey. The community reelected him twice and he served the city until he voluntarily retired in 1951.

While the population had increased four- or five-fold since the turn of the century, the Walnut Creek township still had only one

128

justice of the peace in 1958. That year the election attracted eight candidates: seven men and one woman. The result was a tie between the leading man and the woman. In the run-off the woman won.

Betsy Rahn (Mrs. Leon Rahn), a graduate of the University of California's Boalt Hall, started serving as Walnut Creek's last justice of the peace in 1959. She and her husband had moved to town in 1947, seeking the rural atmosphere for their infant son, Michael. They built their home on Walnut Knolls and lived there until they moved to Rossmoor in 1980.

In 1960 the county superior court answered a procedure filed in 1959, declaring the Walnut Creek Justice Court a municipal court. In 1962 the same court enlarged the Walnut Creek District to include the Danville justice of the peace jurisdiction which added a second municipal court to serve Walnut Creek.

Betsy Rahn's courtroom was in a storefront at East Street and Locust, next door to an automobile body shop. Noise from the pounding was a constant distraction. "Speak up!" the jurist often had to admonish witnesses. Flimsy head-high partitions separated her chambers and the clerk's office from the spartan-like courtroom. A straight-back oak chair served the witness, the rest being metal folding chairs. When Judge Rahn commandeered an oak table from the clerk's office to use for a counsel table, she learned it had been bought by the bailiff with his own money, for him to sit at.

The court's case load was primarily composed of traffic cases. Within three months after taking office, Judge Rahn asked the county supervisors for funds to institute a driver improvement school. The supervisors turned her down. Seeing so many traffic offenders appear before her made her increase her determination. After the supervisors' rejection she appealed for help to the schools, the Walnut Creek Police Department and the California Highway Patrol. Recognizing the need, they all contributed to the cause of better driver education. The police officers taught classes in the adult education program at Acalanes High School. Later, both the Concord-Martinez and the Richmond-El Cerrito municipal courts copied Judge Rahn's program.

In the affluent society of Walnut Creek-Danville, the youthful traffic offenders often pleaded guilty, their parents paid their fines, and the court appearance didn't deter them from ignoring the traffic laws. In her court Judge Rahn required every youthful offender to pay his own penalty. If the juvenile had a job, all well and good. If not, she ordered him to find work. If he came back later and still said he couldn't find work, the judge's own program provided it. Under the "Walnut Creek Municipal Work Program," the city provided trucks, and reserve court marshals working without pay led groups of youth on "clean-up" tours of streets and highways.

Among the numerous awards recognizing Judge Rahn's achievements on the Walnut Creek-Danville municipal bench are five commendations from the American Bar Associaiton. She served as a representative from California on the advisory committee to the Standing Rule Committee for Traffic Court Programs of the American Bar Association. She served five years as chairman of the Municipal Court Judges Association of Contra Costa County.

The Walnut Creek jurist created the first juvenile alcohol program in the county. When critics challenged, "Alcohol education never cured anyone," she retorted, "Some education is better than none."

Alcoholics Anonymous gave her the most support, setting up programs and supplying speakers. The county health department helped too, with time volunteered by county doctors Blum, Kent and Wasserman. Her "Driving Under the Influence School" was the first in Contra Costa County. She saw to it that everyone convicted of that offense attended and, in addition, paid whatever penalty he received.

On their own time, Judge Rahn and her clerk listed similar schools in other counties around the state. When an offender lived closer to another "Driving Under the Influence School," she permitted the guilty party to attend classes nearer his home. Judge Rahn's classes emphasized safety and the negative influence of drunkenness, and showed some of the serious accidents resulting from over-drinking. With her case load increasing along with the rising population, the store front location next to the noisy body shop made hers too difficult a court to work in. Finally Judge Rahn asked County Supervisor Tom Coll to visit her court. The day he arrived her clerk went next door and asked the repairmen to give it their best. They did, and not too long afterward, the county rented the second floor of the Veteran's Memorial Building at 1250 Locust Street and moved Rahn's court there. The second floor was a ballroom and the chairs and tables of the court had to be moved out of the way every time a dance was to be held there.

For a long time the jurist held the belief that too much mystery surrounded the justice system and the best way to dispel it would be to have school classes view the proceedings. Judge Betsy Rahn invited schools to send classes and many did; some even sent a class every month.

Occasionally a youngster appeared in court for riding a moped or a small unlicensed vehicle on city streets. Whenever one too young to be sentenced appeared, she sent him off with a requirement that he write an essay about his experience. They never failed her and she read every one. Judge Betsy Rahn retired in 1979.

For years the fines from the Walnut Creek-Danville Municipal Court often totaled as much as $35,000 a month, and the county could well afford a better building to house the proceedings. Ultimately the county rented a modern building at 640 Ygnacio Valley Road. The municipal court is there now and the current jurists are Michael J. Phelan, Joseph R. Longacre, Jr. and John P. Minney. A fourth court is presided over by a commissioner, Richard P. Calhoun, who handles only traffic violations.

FIRE!

On the morning of July 4, 1922 a warm dry north wind fanned the brown hillsides west of town. It was almost noon when a cry went up, "Fire!" As the volunteers opened the garage door, cranked the Model T to life and rolled it out onto Main Street, people pointed to the billowing cloud of smoke rising from the hills at the end of Mt. Diablo Boulevard.

The driver, Guy Spencer, and his helper, Frank Marshall, stopped the truck where the grass blazed closest to town. Wind fanned grass embers, blowing them south, and within minutes the firemen dropped their empty hoses and beat at the edge of the blaze with sacks wetted with the last of their water.

Already, Chief Raymond Spencer, Guy's brother, had telephoned Lafayette, Concord and Martinez to send men and equipment. The fire jumped roads and lighted creosoted power poles, as fence after fence fell. The billowing cloud darkened the noon time sky as volunteers and farmers alike feverishly beat at the burning grass. The chief sent out calls to Oakland and Berkeley for fire engines and equipment. They came two hours after the first cry went out, but only at eight in the evening, over in Moraga Valley, did the weary firemen lay down their tools.

The fire consumed twenty-one square miles of Contra Costa County. The possible destruction of Walnut Creek was averted, only by the wind's direction.

Even before this near calamity, early in 1922 at a council meeting, the town's fathers made it clear they had no plans to finance the volunteer fire department and didn't know who was the head of the organization or who owned the only usable piece of equipment. No evidence of registration existed, and most volunteers doubted anyone had ever registered their truck. The Ford Model T, hand-cranked, ran well and the two twenty-five-gallon tanks in back held water which the pump shot out in a steady stream until emptied. The truck carried hoses to connect to Main Street's two-inch hydrants.

The council put the question to the Farm Bureau since the truck answered calls in the rural area too. They answered, "We don't know." The final judgment on who owned the fire equipment revealed that it was all bought by public donations and that Theodore Berling, the moving picture operator, had contributed more than anyone else.

On August 26, 1922, after the near loss of the town, the council authorized a volunteer fire department and contributed $3,000 to modernize it. The council also appointed the first fire chief, George Belem.

In the decades before 1920, fire insurance rates were admittedly high both inside and outside the city limits. Complaints to the insuring companies brought the obvious answer, "When you have modern equipment to fight fires your rates will come down." As early as June 4, 1924, the council discussed the need for a tax-supported full-time fire department. The answer was always, "The only way we can afford one is to tax property outside the town as well."

Credit for the department which eventually brought down the rates, the Central Fire Protection District, properly belongs to the veteran teacher and town mayor, E. B. Anderson. In his late years, tall and straight, with a head of white hair, Anderson led the support for the district at council meetings.

About 1936 a fire almost destroyed the town's business district. One dry fall day the usual fire smoldered among the refuse at the city's dumping grounds. The dumps were where the armory is today, and the sewer farm was next to them.

Chet Arthur remembers what happened. "In mid-afternoon the caretaker decided to burn some weeds along the banks of Walnut Creek. 'The wind shifted,' he later defended himself. A brisk wind blew burning weeds toward the backs of the Main Street stores. Sparks feeding on dry grass and debris grew into flames that licked at the wooden buildings.

"Brush, between the creek and the buildings, all the way down to Duncan, blazed up, fanned by sixty-mile-an-hour gusts.

"Fearing the whole business district would go up in an inferno, every able-bodied man in town rushed to help the two firemen. Shovels, hoes or wet sacks were in every man's hands. They shoveled or scraped glowing cinders and hot ash away from the buildings."

A call for help went out to Concord, Lafayette and Martinez. Desperate for assistance, they appealed for tank trucks with long hoses. Even by evening the dry hot wind kept the smallest embers alive.

But their efforts saved the town and the next year the council moved the dumps farther away.

Walnut Creek Population

1891	400
1897	450
1908	400
1914	500
1920	538
1925	City limits expanded
1926	800
1930	1.014
1940	1,587
1950	2,420
1955	City limits expanded
1960	9,903
1970	39,844
1984	59,095

In September 1939, during an absence of Councilman Ernest Nottingham and his family, his house on Oakland Avenue burst into flames. Even though the fire department responded promptly, nothing could be saved from the structure. The family's two dogs perished

134

inside the house. The firemen could only keep the two adjoining dwellings from catching on fire.

Not until a state law became effective in 1926 was it lawful for a community to encompass surrounding lands in its taxing authority. In 1926 the county board of supervisors authorized a thirty-two-square-mile area, with Walnut Creek as the hub, as the Central Fire Protection District.

The first fire house for the new district still stands. It is the two-story building at 1516-18 Bonanza, now the Yarn Basket and La Ultima. Today, in 1984, by looking up at the rear of the building, one may see the three-story hose-drying tower still there. Above it is the two-story steel tower on which the siren whined out the location or type of emergency: one blast, out of town; two blasts, in town; three blasts, accident; four blasts, need a doctor.

As early as 1961 officials recognized that they could effect economies, efficiency, and better all-round protection by combining the fire districts covering Concord, Pleasant Hill and Walnut Creek. This became a fact when the Mount Diablo Fire Protection District merged with the Central Fire Protection District and became the Contra Costa County Consolidated Fire Protection District on December 29, 1964.

Only forty years elapsed between the hand-drawn "engines" and the best modern motorized equipment available.

Office of Contra Costa Courier and Ramona Theater, ca. 1917,
on east side of the 1400 block of Main Street.

MORE NEWSPAPERS

The first two newspapers in Walnut Creek have already been mentioned, each having printed no more than seventeen weekly issues without showing a profit. Prophetically, each started in March, one in 1882 and the other in 1894.

The third weekly to appear has changed hands four times and has grown from a four-page paper to a daily of forty pages or more with a Sunday edition of over one hundred pages, with a circulation of over 90,000 copies.

George C. Compton published the first edition of the *Contra Costa Courier* in May 1911 when the town's population numbered less than 500. At the same time, six miles away, in Danville, C. H. King struggled to make his *Danville Journal* a going concern. The two publishers found advertisers tight with their money and subscribers too few for both papers to survive. Both weeklies were marginally profitable for a longer time than their predecessors and continued publishing independently until just after 1917.

A capitalist from New York and Michigan who lived in Alamo bought the two papers, merging them into one, *The Contra Costa Courier-Journal*. Colonel William White built a new building to house the paper on the east side of Main Street opposite Cypress. He kept the paper going until 1921 when he sold it to his editorial staff, Maude Silver and her husband, a retired dentist. Mr. Silver's health was not very good, and his wife was the backbone of the staff.

After her husband died in 1940, Mrs. Silver published the weekly alone for another three years. She sold it to a very capable young man, David Newsom, in 1943. At the time Newsom was business manager of the *Richmond Independent*.

Newsom published *The Courier-Journal* until July 1947, when he sold out. He joined the United States Diplomatic Service, ultimately serving as ambassador in several Far East countries. Newsom eventually became the United States undersecretary of state for Africa, then for the Middle East and finally became the undersecretary of state for political affairs, the post immediately below the secretary of state. Upon Newsom's retirement, Colonel Romulo, long-time foreign minister of the Phillipine Islands, said of the one-time Walnut Creek newspaper publisher, "David Newsom was one of the best ambassadors the United States ever had."

Dean Lesher, a Harvard Law School graduate, bought the *Courier-Journal* in July 1947, establishing his office at 1605 North Main Street. Lesher, born in Williamsport, Maryland practiced law in Kansas City, Missouri during the 1930s and early '40s. As general counsel of his law firm, he represented a newspaper broker and from that connection first bought the *Nebraska Daily Tribune* in Fremont, Nebraska. He lost money on the Fremont paper and became curious about the publishing business in growing California. He came west in 1941 and bought the Merced daily, *The Daily Sun-Star*. Six months later he sold his Nebraska paper.

When Lesher bought the twelve-page, twice-weekly *Contra Costa Courier-Journal* in 1947, it had a circulation of 2,000, and five years later, in 1952, the circulation had grown and the paper needed larger quarters. Lesher built a building, which with later additions covered 25,000 square feet, at 1950 Mount Diablo Boulevard. At the same time he renamed the paper *The Contra Costa Times*.

Lesher, never an editor himself, lost money on his venture here for the first fifteen years. An absentee owner, he always hired his editorial staff. He started with eight employees in 1947 and now, thirty-seven years later, he employs a total of 1,070 people, each of whom works twenty hours a week or more. The paper's 2,000,readers in 1947 have grown to over 91,000 in 1983.

Mr. Lesher reports, "The Times has won more awards than any other paper in the nation."

In 1975 Lesher built a new building at 2640 Shadelands Drive, installing the most modern four-color presses available. His 1947 forecast proved correct: "Walnut Creek can't help but be the hub of Contra Costa County."

The first time the National Newspaper Association ever gave an award for anyone's contribution to the newspaper publishing business, President Reagan made the award to Dean Lesher. He received the recognition at ceremonies in the White House on March 10, 1983.

Contra Costa County Newspaper Acquisitions by Dean Lesher

1958	*Daily Ledger*, Antioch, from Al Flaherty
1963	Lafayette, Orinda, Pleasant Hill and Walnut Creek *Sun* from Herman Silverman
1966	*Concord Transcript*, from Owens Publications
1971	*Weekly Times*, Pleasanton, turned into a daily
1973	*Valley Times* for Livermore, San Ramon and Dublin
1974-75	Six small weeklies in western Contra Costa County which are now the daily, *West County Times*
1975	Combined the *Pleasanton Times* with the *Valley Times*
1979	Bought *The Daily Post Dispatch* in Pittsburg
1981	Established *This Week*, a shopper in Solano and Napa counties
1983	Bought the *Sonoma News Herald*, the *Sonoma Buyer's Guide*, and *Sonoma Business Magazine*
1984	Contracted to print the *New York Times'* national edition for the Northwest, initially a thirty-six-page daily.

Back in the days when the Silvers published the *Courier-Journal*, a rival publication appeared in Walnut Creek.

An Oklahoma native, and now a *San Francisco Chronicle* reporter who had hankered for a weekly paper of his own, he made his dream come true in 1931, in spite of the times, the lowest depths of the Great Depression.

Lyman Stoddard and his wife Alda, owned walnut acreage in Alamo from where "Mike" commuted daily, via the Oakland, Antioch & Eastern Railway (later the Sacramento Northern) electric line to San Francisco.

After a distinguished career on *The Chronicle* Stoddard retired from that paper and began publishing his, a paper without a name, on August 20, 1931, from an office at 1388 North Main Street, Walnut Creek.

As a promotion he staged a contest, open to everyone, to win a prize by submitting the winning name for his publication. A marine editor on his old paper, the *San Francisco Chronicle* won the prize by suggesting, *The Walnut Kernel.*

Stoddard's *Kernel* succeeded in spite of the hard times in the 1930s and grew into a seven-column, eight page weekly.

Lyman's and Alda's enthusiasm turned them into as active boosters as the center of the farming community had. They loved the small-town spirit of Walnut Creek. The City had just counted 1,014 men, women, and children within its one square mile borders for the first time. Furthermore, only a year before a gas company had built a pipe line and was delivering natural gas to the town. So there were topics to be proud of and his readers eagerly looked forward to his weekly column which epitomized the small town spirit he prized so much. They reached for his "Overheard on Main Street" first, and often chuckled at the simple foibles of others like themselves.

Over the years Lyman Stoddard published three other local papers, publishing four weeklies in all: *Contra Costa Shopper, Concord Journal, Pleasant Hill Post,* and of course *The Walnut Kernel.*

Lyman Stoddard Jr., the youngest of three children, became a printer in the 1950s and eventually shop foreman for his parents.

An area Printers Strike in 1957 started turning the tide against *The Kernel.* The biggest competitor, Dean Lesher's *Contra Costa Times,* had resources beyond those of the Stoddards! Lesher defied the unions, kept publishing while the weekly had to submit to the union's demands. *The Kernel* began losing advertisers and never did recover its former leadership.

Alda Stoddard died in 1963 and Lyman Sr., a year later. Lyman Jr., continued publishing the paper but eight years after his father's death he sold the publication to an Oakland organization. Within a year and after forty-one years *The Walnut Kernel* closed down in 1972.

WALNUT CREEK HOTELS
AND THE AUTO COURT

*O*n 1882, J. J. Noones advertised the Walnut Creek & Mount Diablo Central Hotel for sale. This is the year Antonio Botelho bought the "island" from Mrs. Fales and turned the hotel into his residence.

In later days when the utilities, Pacific Gas and Electric Company and the telephone company brought service to the area, 1910-1915, construction crews needed a place to eat and sleep. The Rogers Hotel was too expensive, so Mrs. Pine's boarding house took care of the crews.

The boarding house at 1517-21 North Main Street served them good wholesome meals, packed their lunches, and became their home away from home.

Mr. Alden, from Livermore, bought the property from Mrs. Pine and renamed it the Walnut Creek Hotel. Before he had it long, Mr. and Mrs. Eugene Costaldo, also from Livermore, bought out Mr. Alden. In 1925 the ground floor contained the kitchen and dining room, and the upstairs rooms were rented. In January 1932 the Costaldos remodeled the downstairs, reducing the size of the large kitchen, making two dining rooms, one for the general public and the other for banquets and parties.

Their chef became noted for the quality of the meals he served. In spite of his never-changing menu, he repeatedly did make Thursday dinners different. On that day of the week he served pork chops. Crowds of people drove out to the country just to eat at the Walnut Creek Hotel because of its excellent meals. A waitress who worked there and wishes to remain anonymous remembers: "The cook didn't just rinse the vegetables, he *scrubbed* them. The only complaint I can remember came from the foreman of one of the work crews. He complained to me about the dry cheese sandwiches Mrs. Costaldo made for his men, 'Gee, don't you ever make anything else?' She made the same ones day after day but after his complaint she let me make them and I gave them some variety."

Al Peronetto bought out the Costaldos and operated the hotel for eighteen years. Eventually Peronetto's rooms remained empty once the traffic from Oakland and Berkeley rolled through the Caldecott Tunnel to Walnut Creek; the ride was so short people didn't need to stay over.

Fewer and fewer diners came to his dining room and finally Peronetto had the old building torn down. He replaced it with a basalt block building and this time he put in three stores on the ground floor, 1517, 1519 and 1521 North Main. He built ten bedrooms upstairs and rented them by the month. As soon as he filled the building with tenants Peronetto sold out. The site has changed several times and today it is prime Walnut Creek commercial property occupied by Dandy Dogs and Ming Quong.

In the 1920s many people bought automobiles for the first time. The Model T Ford sold for $600 to $800 and it really started the rush for every family to own a car. People had been accustomed to taking the train when they went on a vacation. Now they commenced riding in their own vehicles. The spirit of adventure and daring was shared by those early motorists. Fewer than half the highways were paved in 1925. The first in Contra Costa County were the Martinez to Crockett and the Franklin Canyon roads. Both were paved in 1919. However, the novelty of going places in one's own auto overcame any deterrent posed by dirt roads.

Hotels charged from three to five dollars a night in many cities, and thrifty vacationers sought less expensive lodging. Whether the need created the auto court or the auto court created the demand is moot, but in the late '20s many travelers looked for one-dollar accommodations as the best they could afford.

The auto court was a series of one-room uncarpeted cabins with a

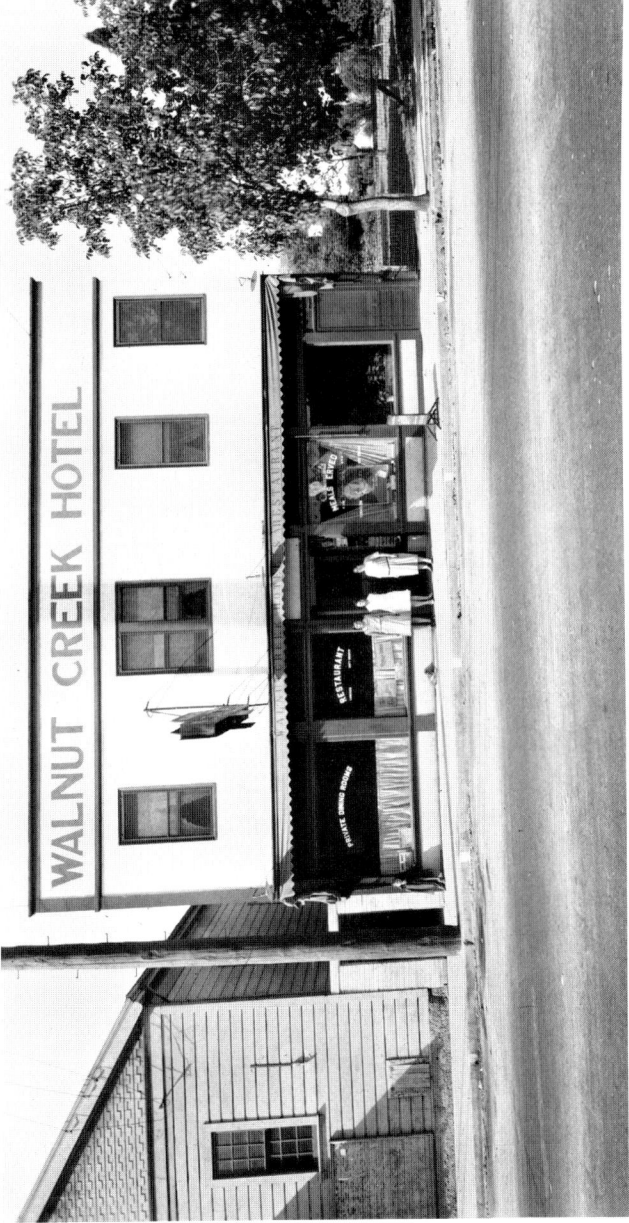

Walnut Creek Hotel, ca. 1930s.

carport adjoining each. The room usually contained a double bed with mattress, a small table and a chair. In one corner a one- or two-burner gas plate alongside a sink comprised the kitchen. In another corner a partition enclosed a wash basin and toilet. A window with the simplest of curtains completed the furnishings. Guests brought their own linens for bed and bath and there may or may not have been a rug beside the bed.

However, the auto court was affordable and Walnut Creek had two of them. One remains, and thousands drive right past unknowingly at 2044 Mount Diablo Boulevard. Grace Sommers of Rossmoor recalls the White Spot and how her parents came to buy it.

"My parents, Henry and Tillie Dick, lived thirty miles from the nearest railroad at Lustre, Montana. They homesteaded on an Indian reservation where they opened a general merchandise store and a post office.

"In the early '30s they moved to Walnut Creek and bought the White Spot which had (it's still there) the owner's cottage out in front, but only four cabins in back (ten now). They rented them out at one dollar a night but charged fifty cents more if they had to furnish the bedding and make up the bed. We had a lockup roadside stand out front where we sold many staples and where our tenants could get some of the food they needed. My folks added four more cabins in 1935.

"We used to be able to look all the way downtown from the White Spot in those days—there was hardly any building to block our view then."

Mr. Williamson, the present owner, says, "A couple of years ago the city asked us to take down the sign which said, 'White Spot.' They thought it discredited the city's image." The White Spot is still there in 1984 though its tenants rent by the month now rather than by the day.

White Spot Auto Court, 1984.

MEMORABILIA

One Walnut Creek success story involves a boy brought up on his father's goat dairy at Napa where, in 1921, he helped milk ninety goats twice a day. Seven years later his father sold the goats and bought land in Biter Canyon, Calistoga, California. For part of his sons' 4-H Club project the father bought a herd of forty-five milk cows.

From 1928 to 1939 the two boys and their father operated a daily delivery route in the Calistoga area. Their project quickly grew into a profitable enterprise. In summer they processed as many as 2,800 quarts of milk a day.

While on his route one day, Dick slammed on his truck's brakes at the sight of a slender girl in a gingham dress standing on the porch of her parents' home. Spellbound, he gawked at the young lady, unable to say a word. Within minutes he vowed, "Someday I'm going to marry that girl!" Before too long he got up nerve enough to introduce himself to Alta, and eventually he did marry her. In years to come they made a loving team and worked hard and well together to achieve their goals.

Before they came to Walnut Creek, Greyhound Bus Lines had its station at the Colonial Kitchen, a restaurant on the southwest corner of Main and Mount Diablo (Great Western Savings now). It was a good thing only six buses a day served Walnut Creek before 1940 because there was no on-site parking at the Colonial Kitchen. Meantime Dick and Alta Lommel had moved to Walnut Creek from Calistoga, bought the northeast corner of Main and Civic (Hibernia Bank today) and built a creamery. Greyhound saw the big field left over after Dick's construction and sounded him out about making him their agent.

The Lommels paid only $500 down on the corner and committed themselves to a fifty-dollar-per-month payment. They borrowed $6,000 to build the creamery, and opened it for business on July 4, 1939, two and a half years before Pearl Harbor.

Dick and Alta did take on the Greyhound agency when only six buses a day came to Walnut Creek. They sold tickets along with ice cream cones, milkshakes and other dairy products. The first few months they sold enough tickets to earn ninety dollars a month in commissions, a welcome sum to help with their monthly payment.

Their creamery business grew faster than even they anticipated. They hired a few young women and later a few more and eventually had twelve on the payroll. Years later Dick would proudly say, "We never laid off anyone because of slack business the entire time we had the creamery." Both the Lommels stayed on the job, many days working twelve to fourteen hours. Then, in 1940, the Sacramento Northern discontinued running passenger trains and more travelers than ever turned to Greyhound. World War II broke out in the Pacific and military personnel rode the buses in untold numbers. From the six buses, now 125 a day stopped at their station. Their commissions ran to "several thousand" a month. Dick and Alta's creamery turned out 4,000 to 5,000 gallons of ice cream a month, over 50,000 a year.

The Lommels were happy and cheerful hard workers. They worked from early to late without regard for the hours spent at the creamery. They took only a few vacations but they enjoyed people and what they were doing.

Lommel's Creamery became known in the creamery trade as the fifth largest independent ice cream distributor in the western states. On summer days they served from 5,000 to 8,000 cones. In their last year they served 350,000 ice cream cones and 100,000 milkshakes.

In March 1974 Dick and Alta gave their business to their daughter and son.

The Lommels built a large home on Lakewood Drive where they still live.

In retirement the couple worked almost as hard to achieve a goal which surfaced belatedly. Although Dick's father was Swiss and his paternal grandfather German, his perception of a need for better understanding among people worldwide could hardly be traced to them. Some inner motivation moved the couple to do what they could to further unanimity among nationalities.

Dick, long a Rotarian, accepted the chairmanship of the local club's International Relations Committee. In addition he was appointed a director of the International House at the University of California and for ten years he assisted the American Field Service in finding Contra Costa County homes for foreign students.

The Lommels' conviction that they should aid young people of every color and origin grounded in the concept, "People come from a single source and we are fundamentally more alike than unlike." They believe that young persons returning to their homelands will spread the good word about the United States faster than anyone. The Lommels are convinced that if we each put more effort into a positive approach, finding ways *we can get along* with people, regardless of race, color or creed, the world will be a much happier place. With that in mind they have made their home a sanctuary for students from thirty-six countries.

They took such a personal interest in these individuals whenever they had problems, that over the years scores have remained in residence; in one case a student stayed for seven years. The Lommels fully believe the first impression, the initial contact, is the one which is heard most often back in the visitor's homeland. So hundreds of new arrivals, with indefinite destinations, spent their first nights in the United States in Alta and Dick's home.

The Lommels recall the Soviet student sent here in the first group of twenty-five Russian exchange students. Yuri Boshilov would not accept the idea that his host was entertaining him at dinner for several nights, of his own volition. Yuri pointed to the half-dozen automobiles other guests arrived in. "They are party people!" he declared, knowing that only Communist officials could own such cars in Russia. The next day Dick drove him to the Sacramento Valley and together they inspected a tomato harvester, saw an automatic milking machine in a dairy, and a walnut huller in a plant processing nuts.

149

When the Russian student returned for a visit two weeks later Dick found him an exuberant enthusiast for things American.

Anyone who has shared in this international experience, no matter how briefly, won't fail to know the affection and love which grows between host and guest. The Lommels, in complete modesty, claim they have received more from their experiences than they have given. From their guests, many now mothers and fathers back in their native lands, the hosts still receive warm letters. Some went home ten years or more ago and yet words of gratitude still cross the oceans. From Brazil, Thailand, the Phillipine Islands and even from Yuri Boshilov back in the Soviet Union, Alta and Dick receive letters reflecting the love given them in years past in Walnut Creek.

From the day in 1878 when Dr. J. E. Pearson opened his pharmacy on Mount Diablo Boulevard, the town has never been without at least two drug stores. Samuel Johnson competed with Pearson in those days, and their successors have kept the rivalry going.

Theodore "Ted" Wiget opened his drug store in the 1300 block of North Main Street in 1913. Like others before him he carried merchandise other than drugs. Ted's brother Bert farmed in Ygnacio Valley and raised a son, Bud, who won national honors in outboard motor competition.

On August 16, 1944 a newcomer to Walnut Creek opened a pharmacy at 1395 North Main Street. Marshall Maguire was the new man's name. He had recently received his pharmacist's license by examination, having no college degree. (Maguire couldn't go to college because he hadn't graduated from high school.) Serving his apprenticeship under experienced men, he learned his trade proficiently and passed the state examination.

Maguire operated his Main Street store for seven years. An extrovert, aggressive and tasteful, the ruddy-faced, red-headed druggist resented the necessity of carrying such non-drug merchandise as candy, stationery, periodicals, gift items and tobaccos. In 1954 he moved to 1428 Locust Street, where he shed himself of most of the unwanted lines. He opened specialty shops to sell the non-drug merchandise: the Pen Shop to sell stationery, pens, pencils and writing materials and the

Camera Shop to take over his photographic merchandise. In the new drug store he did not have a soda fountain or a supply of alcoholic beverages. He had rid himself of the tobacco and periodicals and now he could devote himself to filling prescriptions and selling drugs.

Maguire offered twenty-four-hour prescription service, a benefit not offered elsewhere in the community.

The pharmacist sold out to John Norvik after seven years and subsequently Norvik sold to Newell Pharmacy. In 1984 Newell Pharmacy has Marshall Maguire's 1954 telephone number. Newell's "Yellow Page" advertisement in the 1984 telephone book still carries the notation, "Same as Maguire's Pharmacy."

Maguire sold out before chain stores moved into the drug business, but in retirement he is anything but inactive. Until 1971, Maguire made himself available to fill in for any druggist in need. Meanwhile he and his wife, Dorothy, have put their backs to the wheel for many causes in the city's last quarter century. He served as president of the Walnut Festival Association and for many years as head cashier. Currently he serves as head cashier for Art on the Main and for Concours d'Elegance, the John Muir Memorial Hospital benefit program at Heather Farm.

Marshall Maguire was elected president of the Walnut Creek Historical Society one year and served on its board for many more. He and Dorothy planned and staged dozens of programs for that society. He has served on the Contra Costa County Drug Abuse Commission for a number of years. For twelve years Maguire has been a member of the cast of the *Razzamatazz*, the annual play staged to benefit the Walnut Creek Historical Society and its Shadelands Museum.

A popular member of the Elks Club, Lions, and of the festival association and historical society, Maguire enjoys his retirement with his wife Dorothy, and his two daughters' families.

One Walnut Creek success story involves a World War II sailor, newly discharged at Bainbridge, Maryland in 1946. Tony Lupoi had aspirations for medical school but came to Walnut Creek instead. This account begins with his uncle, John Lupoi, from Sinopoli, Italy.

As Tony tells it, "My father and his brother made their way from Italy to McKeesrock, Pennsylvania soon after 1900. After one winter there Uncle John rode the rods under freight cars to a warmer place he'd heard of—California. He arrived here penniless, no friends and no job. For several years he made a living picking fruit in valley towns from Fresno to Vacaville.

"Later, somehow he had two dairies, one in Tracy and one in Lafayette. He lost first one and then the other. Then for a number of years he eked out a living driving a team and wagon from the Tracy area, hauling produce to Oakland for commission merchants there. He worked for almost nothing, but the merchants trusted him. They would give him cash in advance to pay for the loads he picked up for them."

Tony pointed to North Broadway Street. "Farry Granzotto lived over there. He let Uncle John live in a little cabin behind his house. One of the Stows nicknamed Uncle John 'Caranza.' My uncle couldn't read or write and had never corresponded with my father. Mrs. Granzotto offered to write to relatives for him at the only address he knew, back in Italy. She did and eventually a reply came giving him my father's address in Pennsylvania. So, about forty years after he came west, Uncle John went to McKeesrock for a long visit and during that time I received my discharge from the navy."

Tony reluctantly discussed his years in the service. His experiences involved becoming an "operating room technician." He joined up in 1942 and did duty at Aei Naval Hospital in Honolulu. He also served on submarines, and at the request of Dr. Norman Klein, the commander assigned to the submarine base at Midway Island, went to work in that dispensary. While there an accident befell Tony which nearly cost him the sight of one eye. An enlisted man jolted his arm as he picked up an open container of carbolic acid and some of it splashed on his face and right eye. From his operating room experience he knew he must neutralize the acid quickly with alcohol, but the only such remedy in sight the instant he needed it was a bottle of medicinal whiskey. Tony literally bathed his face and eye in it and hoped for the best. The early diagnosis the doctors reached was that the eye must be removed. Fortunately they delayed and ultimately the eye healed itself. Tony recuperated at Pearl Harbor and six months after the accident returned to duty without any lasting damage.

"Uncle John was at my father's when I came home and he asked me to come out to Walnut Creek with him. I married Dorothy Jankowsky first (July 1946) and seven days later left with my uncle. Dorothy came a few weeks after. Meanwhile we lived at the Las Palmas Hotel (formerly Rogers Hotel) in a basement room. I think we paid nine dollars a month rent.

"Uncle John bought an old truck and on a Monday morning we'd drive down the valley buying whatever produce was in season. We'd bring it back, and from Wednesday through Sunday we'd park under a shade tree on Mount Diablo Boulevard west of Bonanza, until we sold out. That property out there was selling from one month to the next so we couldn't be sure where we'd park each week."

Tony reflected, "The truck and Uncle John got old about the same time. One day he said, 'I'm retiring tomorrow,' and he did. I went out and bought an army surplus truck to haul with and Dorothy and I bought a house up on Buena Vista. Uncle John, ill much of the time, lived with us there for the rest of his life.

"I gave up selling from the truck in 1951. There was an old house on this place and another behind it where Mr. Cameron lived." He referred to his property on Ygnacio Valley Road at Civic where he has his store today. "Through the realtor, Joe Cavallero, I bought this property for $15,000. At that time I sold produce all over the area. There was a saying in the trade out here, 'No matter where you bought it, Lupoi had it first.' Restaurants, hotels, hospitals and schools—from Concord to Danville—all used to buy from me. From my years of contacts I knew who I could count on to sell me fresh, quality produce, and my customers were sure I would have the best for them. Even Hagerstrom and Purity markets bought from me. The chains were my competition but the old saying saw me through: 'Quality will be remembered long after price is forgotten!'"

Tony speaks of the early days of his Ygnacio Valley store. "I only expected to use it as an office for my wholesale business but we added groceries and dairy to the produce and stayed open more hours as the months passed. The retail business grew so big back in the days before convenience markets [that] on weekends and holidays we'd sell truckloads of bread and milk."

Tony speaks of his and Dorothy's two children. "Our daughter, Judy, and her husband are in business for themselves. They own a nursery in Oren, Utah."

With pride Tony tells of his son John's career in health services. "His company is Sport Health, Inc. in Walnut Creek where they prescribe programs to maximize good health."

Predictably, Tony has invested in rental real estate in Walnut Creek. While he doesn't have to work so hard any more, now that he has six or seven employees, he still gets up at 3:00 A.M. six mornings a week. His day ends at 6:30 each evening. He fully believes, "The one who has the most luck is the one who works the hardest."

It may not seem fair to single out any one teacher who has served the youth of Walnut Creek for special attention. Yet, the qualities this teacher showed are the same ones which must be attributed to scores of other self-sacrificing classroom leaders over a century. So, to point out his qualities is to emphasize what parents should be aware their children face in many of the teachers they see daily.

As an ex-Marine and a former football player, California-born Elmo Giulieri came to Walnut Creek in 1947. The only male teacher in Walnut Creek's grammar school, he taught fifty eighth grade students and received $3,000 per year. He was always called on to set up chairs for assemblies, supervise the traffic-control monitors, coach all the after-school sports programs and chaperone the dances.

Giulieri started back to school himself in 1948 to work for his administrative credentials. His wife and three daughters seldom saw him at home in the evenings.

The students remember him well. One said, "Everybody really looked up to him because he was a kind of father figure." Another, "He was always fair and he kept order with authority." Again, "He was a Vince Lombardi type . . . a good old-fashioned teacher [and one who was] always there to listen to you."

In 1951 he served as principal of both the Walnut Heights and the Parkmead schools, with both on double sessions. He recalls, "I'd start out at one school in the morning and get that school organized and then go to the other . . . the next day I'd reverse the order." He wanted to know the name of every student. " . . . I don't know how I did it but I'd know every kid at school—the good ones as well as the bad ones."

Meanwhile Giulieri commuted to the University of California, Berkeley, working on his master's degree. He became involved with the Recreation Commission, serving as summer playground director, and refereed at high school basketball and football games. He served the county as commissioner of athletics for two years and as a member of the Recreation Committee for seven. In 1961 he was named director of special services, in charge of the pioneer program designed for handicapped children.

Giulieri admits he was lucky. "I was fortunate to have a wife and kids who were understanding." He went to summer school for three years when others took vacations, and he went to school at night and on Saturdays. In the spring of 1963 the principal received his appointment as superintendent of Walnut Creek schools.

Teachers remember him with different words but all with the same feeling. One praised him, " . . . the latitude he gave us to develop new programs, tempered with caution." Another, " . . . the professional freedom you felt when you worked under the guy, yet you still knew you had a boss." One teacher said of him, " . . . seemed like he remembered when he was a teacher. He always had time to listen to you no matter how busy he was. He didn't mind if you came in and cried on his shoulder." "A very compassionate man, a warm person, always a gentleman . . . " reports another.

Such is the caliber of one Walnut Creek teacher, and he is no exception. Many devoted, unselfish, considerate and concerned women and men have given and continue to give to our children more than we know and more than we expect of them. Fortunate indeed are the parents and students of Walnut Creek.

A lady who has been honored with Walnut Creek's "Man of the

Year" award is the great-granddaughter of one of the area's early pioneers.

David Glass, born in Pennsylvania, came to Placerville in August 1850. In November he left the mountains and came to The Corners and established his family in a cabin near Rudgear Road and San Ramon Creek. For a short time he sold staples from his house but soon moved to a farm he bought near Danville.

Lucille Glass Mauzy was born in the San Ramon Valley. She has been active on behalf of causes concerning the young throughout most of her adult life. She took a leadership role in the PTA and Youth Welfare, and has been a delegate to the Governor's Conference on Education and Juvenile Delinquency Prevention.

While taking an active part in the plumbing contracting business started by her husband's family, Mauzy Plumbing, founded in 1913, she also raised two daughters.

She devoted more time to education than any other single activity. At one point she was one-half of the team sent by the county to Sacramento to help develop the Comprehensive Master Plan for Special Education. However, her twenty-four years as an elected member of the Contra Costa County Board of Education has been her greatest contribution. She served from 1955 to 1979, during which she was twice elected president of the board.

Lucille Mauzy has received literally scores of honors for her work with youth organizations; the Birth Defect Foundation and the Juvenile Hall Auxiliary are but two examples.

When Mrs. Mauzy retired from the county board of education her colleagues honored her by renaming the Valley Special Education Center in Alamo the "Mauzy Special Day Care Center."

John Nejedly has been quoted in connection with his part in providing such needs in the community as a dependable source of high quality water, an adequate sewer system, and finally, the establishment of a needed community-wide hospital. There is another need he became aware of when he was elected county district attorney, and the story of his actions needs to be told.

When he was district attorney, Nejedly bought some acreage near Gold Lake in Sierra County. He tells why:

The district attorney's office provided little in terms of improving socially those convicted of crimes—we kept sending them to jail and jail made them worse—we weren't changing them at all. So a group of us began focusing on their pre-criminal behavorial patterns. We wanted to find out what their life-styles were, what conditions might get them into trouble. One of us would volunteer to help an individual with his math, civics, English or whatever was taught in their schools. We would go to their homes and community meetings at night and try to get a person-to-person relationship established. The kids were sharp. When they found out the volunteers could have been home with their families but chose to be with them instead, they sensed something positive.

When we opened the camp near Gold Lake we had a lot of help. Some companies who helped us financially were Dow Chemical, Standard Oil and Chevron, DuPont, Johns-Manville, Stauffer Chemical, Shell Oil and Phillips Petroleum. We had a great group of people who helped. Phil Heraty was one. Joe Silva, chairman of the board of supervisors, was our cook. Ed Lindshied was another. Mrs. Melba Lindshied was the craft director. Orrin Allen from the juvenile department was one of our directors. John Davis, the county probation officer, was another. The Sierra County people out of Johnsville gave us a lot of help too.

We had a cosmetic surgeon provide cosmetic surgery. A dentist did dental work on some of the children, and of course we had a doctor all of the time. We tried to find out what was affecting these young people psychologically. Many of them, previously delinquents or pre-delinquents, blossomed into human beings. One boy in our camp program was injured, and when Joe Silva and I went up to visit him the boy broke down crying, "I never thought anybody cared!" He just couldn't believe two men would drive 400 miles just because of him. He emerged into the world. Now he is an accountant at Standard Oil making more money than I ever did. Before he came to camp the principal at Pittsburg High was going to expel him, but because of the adult assistance the boy was getting, he let him stay.

157

I gave the property to the Boy Scouts a few years ago, but they let us use it for handicapped children six weeks a year. The Concord Rotary club just gave us [1983] $700 to sponsor two kids at our summer camp. We have an O'Hara camp event, for handicapped kids, for two weeks each summer. Kids with physical disabilities come up here and have a life experience they'd never have otherwise. We take about twenty-two or twenty-three with staff, but we have about 650 applicants. It's frustrating that we can't take them all. The Quincy-based Plumas County Sheriff's Posse picks them up and drives them to camp and later drives them out. We get a lot of good food from Sid Ross, who represents a number of canners. The Boy Scouts help out too.

HOSPITALS

The pioneer doctors who headquarted here were named earlier, but those who practiced here after 1900 deserve mention. So too does the arrival of the hospitals we take for granted now.

Walnut Creek had no hospital for its first sixty years and for the next forty only the most elementary health care existed. For almost one hundred years Walnut Creek residents had to drive eighteen miles to receive hospital attention. A prejudice existed against going to the county hospital in Martinez. The general feeling around Walnut Creek was, "Only indigents go there so the doctors can't be very good."

As there was no hospital in Concord or Walnut Creek at the turn of the century, Miss Alta Bates took in many patients from over-the-hill as early as 1904, the year she opened her home on Dwight Way for people needing care. Within three years Miss Bates moved to the original hospital building put up for her. It was built on the southwest corner of Regent and Webster streets in Berkeley.

Undoubtedly the first to open a hospital in Walnut Creek was Dr. Blumenburg who advertised his A-B-C Hospital in a local newspaper late in 1909. Nothing came of his venture as far as can be learned. Walnut Creek area residents waited until 1952 for the next hospital to be built in the community.

Dr. C. C. Leech took Dr. Breneman's place in 1897 and was practicing here at the turn of the century. Until his death in 1934 Leech served the town, and during that time he had two female competitors. Dr. Carolyn Cole practiced in Walnut Creek part time in the years 1906 to 1916, and Dr. Louise Oldenbourg, an anesthesiologist, came in 1915.

An East Bay medical man, Dr. Malcolm Goddard, had a large country house near Walnut Creek sometime before World War I. Goddard kept a bear cub at his place, until the bear grew up. His caretaker, Howard Smith, used to haul the cub around in Goddard's car, even downtown.

Eventually the bear grew too big and about the same time Smith left Goddard's employ. He went to work driving the first auto bus between Walnut Creek and Oakland. It had open sides, a top and hard rubber tires. The bus made so much noise that before you saw it, you could hear it coming.

Goddard and his bear left Walnut Creek at the same time. The doctor sold his house to Charles Howard, the father of three sons who became pillars of the community: Bruce, Harmon, and Peter.

During World War I Walnut Creek residents relied on a single dentist, Clifton Henderson. He established his office on the second floor of the Stow Building after the Masonic Lodge vacated the building.

Early in the 1920s a warm-hearted lady, a midwife, opened her three-bedroom home to expectant mothers. Two weeks was the customary post-delivery convalescent period in those times.

Norman Wilson's mother and Ted and Forrest Wilson's grandmother, of medium height and slightly stout, was known all over Walnut Creek as "Granny Wilson." Her single-story house was set back on a rise north of Mount Diablo Boulevard at about number 1950. After the doctor delivered the baby, Granny cared for mother and child. She usually had room for one mother and child at a time, but occasionally she made room for two. For a while, after her daughter-in-law passed away, she had her two grandsons to raise as well. They were live-wires and frequently got into mischief. A younger lady, the kind who always responded to calls for help, and who wishes to remain anonymous to this day, recalls the boys. "They were playing in a closet, apparently with matches, because they set the closet on fire. Granny called me, 'Please come over, those kids are driving me crazy!' I rushed over, smoke pouring out from somewhere, and those two kids were perched up on the roof!"

She recalls another incident. "Granny was mixing pancake batter one day. She had put it on the griddle when she called me for help. When I got there batter had exploded and stuck in little gobs all over the room. She found the empty box which explained what happened. When Granny was distracted those two kids emptied a whole box of popcorn into the batter."

So, with the exception of Granny Wilson's care for mothers with babies, Walnut Creek residents looked elsewhere for hospital care. Concord opened its first in 1930, a six-bed single-story bungalow. In 1935 an addition accommodated ten more patients, and only after 1946 could the Concord Hospital take in as many as thirty-eight patients. As the population grew in Walnut Creek, Alamo, Pleasant Hill and Lafayette, doctors sent more and more of their seriously ill patients to Herrick and Alta Bates in Berkeley and to the Oakland hospitals on "Pill Hill." Doctors lost time driving back and forth when they might have been seeing office patients.

In the early 1950s industrialist Henry Kaiser, who lived in Lafayette, became aware of the lack of hospital care in this area. He took action.

Kaiser's first choice of a site lay between Las Lomas High School and Newell Avenue on the east side of South Main Street. But because the city refused to pay for the bridge across Walnut Creek, and he wouldn't pay for it, Kaiser rejected that piece of property. At the time he was considering it, early 1952, that side of South Main Street was undeveloped; Capwell's, the first store, was not built then.

Mr. Kaiser's second choice was Ted Counter's Art and Garden Center across Main Street from the high school. Counter offered it on the market at $75,000 but when he recognized Henry J. Kaiser stomping across his acreage he raised the price to $100,000 and that is what Kaiser paid.

Jack Chapman, Kaiser's first administrator in Walnut Creek, reminisces at some length over those early times. "I think the Art and Garden Center was a little over five acres . . . they had a tea room . . . The Counters lived upstairs and the place was just full of things . . . it was like a museum. He was a collector of Indian lore." The property had numerous old outbuildings and Chapman eventually used most of them for storage or offices. "There was an old barn over in the corner of the property and they used to sell furniture there. I was told that was where radio station KKIS started . . . We took possession in May of 1952 and conversion started on the old Newell home right away. We turned it into a clinic and had it ready by August 4, 1952, in less than ninety days."

Shadrack Walker, a gardener from Alabama, was Chapman's first employee. Walker felt it important to save as many of Counter's plants as possible, and Chapman agreed.

June Gorman, the receptionist, was his second employee, and the third was the director of nursing, Maureen Rickey. Chapman remembers Maureen well. "She was an inventor. She created a device that is widely used throughout the United States. It is a little machine which tabulates, instead of counting every one by hand, the number of capsules of drugs put through it.

"Lenore Crane was my secretary. Our three physicians when we opened were Dr. Wallace Cook, Dr. Fred Pellegrin, and Dr. Steve Thomas. The first day we opened we had only five patients. We wondered if anybody was ever going to come in.

"Shortly after we opened construction started on the permanent clinic. Originally the hospital was designed for sixty beds. Mr. Kaiser lived right in Lafayette at that time and he would come over practically every day. It seemed like he was over there all the time.

"We opened the hospital clinic on September 9, 1953, although we had the new clinic running since May thirty-first."

Actually, the hospital plan was worked out in Henry J. Kaiser's living room. Sidney R. Garfield, M.D., medical director of Kaiser Foundation hospitals, devised a decentralized nursing station floor plan to save nurses as many as seven out of eight steps a conventional floor plan would require. With the architect, Clarence Mayhew, Kaiser and Garfield added all the modern aids to improve hospital care and added a number of beneficial ideas of their own.

Jack Chapman remembers the opening. "We had a preview for the public. It went on for two weeks, every night, 35,000 people marching through the hospital. They were very interested in the operating room . . . in the patient rooms they would sit on the beds, they were electric you know and we were the first to ever get that kind . . . the draperies opened and closed by a switch at bedside and everybody wanted to work them . . . it was rather wild."

Chapman relates that initially about 40 percent of the beds were filled by patients of non-Kaiser doctors. The hospital opened with seventy-six beds. He speaks about the problem of getting local people to accept this hospital. " . . . All of them had been going to Oakland for years, or wherever they commuted to work . . . and here we were with this funny little thing . . . "

Gradually membership picked up and within five years only staff doctors could admit patients for Kaiser care. The hospital still didn't own the 2½-acre corner of South Main and Newell. Joseph Sherman and his wife owned it and had a handsome Spanish style home there. They employed an English gardener and his wife, who lived in a tile house out in back. The Sherman house is used to this day; the house contains the injection clinic and the public affairs office. The Shermans' large swimming pool sat in the center of their property, under today's two-story medical office building and clinic. A *Look* magazine article of the times shows the hospital and the pool in the foreground. "Mr. Kaiser said that we ought to have a pool as a recreational facility . . . the insurance people said, 'You have to have a lifeguard' . . . so I had to get this great big chair and an umbrella and it seemed so odd . . . I'll bet we were the only hospital in the whole country to have a lifeguard. The kid we hired was the son of a doctor, Dr. Robert King. Later he became a doctor also. It was really kind of a kick to see him return as a physician . . . Doctors, nurses and staff swam in our pool as often as their schedule permitted." Alongside the pool Sherman had built a bar. "It had a soda fountain in it and a built-in beer tap . . . and a big, big fireplace where you could barbecue, and a great big pool house."

Chapman says the Walnut Creek facility was, in 1954, the first health care facility on the Pacific coast to have a microwave oven. "It was at least as wide as a desk with a very small cooking cavity. They were all vacuum tubes . . . Raytheon made the thing. We really attempted to do [new] things. We were the first to serve a kind of a modified diet. We had a breakfast cart with little coffee rolls, and you could plug in the cart as you moved down the hall. We had a variety of fruits and cereals and if you wanted a regular breakfast you could order it."

The first microwave oven sailed around in Air Force radar planes on the DEW line, Chapman believes. "The New York Central Railroad had one and then we got the third and so a lot of people would come out to see . . . how it cooked so fast."

Membership in the Kaiser Foundation Health Plan grew quickly once a few local persons received treatment there and vouched for the service. The two-story medical office building opened in 1960 and the south wing of the hospital followed in 1967.

A three-story addition costing $12 million will open in 1984. It will contain an ultramodern emergency room, nursery, and new intensive care, coronary and radiology units. Construction on this building commenced July 8, 1981.

Jack Chapman left as administrator in 1954 and is now the manager of education and training in Kaiser's Oakland regional office. He still remembers that first day in Walnut Creek when only five patients came through the doors. He shakes his head in wonder at the number of doctors and employees there now. The number of patients admitted in 1982: twenty-six in-patients a day, 9,719 for the year. The outpatient visits came to 1,950 a day, 711,343 for the year.

After only two years (1956) Kaiser's membership had grown so large that there was no room in the hospital for non-members. The area's independent doctors once again found it necessary to send their acutely ill patients to Oakland and Berkeley. Again, it reduced the time they had to treat office callers.

In early 1957 fifty local physicians got together and decided to see what they could do to build a fifty-bed hospital. Meanwhile a smaller group of doctors advanced $6,000 to defray preliminary expenses.

1958 was the year a board of trustees incorporated the Walnut Creek Community Hospital. John Nejedly, named chairman that year, became executive committee chairman the following January. Forty-six physicians and one lay person pledged $80,600 in 1958, and in October they decided to buy a ten-acre site for $31,675. While it may not be entirely fair to point out just a few persons when so many helped to make the facility a reality, two others actively assisted Nejedly in those first days when the ultimate building did not even exist on paper. They were Al Layton and Dr. Frederick Hanson.

In the summer of 1959 Mrs. Harmon (Joan) Howard led the organization of a women's auxiliary to assist the board with its fund raising activities and other needed volunteer services.

Also during this summer, believing a more appropriate name would better serve an area-wide facility, the hospital held a contest among school children in central Contra Costa. As a result, the board chose the name "John Muir Memorial Hospital."

Fund raising brought in only $218,000 by the end of 1959, toward a goal of $750,000. Trustee Al Layton advised his board in mid-1960 that some government money might be available if the plans were increased so as to build a 150-bed hospital. Estimates came in placing the cost of such a facility at about $4 million.

In 1961 the board submitted its request for state assistance on the larger plan, which provided for future expansion to 250 beds. Layton orally pleaded John Muir Memorial's case before the Hosptial Advisory Council in Los Angeles, and as a result, on February 20, 1962 received an allotment of $2,482,174 in state funds. Layton also received a commitment for a $1.2 million long-term mortgage from four banks. At this time $250,000 in contributions were on hand. Thus, with almost $4 million available, the building committee went to work.

David Zuckerman chaired that group and Ray F. Farwell (administrator of the Swedish Hospital in Seattle) was hired as consultant-administrator.

Construction of the John Muir Memorial Hospital started on April 8, 1963 and was completed in March 1965. The hospital opened to serve the community in April 1965.

The hospital was the first high-rise building built in Walnut Creek. It was the first in the county to build a cardiac care unit. John Muir

Memorial Hospital has a gymasium for patient rehabilitation. The hospital's equipment includes a CT head and body scanner. It also operates hyperbaric oxygen therapy (the administration of 100 percent oxygen at increased pressure, which helps burn cases, carbon monoxide intoxicates, gas embolism, etc.) twelve hours a day, averaging 100 treatments a month. These are only a few of the advanced treatment processes used by John Muir Memorial Hospital.

The hospital has been a 262-bed facility since major expansion in 1975. It employed 1,140 persons in 1983 and has an ambulatory care center for out-patient services which provided for some 56,000 visits in 1982.

John Muir Memorial Hospital is owned by the public. It is a non-profit organization and no person or group can benefit financially from its successful organization.

LAW AND ORDER

The offices of constable and town marshal were easily confused. A constable was elected as the enforcement officer of the justice court, presided over by the justice of the peace. Normally felonies were investigated by the county sheriff's office. The town marshal served only the community which hired him. Walnut Creek hired a marshal only at intervals, having insufficient numbers of crimes to warrant the cost of the employee.

All through the village's first sixty years a few misdemeanors brought an occasional charge of such crimes as: "He stole a chicken from my coop." Or "He took some clothes from my line!" Or"This man swore in front of my wife and children!"

The first town marshal, A. N. Paterson, appeared before the trustees' meeting on April 7, 1915, asking to be "supplied with a reliable gun." The trustees told him to buy one at the "lowest price possible."

In August 1917 the trustees hired a night watchman, F. S. Dirion, at fifty dollars a month.

Because fines would pay his salary, a part time traffic officer was hired by the trustees in 1924. He was Lon Buck and the city paid him ten dollars for each day he worked.

Orville Stow served as town marshal in the years 1918-19. Charles Reed well remembers Stow's tolerance when a ball Reed hit went through a window in Stow's house. "Orville Stow was a good guy," Charles Reed recently reminisced. "He didn't make a big deal of it by complaining to my parents; he just asked, "Are you willing to pick almonds for me this season and pay me back for what the window will cost me?'

"Of course I agreed on the spot and I did work it off.

"I remember Harry Stow sometimes treating us kids to ice cream cones."

In 1923 the old town jail still stood east of Main Street (what is now Mount Diablo Boulevard). Harry Stow reported to the trustees, "The lockup is uninhabitable."

In 1926 Theodore Berling succeeded Stow as town marshal and two years later, on August 1, 1928, the city appointed him chief of police (the first) and license collector, at a salary of fifty dollars a month. Thirty days later the first speed limit signs went up—fifteen miles per hour throughout town. In 1936 the telephone operator in Bradley's Confectionery would summon the police chief by turning a switch which lit a red light on a pole in front of the store. Even in Berkeley a variation of this practice called policemen to an emergency.

Finally, in 1940 Walnut Creek created a true chief of police. Theodore Berling took the job and gave up his duty as license collector. Serious crime still didn't exist in Walnut Creek in the early 1940s. Occasional petty thefts or stolen automobiles were almost thought of as crime waves. Speeding automobile drivers were the most numerous law breakers apprehended.

There was one murder, whose tangled trail was so well hidden, the killer almost got away with the perfect crime. Strangely enough, this murder was the only one in the first 100 years of Walnut Creek's history. The crime took place in the abandoned Diablo Glove Factory in 1925. This building stood on the hill above the Walnut Creek Cannery (Gemco today) north of Ygnacio Valley Road. The factory consisted of two or three hollow tile outbuildings, a gaunt two-story frame structure with basement and a first floor laboratory.

Shortly after the November 1918 armistice ended World War I, a promoter came to town with what might still be considered a practical idea. He built a two-story frame building where he would employ women to sew rabbit skins into gloves.

He let it be known around town he had a number of one-acre parcels on Walden Road and anyone who bought one from him and raised rabbits on it would always have a ready buyer for all the skins they could deliver.

For a time, his plan worked. He did buy skins and he did hire women who stitched skins into gloves.

One of the purchasers who bought on Walden Road was noticeable around town for his unorthodox style of dress. The man used rouge and lipstick and walked around town with bracelets on his arms. But he too raised rabbits and sold the skins to the glove factory. Many local girls in the early 1920s crocheted designs on the gloves. Mrs. Rushton was the floor lady who instructed the girls and tallied their work. But the factory didn't pay its way and sometime in 1923 it closed.

Before long the Pacific Cellulose Company bought the plant through negotiations with its representative, Charles Henry Schwartz. (Actually, the two were one and the same. Schwartz sold stock in his company.) As long as Schwartz paid his local bills, he sold stock in his venture, but when he went behind in his accounts, local merchants lost interest.

Schwartz had his private laboratory in the rear of his building and his order to employees was to stay out. His stockholders disturbed him, "When will the plant go into operation?" Schwartz claimed he was only a few days away from perfecting his formula to make artificial silk, and the machinery he had ordered from Germany would be arriving at San Francisco any day.

July 30, 1925 dawned to a chilly fog in Oakland, where Schwartz lived with his wife and three children. It would be a long day for the chemist. He arrived in Walnut Creek in good time, bought a new tire for his car at a service station and went to the plant, puttering about his laboratory. Mrs. Elizabeth Hatfield, his secretary, observed that he was very nervous all day, going in and out of his laboratory dressed in "a long yellow dust coat" and visibly sweating.

There was a dog that frequented the building owned by the watchman, Walter Gonzales. Schwartz like the dog—and had always been kind to it—but to everyone's surprise he almost kicked it away from a locked closet door where it had been sniffing. In late afternoon the chemist was heard to telephone H. M. Kleinjung of San Francisco, titular head of Pacific Cellulose. He reported he had just perfected his formula and all he needed now was the equipment he had ordered overseas. Jubilantly Schwartz accepted a dinner invitation from the Alamo stockholder, M. A. Ray. After dinner he told Mr. and Mrs. Ray he intended working late that night and he left them shortly after 7:00 P.M.

Back at the plant he jested with the night watchman and about nine o'clock sent him to buy a package of gum and a flashlight bulb. After Gonzales returned he heard the chemist calling his wife on the telephone and telling her he would be home soon.

Schwartz told the nightwatchman to lie down for an hour or two, that he wouldn't be needed until Schwartz left the plant. After a half hour the uneasy Gonzales left his cot, drawn by a premonition. "Something seemed to take me by the coat lapel and pull me out toward the lab!"

He'd barely left the outbuilding when, in a blinding roar, the sky lit up as thought it were daylight. Plumes of fire shot over the roof. The shattering explosion roared over the sleepy town. Violet flames shot from the lab windows. Masses of acrid smoke poured from the doorway, the force of the blast having blown out the door and frame. Jets of burning chemicals sprayed a terrific background of pyrotechnics over the plant.

Gonzales snatched a fire extinguisher and screamed, "Doc, Doc!" plunging toward the blazing room. The first onlookers, red flames reflecting in their faces, saw Gonzales throw down the extinguisher and run to a telephone. The Walnut Creek Model T fire truck arrived on the scene "scarcely five minutes later." Hooking lines to nearby hydrants, the volunteers quickly had two streams of water pouring into the gaping hole that had been the lab doorway.

"Hurry! Hurry! My boss is in there!" the watchman screamed.

"No man could live through that," a spectator shouted.

With the efficiency of professionals, the Walnut Creek firemen extinguished the blaze in just a few minutes. Strangely, little damage had been done inside the lab. The explosion blew the door out but the windows were unbroken. Some paint was scorched and some of the furniture charred. On the floor, in an aisle between two benches, was a heap of charred fabric, still burning, with something under it which turned out to be a body.

"He was working late! Something must have gone wrong!" lamented Gonzales.

During the grim business which followed, the firemen found $2.69 in coins lying on the floor. Under the body were fragments of a blanket, the remains of Schwartz's shirt, some cards and some keys. Lying across one shoulder was the chemist's watch and chain.

By now the coroner's men had arrived and they agreed the body was indeed that of Schwartz, presuming that he had died only an hour or so before, although rigor mortis was already pronounced. The body was burned beyond recognition, but Schwartz's dentist in Berkeley replied affirmatively to the question, "Did Dr. Schwartz have a molar missing on his lower left jaw?"

"It is all so impossible," sobbed Mrs. Schwartz, brought to the scene by friends. "And him just now on the verge of success."

"He worked too hard!" sympathized Gonzales. "The last time he sent me on an errand he looked wild-eyed. I said to him, 'Doc, why not quit now and go home and get some sleep.'"

As Guy F. Spencer, chief of the Walnut Creek Fire Department, came to inspect the scene the next morning, he couldn't help noticing Dr. Schwartz's car parked in its usual place, with one new tire, clean of dust and dirt. Descending into the basement he looked at the studding above him and saw bloodstains.

He went back upstairs and found a larger stain, quite fresh, in a closet opening off the laboratory. There were blood stains on the closet walls and some had run into a corner, collecting there and seeping through cracks in the floor. He thought the room sparsely supplied with lab equipment and wondered, "Where does he keep it?"

The presence of blood was not unnatural but its presence in a closed closet was! What about the body found between the two benches with a blanket around it? Could Gonzales have killed the doctor? Officials took the nightwatchman into custody and drove him over to Berkeley where Mr. Edward O. Heinrich had just invented the

171

polygraph, the lie detector. Protesting his innocence, Gonzales took the test and Heinrich pronounced him innocent.

When Heinrich learned a thorough autopsy had not been performed on the corpse, he insisted on one. When he analyzed the condition of the lungs, he decided the man had died before the explosion. The fingertips had been defaced by acid burns, and the eyeballs punctured, preventing identification by the usual means! The man's height had been taller than Schwartz's five feet four inches. The missing tooth did match the chemist's missing molar, but it had been *knocked* out!

Mrs. Schwartz insisted the body was her husband's. "I looked at it for almost fifteen minutes and I should know." The dentist maintained it was Schwartz, and Gonzales was sure it was "Doc." But death was ruled as caused by a blow or blows to the skull, presumably by a hammer. Heinrich could find nothing in the lab which could have caused the fracture. Further, "No real chemist," he said later, "would be fooled by that laboratory. Evidence of experiments is non-existent. I think it is an elaborate front for an insurance fraud."

Mr. Kleinjung, president of Pacific Cellulose, rebutted, " . . . the chemist's experiments had been completed to the satisfaction of the officers of the company, and the valuable formula reposes in the company vaults."

Meanwhile Walnut Creek saw a wave of reporters and sightseers flood into town, more than the residents ever dreamed possible. The few restaurants filled for breakfast and stayed crowded all day long. The hotels (two) had every bed filled. The telegraph office at the Southern Pacific station handled messages to east coast newspapers as well as to the north and south. Every dateline read, "Walnut Creek, California."

Finally search warrants went out for Schwartz. But who *was* the dead man? One local laborer called "Portuguese Joe" or Joseph Rodriguez was missing. His friends searched all his haunts and reported him not seen for four days, since the day before the explosion. His intimates prepared to mourn him. Then one day, five days after the fire, Joe ambled sheepishly into town, having been in Oakland for the weekend.

Meanwhile E. O. Heinrich evolved a description of the dead man. The soiled and tattered socks on the corpse's feet, the "tramp-type" blanket around the body, and the coffee "bindle" (a cloth bag which could be rolled up as coffee was consumed), all spelled "hobo." He found religious tracts and a Bible with underscorings on the bench. In the Gospel according to Saint Matthew, the sixteenth verse of the fourth chapter was underscored: "Behold, I send you forth as sheep in the midst of the wolves." And still another read in part, " . . . as ye go, preach, saying the Kingdom of Heaven is at hand . . . "

To Heinrich these clues said "itinerant preacher." He put the description of the body onto the teletype and it came to the attention of an undertaker in Placerville. He reported he occasionally employed an itinerant preacher of that description and they kept in touch by letters. One was overdue now from the man—Gilbert Barbe. Barbe, his friend said, was a shell-shocked veteran of World War I who had given up a white-collar life to take up his mission among workers. So this was the murdered man—and where was the murderer?

Henry Schwartz was now being hunted the length and breadth of California. A few still maintained he had died in the explosion. One of these was a bachelor, Harold Warren, of the Nottingham Apartments in Oakland. Warren had been invited but couldn't accept the dinner invitation of his neighbors, Mr. and Mrs. Robert Heywood. Another couple, Mr. and Mrs. N. B. Edmunds, did attend. The main topic of conversation throughout the evening was the Walnut Creek murder.

During the dinner Mr. Edmunds said he had never seen a picture of the chemist, whereupon his host retrieved one from the Sunday *Oakland Tribune*. By a most unusual and ironic twist of fate, Edmunds had a friend in the Berkeley Police Department, Officer Walter Pidgeon, who had once shown him how to cover up various portions of a photograph and point to other features. He did this now on the picture Heywood had just brought him. It struck him how much parts of the picture looked like his fellow apartment house dweller, Harold Warren, the missing dinner guest. The more he thought of it the more excited he became. Late that night, with his heart in his mouth, he called the Berkeley police. Harold Warren's zero hour came at three o'clock the next morning. Pidgeon and other officers went to the front door of the apartment. The manager went with them and knocked on Warren's door. There was no answer, but someone could be heard moving about. The police rushed the door, but it held. They went around to the rear when suddenly they heard a single shot. They broke down the door easily and found Schwartz unconscious and dying. There was a half finished note, saying in part, " . . . I made a dirty job of it."

Many questions about Walnut Creek's famous murder story were never answered. How did Schwartz get back to Oakland from Walnut Creek the night of the murder? He had taken out an insurance policy for a total of $190,000 in case of accidental death. Suicide cancelled all but $20,000 of it, but how did Schwartz expect to capitalize on the larger sum since the beneficiary was the Pacific Cellulose Company?

The glove factory became a four-unit apartment house, and the town settled down to its amiable, tree-studded, slow-moving self. Before long most people forgot the cold-blooded killing.

Before the murder Theodore Berling was the police department, and when he retired in the late forties, his nightwatchman, Johnny Jordan, succeeded him.

Chet Arthur recalls vividly the experience a new police officer faced early in his duties.

"It was in 1948 or '49 that we had young fellows who liked to show off how fast they could drive their cars. A rookie cop started bragging that he would slow them down. As it turned out, they knew Walnut Creek better than he did. One night they teased him into chasing them and they deliberately turned down a dead-end street. At the end they made sharper turns than he could, and the officer's car rolled over. There were three or four ruffians who planned it."

With every aspect of life in the 1945-1955 period growing in size—population, numbers of stores, numbers of automobiles, schools and churches—the police department also grew. By 1955 there was a chief, three sergeants, a secretary and eight patrolmen. They ran two patrol cars, one a 1954 Chevrolet Belair sedan and the other a 1953 Ford. After five o'clock in the evening the county sheriff's office took all the calls.

In 1957 the city council appointed Lee M. Brilliant chief, and John B. Jordan stepped down to captain, due for retirement soon.

One officer joined the department as a reserve in 1955 and is now Lieutenant John Cashman. He speaks of the department as it was. "Our old cars then didn't have powerful engines and the radios were very old. They had huge tubes and the set almost filled the front seat. They put out so much heat we didn't need heaters.

"Chief Brilliant asked for funds for officer training and for equipment and got them. He had a law degree from Boalt Hall in Berkeley. He led the way to modernization and today we have the most sophisticated equipment available. Brilliant was very strong on public service, education and training. Because of his foundation, those principles carry through to today. He believed officers should become involved in the community and help people, not just arrest them; they should counsel and be available to citizens. Today we are out to help people succeed and assist them. We didn't agree with Brilliant at first, but now we see his ideas were the correct ones.

"Chief Davis and Chief Burke followed Brilliant, and today our chief is Karel A. Swanson.

"Walnut Creek will be known for years for its innovative ideas. We know we are in a favored place—there are many communities in the Bay Area who couldn't do as we have. We operate today with seventy-five sworn officers, approximately twenty-five civilian personnel and a reserve of about thirty people. Some volunteers, largely from Rossmoor, come in and help us with our microfilming at no cost to us. About twenty Explorer Scouts from Post 600 come in and help us with fingerprinting. They also help us at Walnut Festival time. We have volunteers, male and female, who ride with us as reserve officers in the open space program. They ride bikes and horses.

"In the early '50s when we had Mel's Drivein and Hoakies' Drive-In, local kids did a lot of cruising, but in the '60s people

175

came from as far away as Reno just to cruise in Walnut Creek. We even had one Chinese youth gang from San Francisco get into a problem here one night. They ran over two of our local boys and left, saying they'd be back. We checked with the SFPD and found several of them, fourteen- and fifteen-year-olds, had been involved in homicides. We put together a SWAT team to deal with them, but they never came back. Today we are clean as a hound's tooth and we can devote our time to other things.

"In the late '50s and mid-'60s we discovered we had all the drugs around us: LSD, marijuana and the rest. The minute you have daytime burglaries, you have a drug problem. There is more of it here than we can keep up with.

"We have a low homicide rate here. In a sophisticated town like this we don't have the informants to help us that big cities do and several of our homicides are unsolved.

"In our old building we once were holding a dangerous person, though he wasn't armed at the time. He jumped through a window, glass and all, and ran across Main Street, where he stopped a young woman, with a child, in her car, to make his getaway. We took him into custody at gun point and no one was hurt. We've never had an officer killed on duty and we've never taken a life by police action."

Cashman is also proud of the economies his department effects. "While we spend big money for our patrol cars, Chevrolet Impalas, at 100,000 miles we rebuild the engines and run them another 100,000 miles. The last mileage costs us half what the first cost. For our unmarked cars we buy used Hertz rent cars. Our motorcycle officers buy their own and the city leases them back. That way we have the best maintained bikes we can get. Including our Cushman motor scooters, the department has forty-one vehicles."

WATER AND SEWER SERVICE

rom pre-historic days until the present, and no doubt into the future, the location of man's cave, hut or home has been determined by the availability of water. Where water is easily found, people settle down.

While the streams which formed Walnut Creek ran full much of each winter, by the end of summer little water could be had. Hand-dug wells, dug through clay, filled with fresh water. First buckets, then hand pumps drew the water up. Ultimately, elevated tanks supplied a reserve for the hand-pumped wells. And at long last windmills moved water into the elevated tanks. In Walnut Creek two pumps of an earlier day remained in use as late as the 1880s. A five-foot-long arm attached to the vertical shaft of a pump, when turned by a horse walking around and around, lifted water into nearby twenty-foot-high tanks. One served Arthur Williams at his home and slaughter house on Locust and Cypress streets. The other stood next to the town jail, near the twenty-foot-high, five-thousand-gallon tank of Michael Kirsch, the black-smith at Main and Mt. Diablo.

Every householder and shop owner had his own water supply. But not until 1910 was electricity available to power motors which pumped water.

About 1900 Simon Lacassie and his wife Mary bought a 310-acre farm one and a half miles from Main and Mt. Diablo streets. Lacassie bought the place for its springs which fed water to his pasture. At the request of water-hungry neighbors nearby, the farmer developed his supply and sold them water, augmenting his income. Within five years he laid three-inch pipe from his springs to a 15,000-gallon tank he had constructed at an elevation of 300 feet above sea level.

Lacassie bought meters and laid pipe to about twenty-five customers on the northwest corner of town. Elliott Mauzy remembers Simeon Lacassie well. "He was a nice old man. He'd sold off much of his land when I knew him; he didn't farm then. I used to repair his meters for him. He didn't have much water in summer then." A test in 1917 showed Lacassie's springs fed only twenty gallons a minute into his tank. In 1915, after he died, his widow offered to furnish water for the horse trough in front of the town hall for thirty dollars a year. When she finally submitted her bill, the trustees ordered it cut to twelve dollars. Mrs. Lacassie returned their check, writing, "My price is $30." The city turned to the Walnut Creek Water Company, owned by Mr. J. B. John. Apparently his supply was no more dependable than Mrs. Lacassie's because when he sent his bill for twenty-five dollars three months later, the city clerk returned it, adding, " . . . bill for $25 [is] held up for payment because of poor service."

Mrs. Lacassie offered to sell the city her sixty or sixty-five acres for $300, and the trustees refused her offer. Later they sent an inspector out to appraise the property and she drove him off.

Mr. John's wells were on property now owned by the Walnut Creek Elementary School District on Walnut Boulevard. He used gasoline engines to power the pumps, one in use and one on standby. Fortunately many private wells still supplied some businesses and homes, because John's supply never would have provided the town's needs. The Central School well went dry and John had the school hooked up to his line. Even in 1915, after electricity made electric pumps available to him, he was in trouble. The trustees decided, "For failing to furnish sufficient water for street sprinkling purposes the city clerk is instructed to make a just deduction from the Walnut Creek Water Co. bill." A week later they ordered a 24 percent deduction.

Mr. John offered to sell the city his water system for $17,500 on December 10, 1919, but the trustees ignored him. He abandoned his company and the city started operating it. In 1923 ninety-six meters were in use.

In November of 1925 John again offered to sell his sytem, this time for $6,500, and again the city ignored him.

A year later, in November 1926, the city notified the owner they wanted to abandon his water system, but they kept on using it for another year and a half. Finally on April 16, 1928, the city paid John $500 for his water company. That fall the record shows, " . . . some wooden water pipe [is] still in use but [it is] in bad shape and will be replaced with three-inch iron pipe."

Within two years the city spent another $500 on the old Walnut Creek Water Company system and from then on they made a small profit on the sale of water. Yet the supply remained so bad that when in 1936 the town council put before the voters a proposal for a $38,850 bond measure, in part to drill new wells and replace the antiquated pipe, only twelve out of 260 voters were against the measure.

But the old problem of poor service wouldn't go away; it remained to haunt the city council and the city treasurer. From 1930 to 1940 the population grew 57 percent and with it so did the need for water. Finally the California Water Service Company of San Jose agreed to furnish water and the city was happy to have them step in.

Ex-State Senator John Nejedly, Walnut Creek city attorney at the time, puts the water problem in perspective. "Getting water was the number one problem here in the developing days. Part of the city was served by the California Water Service Company out of San Jose, but they couldn't supply our needs for expansion and some of it came from the city's own water department. Senator George Miller got a bill through the legislature whereby the East Bay Municipal Utility District, if serving an incorporated city, could automatically serve an annexed territory. This wasn't possible before Miller's bill passed.

"This bill is what broke open the development of Walnut Creek. Ygnacio Valley is the biggest example. We took in Burgess' Homestead and Lakewood tracts even though he had a water system of his own. We took in Lawrence's slaughter house property. Paul Lawrence made us a partial gift of his interest so we could get to the John Muir Hospital site. Then we got to Eichler's subdivision (San Miguel) and just kept on annexing and supplying EBMUD water."

John Nejedly takes pride in his role by which the enlarged community receives a plentiful, dependable supply of clear mountain water, due in part to the 1951 legislation which permitted the utility to serve Walnut Creek.

A functional part of every community is the disposal of human waste. In Walnut Creek's early days every house and business establishment had an outhouse. For kitchen waste a sump helped filter water through rock or soil strata. As inside toilets were built, 1880-1890, sewer water drained into cesspools, an earthern or wood lined area where solids were eaten by bacteria and where the liquid seeped out through the soil. An improvement came in the form of septic tanks, the addition to a cesspool of a drain field where the water drained away more quickly, increasing the capacity of the system. Finally, communities built sewer systems by connecting each house or business to large pipes which led to a large sewer farm, in early design much like oversized septic tanks.

Residents in Walnut Creek supplied their own means of sewer water disposal until the 1911-1914 era. The city population grew to 500 in 1914 and only a little imagination allows one to realize that many cesspools and septic tanks, in a town with private wells, posed a threat of contamination to the community. The newly-elected town trustees passed their sixth ordinance on January 1915, which read, "Every person . . . owning . . . real property . . . upon which improvements have been constructed . . . within 200 feet of any existing public sewer shall connect such improvement to such sewer." In June of that year Philip Schuyler, who constructed and owned the sewer system, reported to the trustees on its construction, capacity and cost.

He located it near the town dumping grounds, on the north side of Ygnacio Valley Road (now Civic Drive) and east of Walnut Boulevard and served the community for a fee.

R. N. Burgess gave his sewer system, which served some of the Homestead area, to the city in January 1917. He included a large septic tank, but it was in such poor condition the trustees noted in an early meeting, "It needs repairs at once."

The grade of downtown Walnut Creek was quite flat; it had no slope to it before engineers graded the streets in the 1920s. Every rainy season several locations remained flooded. One of them was around the present city hall where a foot bridge crossed the swamp from Main Street to the present library.

Across Walnut Creek, in the area around Mt. Pisgah, along Sierra Drive and Walker Avenue, a pond formed where children poled rafts, fantasizing they were on San Francisco Bay.

Georgana Duncan, now Mrs. Nick McNamara, daughter of the justice of the peace, smiles as she relates memories of her childhood. "During especially rainy winters the low lands near the Southern Pacific station would flood just west of the tracks. We named it Turtle Pond. Boys, and girls too, would construct rafts and ply the water, playing Robinson Crusoe. One winter the pond froze over and although none of the locals knew how to ice skate, we had a great time just sliding around."

She remembers another result of flooding. "In the early 1900s the two bridges across Walnut Creek were made of wood. Several times during severe winters both the bridges were washed away. Men made rope bridges which we used to cross on to get food and other necessities."

Even though the community grew very slowly after 1914 and before 1920, additional sewer lines were installed even more slowly. In 1918 there was still none along Mt. Diablo Boulevard and along Bonanza Street. Little attention was given the problem for another ten years in spite of the council's awareness. On November 3, 1926 in a meeting the council noted the poor condition of the town's sewer lines and the big septic tank. At last, in 1928, the city spent the money for a new sewer farm.

Unfortunately the builders couldn't foresee how the community would grow, and before long the need did become apparent for even larger facilities. Relief came when the council proposed a $50,000 bond issue to the voters for both sewer and water improvements. One-third of the money went for another sewer plant which became operational in mid-1937.

If the area hadn't continued to grow this would have been the end of the sewer story. However, at World War II's end, men and women with the military service who had passed this way to the Pacific returned to make Contra Costa their home. The demand for housing overwhelmed the local community to the bursting point. It simply lacked the ability to serve the need for sewers and water for subdivisions fast enough.

John Nejedly, Walnut Creek city attorney at the time, recalls the battle to build an area-wide sewer system when it was desperately needed. "Homes were cheaper out here and people were developing land where it was cheaper. In Danville, for instance, they were dumping their effluent into San Ramon Creek, which ran all through the valley to the bay. Thirty-two individual sanitary districts in our end of the county were disposing of theirs the same way, which finally led us to form the Central Contra Costa Sanitary District. Instead of a small line to take care of Danville's need, for example, we put in a thirty-eight-inch line. We were looking ahead, but all along the way the local improvement districts fought us. We put in a large line to serve all the way from Tassajara and Alacosta, to take all the drainage which could flow by gravity from the Alameda County line. Walnut growers fought us but it was obvious they would subdivide before long, though they couldn't see it. Actually, after the line was in operation they subdivided so fast the line was paid for within three years. The valley and the country all around us just went boom after that."

The year was 1946 when the Central Contra Costa County Sanitary District took over all the local improvement districts.

When shopping in the stores comprising the Broadway Shopping Center, one is unaware of the streams which flow underneath. Until 1957, both San Ramon Creek from the south and Las Trampas Creek from Lafayette flowed through town and merged to become Walnut Creek, or as the Mexicans named it, Arroyo de las Nueces. They still flow together and where they meet today they make a single stream. They are out of sight, confined to a large box-like culvert.

For half a century Antonio Botelho's home sat between the two streams on the gore of land they formed. Botelho had a small bridge over Las Trampas Creek that he used to reach his house. Botelho's land escaped the early twentieth century developers because other parcels could be built on more easily, having no water courses to bridge.

The influx of homeowners to the area in the late 1940s increased the demand for downtown commercial building sites. South of Mount Diablo Boulevard, on the west side of South Main Street, the Permamente Foundation built the Kaiser Hospital in 1953. Emil Villa built his restaurant on the same side, and across the street the Acalanes School District erected Los Lomas High School. Back across South Main, diagonally across the street from Kaiser, the only building where Botelho's house had stood was a Safeway store. (Home Savings is there now.)

When the construction started on Botelho's "island," H. C. Capwell bought land and contracted for its own building. The McDonald Company built most of the other stores. Lucky Stores occupied a market on land that Bullock's occupies today. Although construction actually began in 1950, it proceeded at a slow pace. The need to cover the creeks with buildings and parking lots became apparent by the mid '50s.

The City of Walnut Creek built the first culvert. They enclosed Las Trampas Creek with a twenty-five-feet-high by forty-two-feet-wide box with a separator down the center. That enclosure runs under the two-story parking lot to meet San Ramon Creek, under Mt. Diablo Boulevard. The city completed its job in 1958, and work on the stores above the culvert started soon after.

Some people might wonder what happens to the water in Tice Creek. This stream cuts across Tice Valley Road east of Rossmoor and meanders through backyards and under paved roads until it emerges into view and empties into Las Trampas Creek only 100 feet west of South Main Street.

The United States Corps of Engineers designed the culvert that forced San Ramon Creek underground, as well as the enclosure of the Walnut Creek from the junction of the two smaller streams, under the Bank of America parking, to where the creek comes out in the open at Lincoln. Contra Costa County's Public Works Department completed the culvert during the winter of 1971-72.

Oakland Rotary Club visits Walnut Creek in 1914. They meet at the Oakland, Antioch and Eastern Railway station. The view is up Trinity Avenue.

ELECTRICITY AND ELECTRIC TRAINS

The first home wired for electricity as it was being built was Joseph Silveira's house on Locust between Mt. Diablo and Olympic.

The E. Ignace store on Main Street, a general merchandise store, built of brick by James M. Stow, was the first commercial building to have electric lights. They were turned on in November 1910.

In late November, lights in the Presbyterian Church glowed for the first time. Six lighted the main hall, one shone over the front entrance, and another lighted the inside of the horse shed.

On December 5, 1910, the *Daily Gazette* of Martinez noted, "The Walnut Creek Meat Market has put in electric lights and an electric motor for grinding and chopping . . . Mr. Eugene Sweet has his store lighted by electricity. A. C. Cameron has had electric lights put in his harness and blacksmith shop. The Rogers Hotel is now lighted by electricity. Within the next few days the city hopes to have lights on Main Street."

The same newspaper states in its January 6, 1911 edition, "The Stow brothers are being kept busy wiring houses for electric lights. They have just finished wiring the Masonic Lodge (in the Stow building), Dr. Leech's residence and are now working on Mr. Burpee's building.

In Walnut Creek as elsewhere in rural communities, electricity replaced coal oil (Standard Oil Company branded theirs Kerosene) for illumination. In cities it took the place of gas manufactured from coal. Both barely survived a half century of popularity. They had replaced animal fats and whale oil in the decade of 1855-1865.

In the days before 1910 most families around Walnut Creek had a farm animal or two to feed. Leaving home for any length of time called for advance planning. A trip to Oakland, only a day-long venture, meant most farmers would have to drive their buggies, and in their absence someone else would have to care for and feed their animals.

Only the rich used automobiles in the days before Henry Ford massed-produced his Model T. Until then the steam train gave Walnut Creek residents the quickest service to Oakland or San Francisco. But the train left at 7:00 A.M. so the milking and the chores had to be done early. Any later departure would mean the passengers couldn't return the same day.

In 1910 Walnut Creek was without the fast, frequent suburban electric train service that some other Bay Area residents took for granted, one north and one south of the bay. In their communities the electric trains whisked passengers swiftly and comfortably between numerous stations.

Regularly, every hour, electric cars ran between Petaluma, Santa Rosa and Sebastopol, stopping at scores of avenues in between. With stations spaced so closely, travelers flocked to the electrics, leaving the Northwestern Pacific's steam trains.

In Santa Clara County, where steam trains went to Los Gatos only twice a day, another electric line gave people the opportunity to ride to San Jose, Santa Clara, Los Gatos, Saratoga, or Mayfield (Palo Alto) any hour of the day they wished. Clean, fast, and frequent cars brought a sense of a new age to the ordinary citizen in the days before he could afford his first automobile.

Walnut Creek received good news. It would have electric trains simultaneously with the first electric power line. The Great Western Power Company strung wire from Big Bend, Plumas County, to Oakland in 1909. By 1910 they supplied electricity to Concord and the electric railway via a substation at Clayton.

The Oakland and Antioch Railway landed its construction equipment at Port Chicago, then called Bay Point, in 1910. The first electric car rolled out of Bay Point, bound for Concord, on February 13, 1911.

Construction as far as Lafayette went well with rails laid that far by summer. Stations south of Concord included Kilgore, Meinert (where it crosses Oak Grove), Bancroft, Las Juntas (where it crossed the Southern Pacific line, approximately three blocks northeast of today's Pleasant Hill BART station), Moore, Walnut Creek, Saranap (at today's junction of Tice Valley and Olympic boulevards), Reliez and Lafayette. Regular service between Walnut Creek and Port Chicago commenced about May 1, 1911. Difficulties boring the tunnel through the Oakland hills delayed service to Oakland and San Francisco until March 1, 1913.

To carry passengers to San Francisco before March 1913, the Oakland and Antioch Railway made an agreement with the Santa Fe Railroad. The electrics took their travelers to Port Chicago, where passengers climbed aboard Santa Fe trains to Richmond. Connections could be made five times a day. Riders enjoyed a picturesque, relaxed voyage on the Santa Fe ferry to San Francisco's Ferry Building, taking two hours nine minutes on the fastest run and two hours fifty-nine minutes on the slowest.

In March 1913, a year before Walnut Creek incorporated, electric trains ran through the Oakland hills. The route brought trains from Walnut Creek, through Moraga and the 3,600-foot tunnel, down Shafter Avenue to Fortieth Street. There, it joined the Key System tracks and ran out into San Francisco Bay, to the ferry terminal on a mile-long pier. The boats docked at a terminal built a half mile west of today's Bay Bridge Toll Plaza, where the train's passengers walked aboard a ferry boat for the ride to the Ferry Building.

Ten trains ran daily schedules through Walnut Creek. Six went to Sacramento, the others to Concord. From Walnut Creek the ride to San Francisco took one hour and ten minutes, including the ride on the ferry.

The steep grade from the west portal of the tunnel through the Oakland hills to the crossing of College and Shafter avenues necessitated two special orders to trainmen:

1. Conductor must ride front end of passenger trains between

Havens and Rockridge and take up slack in hand brake and be ready to use same if necessary.

2. All trains must be preceded by a flagman when crossing College Avenue and Shafter Avenue.

The first train of the day blew its whistle going through Walnut Creek early in the morning, loud and long enough for demands to be made on the mayor to write the railroad and stop the nuisance.

That train left Oakland before 5:00 A.M., dead-heading to Concord with mail and newspapers. There it turned around, terminating its run at Walnut Creek, where the crew ate breakfast and readied the train for its 6:20 departure with commuters.

The waitress who asks to remain anonymous tells this story. "I worked for Mr. and Mrs. Costaldo who ran the Walnut Creek Hotel at what is now 1519 North Main Street. As that train went through Walnut Creek about 5:00 A.M. the motorman blew his whistle to be sure his breakfast would be ready. I would get up when I heard the whistle, as the cook did too, and go around the corner to the hotel, fill the coffee urn and turn it on, and get the three trainmen's breakfast table set. They had the same thing every morning, always fried eggs, bacon, fried potatoes, toast and coffee. By the time the train got back from Concord I'd have their meal on the table ready for them. But how the neighbors complained about that whistle!"

In 1911 a branch line served Walnut Creek residents. The Walwood Branch began running from Meinert Station to Hillside, 3.6 miles south of Meinert Road along the west side of Oak Grove Road. Its purpose was not so much to bring better transportation to Ygnacio Valley residents, but to haul gondolas of limestone destined for the Spreckels Sugar Company in Monterey County to the Las Juntas transfer point on the Southern Pacific. A spur to the quarry left the Walwood Branch at Valley Vista and Oak Grove Road, running up the hill on Valley Vista to where the Boundary Oaks Restaurant is now.

On two occasions, three weeks apart, a motorized wooden passenger car went up the hill to the quarry to tow a loaded fifty-ton gondola down the grade to Oak Grove Road. Each time, the heavy gondola behind the electric car overpowered the brakes of the car in front, pushing it out of control down the hill. At the sharp turn at Valley Vista and Oak Grove, the cars jumped the tracks, and each time the gondola crushed the lead car into kindling. In both wrecks the three crewmen jumped from their speeding car in time, suffering painful but not critical injuries. The quarry solved the problem by installing a drum at the top of the hill from where a long steel cable pulled the cars up and lowered them down the hill.

Not enough passengers rode the five trains a day on the Walwood Branch and in 1915 the service was cut to two. In 1920 both quarry and the branch line were abandoned.

The eight-mile Danville Branch was a more profitable one. This route left the main line at Olympic and Tice Valley Road in Walnut Creek at a station called Saranap. The station took its name from the wife of the president of the San Ramon Valley Railroad (Sarah Naphtaly) when the branch was incorporated. Conductor William French and motorman Frank Flautt took the first scheduled train over the Danville Branch on June 2, 1914.

Originally, this branch prospered due to the development of the country in the Mt. Diablo Park area. The Mt. Diablo Scenic Boulevard Company established a residential tract and built the Diablo County Club four miles east of Danville. In addition to the branch shuttle service to Walnut Creek, the Oakland, Antioch and Eastern operated regular main line trains to Diablo on weekends, from the Key Route Pier in Oakland. Some cars were cut off at Saranap and went on to the country club. The Oakland, Antioch and Eastern referred to these trains as "Million Dollar Specials." Not only main line equipment ran in this service; on one occasion William Randolph Hearst's private car reached the country club via the Danville Branch, in the summer of 1916. It was hauled by a passenger motor-car and departed the country club days later on the same route, Diablo to Saranap to Port Chicago.

Special trains ran on Sundays and holidays for the R. N. Burgess Company, which sold land adjacent to the country club.

During World War I another notable special was "The Riveter."

189

This train started from Danville, picked up shipyard workers at Walnut Creek and other stations along the line and took them to the shipyards at Port Chicago. This special ran as a five-car train between Port Chicago and Saranap, where three cars remained all night. The morning train hooked onto them again and the five cars filled on the way back to the shipyards.

The vice-president of the Oakland, Antioch and Eastern was farmer Samuel L. Naphtaly. He owned 700 acres of Walnut Creek's Tice Valley (now Rossmoor) and grew wine grapes and pears. As president of the Danville Branch, he used his influence to build the branch and lease it to the Oakland, Antioch and Eastern. He had a spur built into his farm, to his fruit packing shed and small winery. This spur went into the farm for several hundred yards along what is now Rossmoor Parkway.

Elliott Mauzy, the retired local plumbing contractor, best remembers the Danville branch for his weekend rides to the Diablo Country Club, where he would caddy. James McGeehon, a retired earth moving contractor, recalls how he and his friends used to hitch rides to and from the country club for the same reason. He has one memorable recollection.

"On a Saturday morning several of us jumped on the car as usual, just as it started rolling from Saranap. We would hang on the back end from any of several protuberances and get free rides all the way to the country club. This particular morning one friend had his hand right under where the conductor slammed down the hinged steel plate, the floor over the steps. My friend's fingers were in the wrong place and the steel plate cut off several at the first knuckle."

The Oakland, Antioch and Eastern became successively the San Francisco-Sacramento Railway and the Sacramento Northern. It pulled scores of cars, loaded with walnuts, from the Walnut Growers packing plant in Walnut Creek every year. In fruit season they often rolled ten carloads of pears a day to eastern markets. The trains brought in lumber, gasoline and building materials.

Beginning in 1913, San Francisco-bound commuters chose between two early morning trains; one left Walnut Creek at 6:33 and the

190

other at 7:30. Peter Howard recalls his solution to missing the return commuter run from Oakland. "My father, brothers and I would leave the office on the Estuary for the Fortieth and Shafter station. We'd plan to catch the 4:30 departure. It would arrive back in Walnut Creek at 5:23. Occasionally we'd miss it and unfortunately the next commuter train didn't leave until 5:50 and didn't get here until 6:30.

"Our solution was to ride the "Meteor," the Sacramento Express, which left at 5:07 and flew through Walnut Creek without stopping at 5:42, but did stop at the Southern Pacific crossing at Las Juntas four minutes later. The conductor would let us off there and we'd walk back home. It wasn't much longer from Las Juntas than it was from Walnut Creek. We beat waiting for the next commuter by about forty minutes."

Passengers from Walnut Creek went directly into San Francisco over the lower deck of the Bay Bridge from January 15, 1939 until June 30, 1941, cutting ten minutes from the already fast service. All passenger service over the Sacramento Northern ended on the same date in 1941.

Gradual abandonment of the Sacramento Northern in Contra Costa County led to the dropping of all freight service (except from Walnut Creek to Pittsburg) on August 10, 1958.

William Rice home, later the Fish house, and still later R. N. Burgess' Homestead. Home was built on the site of Francisco Garcia's adobe.

LAKEWOOD'S BURGESS

The developer of Lakewood, the finest subdivision in the town's first century, grew up on his father's hog farm in Danville. After he left the farm he bought and sold thousands of acres of farmland, built hundreds of buildings in San Francisco and Oakland and secured a contract, with a $2.5 million advance, to build a shipyard and ten freighters for the United States government. But as fortunes sometimes go, his faded too, and his Lakewood Estates saved him in his late years.

Robert Noble Burgess, the son of a minister who moved to San Francisco from Saint John, Nova Scotia, before the boy entered grammar school, remembers the city by the Golden Gate for his first grade classmates' taunts. His mother dressed Robert in knee britches, a white starched shirt with an Eton collar, a dark blue jacket and a Scottish cap. The locals, many clad in overalls, jeered him and called him "Freak!" and the youngster fought many a sandlot battle defending himself.

Leaving San Francisco soon after Robert's first year of schooling, the boy's father accepted a call on May 22, 1886, to take the pulpit of the Danville Presbyterian Church for $1,000 a year. To help make ends meet, the senior Burgess bought twenty acres and started raising hogs. Eight years old at the time, Rob helped raise the animals and by the time he graduated from grammar school, in 1893 at age fifteen, he often rose at 2:00 A.M., loaded the wagon with shoats for market, and drove them into Oakland. When slaughter time arrived, Robert wrestled the pigs to the ground and cut their throats.

By the time he reached seventeen Burgess discovered how to light the fuse of ambition; how to turn hopes into realities. He took advantage of bankers willing to lend money. But he didn't learn the inherent dangers involved.

He first recognized the opportunity to go into business with very little capital. He saw the chance to make money by buying fresh fruit from the growers and then drying it and shipping it in carload lots to the eastern market. When he looked into buying the necessary machinery and lumber to build a plant, he learned the suppliers would deliver what he wanted and would wait until the end of the season for their money, and the local bank would advance him the money to pay the farmers.

With a partner, the eighteen-year-old Burgess formed the company, Burgess and Noble, rented 100 feet of the Southern Pacific freight dock at Concord for a processing plant and ten acres at the rear of the station for a drying yard. All on credit, with no money down, he took delivery of a double prune dipper, steam boiler and steam engine, elevator and prune grader.

The partnership had the first telephone in Concord, when none existed in either Walnut Creek or Danville. They bought prunes from the Bancrofts and Pennimans in Ygnacio Valley and from orchardists all the way east to Knightsen. The company paid the lumber dealer, the equipment manufacturer, and the fruit growers, but after two years living over his office, Burgess dissolved the partnership when creditors started pressing his partner, Noble, for his personal obligations.

Next, when Burgess was only twenty years of age, the California Beet Sugar and Refining Company hired him to manage their camp at Hookston. The camp hired as many as 600 Japanese farm hands and used up to 160 horses in growing their crops. The company leased 370 acres from James Hook and between one and two thousand acres in the flats between Hookston and Pacheco. At harvest the employees loaded from fifteen to twenty carloads a day at the Hookston Station (corner of Bancroft and Hookston roads).

While working for the California Beet Sugar Company, Burgess reminded himself many times he could do better if he grew these same crops for himself rather than for someone else. His chance to prove it came soon enough. February storms in 1899 washed out roads and filled channels with debris and flooded farm land all over Contra Costa County. Discouraged at losing their crop, his employers made it plain to him they would not finance any improvements and he would have to plant again without leveling any more land.

He broke away from the company when the mortgage holder offered him the 240-acre San Miguel Ranch, five miles closer to Walnut Creek. The London and San Francisco Bank claimed the property was worth $15,000, but because they were liquidating all their real estate holdings, they would rather have him pay $500 down and give them his note for $7,500, which he was eager to do.

Recognizing he could make more good buys like this just for the looking, he vowed he would do just that. But before he could start, the April 1906 earthquake and fire brought San Francisco to its knees. People poured across the bay the buy homes. Always the opportunist, he turned his attention to making quicker money. Burgess bought forty lots on Oakland's Telegraph Avenue, between Forty-fourth and Forty-fifth streets. He teamed up with a man who had all the money he would need, Henry C. Morris. Morris offered to finance all the homes Burgess could build, for 40 percent of the profits.

Now with financing assured, he formed the R. N. Burgess Company in 1907, hired a builder and, at only 10 percent down, sold his houses as fast as he could put them up. Burgess bought a block on Forty-ninth Street, lots on Lake Merritt's Adam Point, Linda Vista and Piedmont. He cleared about $35,000 for himself and bought his first auto, an Elmore.

Burgess built five handsome homes for William Randolph Hearst's architect, Julia Morgan. Morgan, at the top of her profession, built for wealthy, influential people. Later, her clients became prospects for some of Burgess' financing.

The panic of 1907 interrupted his plans to build more houses. Mortgage money wasn't available in the usual places. When Burgess formed the R. N. Burgess Mortgage Company for $2 million and turned over the deeds to all the lots, houses and farm property as additional security, lenders advanced him money.

In 1908 his company bought the land he had coveted from the first time he saw it. It was the 1,750-acre William Rice Ranch adjoining Walnut Creek on the east and containing, as a small part, what would one day become Lakewood Estates (east of Homestead Avenue). The heirs of William Rice sold him the ranch for forty-five dollars an acre.

He'd finished building in Oakland, and had no immediate jobs in sight. Lonely, without too much to occupy his thoughts, but feeling well off financially, he moved to the new Clift Hotel in San Francisco. On a train trip to Los Angeles soon after his move to the hotel, he sat alone, brooding. Never much of a drinker, except in the company of friends, he dwelled on his situation. Thirty years old! Building homes for others but none for himself? Visions of attractive Anne Fish of Martinez came to mind and wouldn't go away. In the morning he bought her a fine piece of jewelry and gave it to her as soon as he returned north.

The couple married on July 30, 1909 and went on a honeymoon to Victoria, Vancouver, Seattle, Portland, and Crater Lake. On the next May 13, Anne gave birth to Robert N. Burgess, Jr.

Money loosened up and the R. N. Burgess Company borrowed freely. The builder concentrated in San Francisco. He took on bigger jobs than any he had done before. He erected a ten-story, ninety-apartment building. Always interested in good farm land, he extended himself with borrowed money and bought the 3,700-acre Foskett and Ellworthy Ranch in the Concord-Clayton area.

In Walnut Creek he purchased the 300-acre Pringle property. When he planned to build homes in Walnut Creek the insurance companies surprised him. They refused to insure there. "No dependable water supply and inadequate pressure." In self-defense he drilled a well on his San Miguel Ranch and ran a four-inch water main to Larkey Hill, where he built a 100,000-gallon tank, and sent a four-inch main down through the town's Main Street.

Anne furnished the old Rice home, which they named Homestead, on their 1,750-acre parcel, and the couple used it for weekends

R. N. Burgess and daughter at Lakewood, 1932.

and partying. They regularly brought Rob's moneyed friends to the ranch, where he played poker with them, drank and helped them shed the concerns of the world of finance.

One day before the town incorporated, Dr. Leech called on Burgess, saying, "We are threatened with a dyptheria epidemic."

He replied, "Why tell me?"

"Because you are the only man in Walnut Creek who will do something about it. The town's sewer system is so bad it might as well not be there. Effluent is appearing in our water supply!"

So Robert Burgess built a twelve-inch sewer line down Walnut Creek's Main Street and eventually, as people connected to it, received all but $12,000 of his money back.

He still spent most of his time in San Francisco, getting financing for his many projects. He and his wife moved to the St. Francis Hotel, where they sat at the same dining room table for every meal. In town

197

five days, at Homestead for long weekends, they lived a very social life. Anne kept a Chinese cook at the ranch and often filled their three extra bedrooms with important guests.

The developer bought a Marion steam shovel and built the North Gate Road to the top of Mt. Diablo. Once there, the machine backed down about three miles and started a road to the south and west that ended at the South Gate in Diablo, practically Danville.

Carroll Walker recalls a story about Bill, last name unknown, who used to work for R. N. Burgess during World War I. "He worked on the original road up Mt. Diablo. He always came in to Walnut Creek on pay day to celebrate and would go on a big binge. He usually hit all three saloons before he was through and eventually ended up in the livery stable sleeping it off in the straw in some empty stall. The man who ran the livery stable would find him, and concerned about fire, warned him off several times. But every pay day the same thing happened. So he decided to teach Bill a lesson. He found a big empty redwood box and picked Bill up, dead drunk, put him in the box and let the lid down. Of course, it was not air tight, and he figured when Bill woke up he would find himself stretched out in a box. And he did, after a while. When he woke up he thought for sure he had been buried alive and he jumped out of the box scared stiff. He found the owner and threatened to beat him up, but as he began to sober up he got less angry and more scared. He quit his job, swore off drinking and never did drink again. He lit out for Martinez, where he enlisted in the army."

The R. N. Burgess Mortgage Company bought the mortgages Burgess took in payment for his buildings. His business expanded and he needed more money. The $2 million capitalization was not enough so he formed the Western Mortgage and Guarantee Company. This firm received funds not by selling its mortgages, but by selling certificates which represented the value of mortgages. The certificates sold well and money to finance his projects flowed in.

In 1913 Burgess bought the 10,000-acre Park Stock Farm between Danville and Tassajara for $150,000. He did his best to interest William Randolph Hearst in becoming his partner, and Hearst came out to view the farm. However, Hearst rejected the idea, saying almost every

198

Looking north from the Walnut Creek Meat Market's slaughter house toward Ygnacio Valley Road in 1960. The land is now the San Marco development. The transmission tower is at the corner of Marchbanks Drive.

one of his newspapers was losing money. This rejection hit Burgess hard. He had counted on Hearst to relieve him of half the interest and principal payments he faced.

But looking ahead to the opening of the 1915-1917 Panama Pacific International Exposition in San Francisco, ever the optimist, Burgess saw trains filled with upper income people, all yearning to buy homes in beautiful California.

He next bought the 1,300-acre Brubeck Ranch and 300 acres more adjoining it on North Gate Road. He also purchased fifty acres from the orchardist Hutchinson. From H. H. Haight he bought 15,000 acres which included the summit of Mount Diablo. An old policy helped him finanace these purchases. "It was the policy of [the] R. N. Burgess Company to share their undertakings with those who could be helpful," he later wrote in his *Memoirs*.

Burgess' friends built two electric train branch lines, one to the beginning of the North Gate Road and the other to Diablo. Another friend, the president of the Pacific Telephone Company, had lines strung to his new Diablo Country Club and the houses built around it. Burgess erected a fine home for his family there but kept the house at Homestead. The family lived at Diablo for ten years. Besides Robert, Jr., there were four girls: Frances, Suzanne, Nancy and Polly.

When C. A. Cooper bought Horace Carpentier's 6,000 acres, he financed the purchase by forming the Moraga Land Company for $1 million. R. N. Burgess and friends made up the company. Burgess himself came in for 10 percent, $100,000, and received the appointment as sales agent.

Meanwhile at his Diablo home, two Chinese cooks, Sing and Fong, served the meals; a maid and a nurse kept house and cared for the children; a gardener saw to the grounds; and a chauffeur drove Burgess back and forth to the electric trains in Oakland.

Unfortunately, his lots at Diablo sold slowly. At North Gate Road, he planted the borders of the road with palms and olives. Even then very few prospects came and fewer bought his acreage. Over at Moraga nothing sold at all. The fair goers went to the fair, but very few bought any of his building sites.

However, World War I demanded his attention now. Grain and foodstuffs of many kinds were needed in Europe, and that required ships. Burgess thought of the 233 acres bordering Suisun Bay he had bought. Why not build a ship yard there? Off he went by train to Washington, D.C., and in little more than two weeks he negotiated a contract to build a shipyard, ten 10,000-ton freighters, and best of all— $2.5 million as an advance.

He came home and formed the Pacific Coast Shipbuilding Company and was elected its president on January 19, 1918. The firm built eight ways on his land at Bay Point (Port Chicago). To house the yard's workers the Federal Housing Fund gave him $2.5 million to build the town called Clyde. He bought 300 acres between Concord and Bay Point, put in sidewalks, built 100 cottages and a first class eighty-room hotel, with a dining room capacity of 2,000.

During the war, with men drafted and sent overseas, new sales of his homes stopped. Payments on old contracts became delinquent. Interest and principal payments on his many land purchases became overdue. His Moraga Land Company brought him no return. Once the war ended, he received nothing from his Pacific Shipbuilding Company. He shut down the Homestead house and lived at Diablo. One afternoon on his way home from San Francisco, Burgess stopped by for his car at the Oakland garage where he'd housed it for years. The garage man stopped him, "Your car has been attached. I can't let you have it." He telephoned Mrs. Burgess and she went into Oakland to pick him up.

They sold the Diablo house. His creditors took title to all the land he still owned, except for the Lakewood property, Homestead, and forced him into bankruptcy. At his desk one evening he riffled through notes which represented loans to friends and relatives— $55,000.

Not even Homestead survived the storm intact. Fortunately he had deeded the house and fifteen acres to Mrs. Burgess some time earlier, and he retained 140 more. The balance of eighty-five acres went to his creditors. Mrs. Burgess had a forty-acre walnut orchard of her own which escaped garnishment. The income from the walnuts helped take care of their living expenses.

201

Robert E. Green, the one man who worked for Burgess for twenty-five years, stayed on, receiving one dollar a day. Among other things, Green cared for the nursery, the source of all the trees Burgess hoped to plant on Homestead.

Eventually Green did plant the trees on 100 acres. They included eucalyptus, Monterey and Japanese black pine, white and iron back, Australian compact, Arizona ash, albizzia, julubressen, black locust, catalpa and juniper.

Robert Burgess never gave up and tried his hand at many things in search of the end of the rainbow. He went off to Arizona and New Mexico and tried to put together a large sheep ranch operation. At times he thought it would work, but in the end several thousand sheep died in a winter blizzard, and he returned to Homestead wiser, but several thousand dollars poorer.

At one point, lacking any business opportunities, Burgess built a travel trailer and with one daughter retraced the southern part of his honeymoon route: Crescent City, Crater Lake and Klamath Falls. Mrs. Burgess stayed home, caring for an intestinal ailment which plagued her for most of her adult life.

During the 1930s, while the nation was in the grips of the Great Depression, Burgess approached a local bank for a loan on his Homestead property. The bank's appraiser gave it a value of fifteen dollars an acre, and the bank refused to consider any loan at all. Burgess went off to St. Helena, where his knowledge of money sources proved valuable. The St. Helena bank loaned him $15,000. With a hired steam shovel, he drained the lake on the property, smoothed the bottom, squared up the banks, built up the dam, and cut a road around the north end of the lake.

Burgess filed a subdivision map cutting his Homestead acres into 250 building sites. He sold several lots and even built six houses of adobe bricks made on the site. World War II stopped him dead in his tracks. Restrictions put on the sale of lumber, nails, electrical wire and plumbing supplies stopped all but construction essential to the war effort.

However, the shipyard workers in Richmond and Oakland

needed housing, and Robert Burgess, now sixty-three, jumped at the opportunity. As eager as ever, he found a foreman, received government allotments for materials, and just as in old times, he put crews to work building scores of cottages in Richmond and converting commercial buildings into apartments. He even constructed second story apartments over two East Bay theaters.

He made profitable deals and cleared his obligations on the Lakewood tract and deterred further foreclosures of Homestead. This time he didn't borrow beyond his capacity to pay.

People started moving to Walnut Creek once World War II ended. Burgess sold his lots at good prices. In his late sixties now, he sold twenty lots to his son.

Mrs. Burgess died in 1953. Now seventy-five years old, Burgess remained at Homestead for several years, often alone except for his daughters' occasional visits. Most of his San Francisco moneyed people were gone; he'd never made friends in Walnut Creek beyond the few tradesmen he employed.

He spent many evenings, sometimes until two in the morning, shelling walnuts. When he had enough meats he'd go to Berkeley and sell what he had to bakers and ice cream makers.

In his early eighties, Burgess sold the last of his Lakewood lots, the last for $10,000, and moved to Santa Barbara. He died there on January 22, 1965, age eighty-seven.

THE WALNUT GROWERS ASSOCIATION

*T*he importance of the nuts—grown all over the county—to the residents of Walnut Creek is readily evident. Though the harvest barely lasted fifty years, it came at just the right time. In 1920, when the Volstead Act prohibiting the use of intoxicating liquor doomed wine grape production, the town had no industry to employ its people. It had little reason to exist; much less to grow.

Very early in this century farmers learned they could graft the soft-shell English walnut shoot to the native black walnut trunks and harvest a more marketable nut, one with more than double the meat and easier to shell.

Farmers, after they harvested their crop, hulled and dried the nuts, then set out for nearby cities to find stores that would buy them. Horses plodded up the hill to the old high-level tunnel, pulling wagons loaded high with sacks of nuts. On the other side they went down to Claremont and Telegraph avenues to the foot of Broadway. There they rolled their wagons onto the "Creek Route" ferry at the Estuary, bound for San Francisco.

By 1915, though the crop was small by later standards, there was competition enough between growers to keep the price they received unprofitably low. As a result, the idea of all the growers pooling their entire crops and hiring salesmen to sell for them culminated in such a move in 1917. On July 30 that year, sixty growers signed an agreement to deliver all the nuts they raised to their association, the Contra Costa County Walnut Growers Association.

In lieu of taking all of the money received by the association for their crop, the members voted to spend part of the profit to build a processing plant. They constructed it next to the main line of the

Oakland, Antioch and Eastern Railway in downtown Walnut Creek (on Locust, between Civic Drive and Cole Avenue and California Avenue).

By the mid-1920s farmers sold tens of thousands of dollars worth of walnuts and delivered them to Walnut Creek. Whether the crop came from San Ramon, Clayton or Alhambra Valley made little difference—drivers trucked the crop to town for processing. Because they were in town, the farmers bought some of their supplies, food and hardware at least, from local merchants instead of their usual storekeepers. "Since you're going to be in Walnut Creek anyway, pick up . . . " first started many a farmer spending money there. From then on, the wide variety of products available, and the good service, kept many farmers buying from the town's shopkeepers.

At harvest time trucks from all over the county rolled onto the scales at the south end of the building. Here bulk nuts fell into a funnel in the floor and a conveyor lifted them to the top of the building. By gravity, they ran down to sorting tables where, under the scrutiny of women, dark and defective nuts were pulled out. Next, a tank of chlorine wash transformed them into a uniform color. The moisture blown off, they next dropped onto grading tables where openings of certain sizes allowed small, medium and large nuts to sort themselves. Machines branded "Diamond" on the largest and "Emerald" on the mediums. Lastly the nuts ran into a fumigating tank where undetected worms were killed. The last conveyor ran them into storage bins where they awaited orders for shipment, either in bulk or sacks.

The first year about 350 tons of walnuts were delivered. In both 1936 and 1937 the local plant processed 5,600 tons. The peak season was 1952, when 6,600 tons of walnuts were brought to the Walnut Creek plant. The association employed 100 people that season. Production dropped rapidly after 1952 when the combination of die-back and bulldozing walnut trees for subdivisions forecast the future of the walnut crop in this county. The Contra Costa County Walnut Growers Association joined the California Walnut Growers Association back in 1925. By 1956 the local plant was uneconomical to operate—it employed only twenty-five that year—and the association closed it on

August 6, 1957. From that date on all the walnuts grown in Contra Costa County by association members had to be delivered to the California Walnut Growers Association plant in Stockton.

The current Civic Arts Theater was built in 1952 by the association for just under $60,000. They used it as a storage facility only and held nuts there until they could sell them.

One memory old-timers recall, as they wrinkle their noses, is the aroma in town during walnut and tomato harvest during the 1930s and '40s. The odor of chlorine bleach mingled with ripe tomato from the Walnut Creek Cannery wafted over the town. When the wind blew in just the right direction, those living downwind of Dean's Goat Farm on Oakdene Court knew an odiferous combination of three aromas which no one envied.

After the local one-acre processing plant closed the association joined the other three owners of the adjoining businesses to the north (Diamond National Corporation, Farmers Feed and Fuel, and Walnut Creek Hardware) and offered for sale the two and one-half acre lot, bounded by Cole, Locust, Trinity and California. Early-on the Pacific Telephone and Telegraph Company built on the north end. The balance of the property lay vacant from 1957 until 1984 when the complex, Growers Square, was built.

THE DEVELOPMENT OF CULTURE

*I*n the case of the interests which support the intellectual improvement in Walnut Creek, the women have been leaders, not the men, and in many cases without any help from them. For three-quarters of a century the ladies have set the goals. One may only speculate on their motivation, but two definitions of "culture" may give us a clue. In the preface of *Literature and Dogma* one finds, "Culture, the acquainting of ourselves with the best that has been known and said in the world." Or, they may have had in mind the description from *Culture and Anarchy, Sweetness and Light*: "Culture is then properly described . . . as having its origin in the love of perfection; it is *a study of perfection*." Whatever they yearned for or whatever their motivation, the ladies of the community took the lead in bringing us culture.

The growth of culture in Walnut Creek is best seen in the formation of social, intellectual and artistic senses in its citizens. The formation and the amount of activity grew slowly, but certainly very few communities its size can enjoy more satisfaction from their cultural accomplishments over the years than is enjoyed in Walnut Creek now.

The very first evidence of culture, however minute, must have been Barnabas Webb's piano in 1860. In her candlelit parlor Mrs. Webb might have entertained her guests with selections from Beethoven or Bach. When the village numbered no more than fifteen or twenty persons, the Webb piano must have been the center of artistic endeavor.

Fifteen years later, in 1876, churches provided the basis for most social activity. At that time Mrs. Frank Webb taught the Presbyterian Sunday School. Unremembered people led family groups in other churches: the Catholic Church opened first, then the Presbyterian, the Methodist and then the Episcopal Church, all founded between 1872 and 1888.

The violin teacher in Walnut Creek in the mid-1890s was Professor Louis Proll, jeweler by day, and the violin instructor in the evening.

In 1912 the women of the town opened the first library and brought the means for intellectual stimulation.

Ballroom dancing gave the first touch of the social graces to some of the youngsters in the village. Some mothers invited a few couples at a time to their homes, where the young people learned some rules of polite behavior. "Always let the girl go first," or "when the music stops, bow to the girl and thank her for dancing with you." The children danced to Victrola records.

Elliott Mauzy recalls his initiation to dancing about 1927. "Every Friday afternoon after school Peter and Harmon Howard's mother invited anywhere from five to ten couples over to their house to dance. She hired a dancing teacher for us and that's where I learned. Most of us enjoyed it quite a bit."

Private ballroom dancing lessons were offered in town in 1928. At that date, Mr. G. Bartalini advertised in the *Courier-Journal* " . . . two afternoons a week of dancing lessons for $2.50." Two women taught dancing before Bartalini. Gladys Geary held classes on the second floor of a building on Main Street, and Mrs. Robinson gave lessons in the town hall as early as 1920.

Adults in the town had either of two options for a satisfying social life. One was to join a fraternal order, represented by the Masons and Odd Fellows and their auxiliaries. The other was to entertain and be entertained in their homes. The Red Cross and the PTA provided limited social contact for the women, but the majority of families did their entertaining in their own homes.

For the first half of the twentieth century residents seldom went to San Francisco, Oakland or Berkeley to avail themselves of "cultural events" such as the symphony, opera or a stage play. Museum and art exhibits were foreign to Walnut Creek, though in the late 1940s rumblings could be heard of what was to come.

Occasionally individuals with enthusiasm for a particular branch of the arts put together a group to further their cause. One such interest kindled the desires of a brother and sister for a women's choral society in the 1920s. Mrs. Freuler and her bachelor brother-in-law, Artie Freuler, brought several women together in Ed Bradley's home, where they practiced. Information about where and how often they sang is lacking, but more surprising is the almost seventy years it apparently took for any choral society to organize.

Probably the initial cultural site was in a private home on fifty acres of orchard on the northeast corner of what is now the Kaiser Hospital grounds. Mr. and Mrs. Theodore Newell bought the property in 1922. With their two sons, Sid and Mike, they moved into Walnut Creek's largest house. Las Trampas Creek bounded their acreage on the north, and Tice Creek cut diagonally across their orchard. Mr. Newell built a wooden foot bridge across Tice Creek which connected the two halves of his property. But heavy rains in those years washed his bridge away time and time again.

Ted Newell grew pears and prunes in his orchard but surrounded his house with iris and mums. He welcomed children the ages of his sons. In his ballroom he taught them dancing and gave them parties. Newell lived a comfortable, baronial life, but just before the outbreak of the war with Japan, in 1941, he sold his home and surrounding acreage to Mr. and Mrs. Edward Counter.

Mrs. Counter, a positive, volatile and forceful person, gave the community a place to enjoy a touch of class. She turned the house into a luncheon room or a place to dance, or hold a banquet or lecture.

In her home Mrs. Counter served quality food, tolerating only the best. The Walnut Creek Art and Garden Center, as Mrs. Counter named it, operated the luncheon room and four stores stocked with quality merchandise. There was an art gallery, a ceramic studio, a jewelry store and a yarn shop. At times she had a wood carver demonstrating his skills for her guests.

The Art and Garden Center became the town's cultural center in the 1940s. Some organizations met there regularly. Others, such as the Walnut Creek Garden Club, alternated meeting places, one month meeting for lunch at the Art and Garden Center and the next at the Diablo Country Club.

Before 1937 the opportunity to see a first-run movie involved a trip over the Fish Ranch Road to Berkeley or Oakland. The Ramona in Walnut Creek offered less expensive reruns. Finally, on July 30, 1937, the town welcomed the opening of the new El Rey Theater. Searchlights swept the evening sky and crowds thronged to the opening of the theater which would bring Walnut Creek the best of pictures. The double feature they saw that night featured Jean Arthur and Edward Arnold in "Easy Living" and Marian Marsh and Reginald Denny in the exciting mystery drama, "The Great Gambit."

Outside, the flashing lights on the marquee reminded many patrons of similar facades at the best theaters in San Francisco. Inside, gilded lamps, velvet drapes, and cushioned seats took the first nighters into a new era for the town. Comparing the El Rey with the Ramona was like contrasting a new Packard with a Model T.

Upon arriving at the opening, theater-goers passed the new auto showroom next door. Lester Lawrence had opened his agency next to the El Rey the same month, July 1937. Gleaming Chryslers reflected the theater lights, making that fantasy of every movie goer come true: take him into another world where even the best is not too good for him.

Elwood Lawe built the movie house, giving it three times the seating of the old Ramona. A modern projection room did away with the nemesis of the older house; now the film wouldn't break in the middle of a reel and whistling and booing wouldn't be a part of seeing a movie in Walnut Creek.

About the same time Mr. and Mrs. Counter opened their home to commercial ventures in the early 1940s, another Walnut Creek woman made her presence felt in a different way. A thin, wiry, blonde graduate of Mills College, where she majored in art, this lady saw a vacuum in the children's lives. Ruth Howard was probably the most important organizer Walnut Creek has ever seen. She threw herself into cultural endeavors which she never stopped supporting. First, she held art classes, free to children, at her home at 2385 Walnut Boulevard. When

210

the Walnut Creek branch of Oakland Children's Hospital Auxiliary organized in 1940, she was the first to join and she organized the first benefit, which was a fashion show held at the Art and Garden Center. The cause for this benefit was to pay for hospitalization of those children whose parents can only "part pay." Forty-three years later, Ruth's sister-in-law and both their husbands still provide the site for the annual fashion show at Joan and Harmon's home on Walnut Boulevard. Between 700 and 1,000 guests come to this event every year. Ruth Howard died in 1981.

Both the Harmon and Peter Howard families, along with several other couples, sponsored the "Diablo Assemblies" through Las Lomas High School. In the early 1950s they backed three dances a year which gave the young people an opportunity to dress well and mingle in society, as they might be expected to within a few years.

These dances were held at the high school. For adults, this same group offered "The Diablo Cotillion" at the Diablo Country Club. The group the Howards sponsored was the first to use the new ballroom at the Diablo Country Club.

In 1954 Ruth Howard and Mrs. DeWitt Kruger appeared before the Walnut Creek School Board to point out that there was little, if any, art education in the local schools. The result of their action was the formation of the Diablo Arts Association, to sponsor art for grammar school age youngsters. Their appeal to the board brought about the hiring of a teacher to give art classes: Earl Allen. Today he is principal of the Walnut Heights Elementary School.

In 1955 the Diablo Pageant of Arts Alliance encouraged artists to exhibit and compete for prizes. The first display was a humble beginning. From several specialities artists displayed their works in the kindergarten room at the old Walnut Creek Grammar School. Easels and display boards held some of the exhibits out in the school yard. Prime movers of this event were two ladies: Vee Strickl and Evadne Wenker. They labeled this first event "Art on the Main" and the next year artists vied for a chance to display their works at the annual Walnut Creek Art Pageant, held in the city park.

In 1962, Earl Allen was hired to coordinate the seventh annual

211

Pageant of the Arts along with Ron Caya, a San Ramon High School teacher. That year they took the event off the street, moving it indoors, in the California National Guard Armory at 1800 Carmel Drive. They scheduled the pageant for ten days. Two hundred and four contestants vied for awards, and an estimated 2,000 art enthusiasts came to view the show on Awards Night. The last Pageant of the Arts was held in 1963, and the Arts Alliance voluntarily turned the program over to the Civic Arts Commission and Walnut Creek's newly hired director of civic arts.

The year before, at Ruth Howard's urging, the Walnut Creek City Council established the Department of Civic Arts. In 1963 the San Ramon High School art teacher, Ron Caya, was hired at $6,000 a year as director. His instructions were, "to advise the City Council how to coordinate all phases of cultural activities in the city."

The first buildings made available to the arts program by the city were the two surplus quonset huts which stood in Civic Park. Caya opened the first art gallery in central Contra Costa County in October 1963 in one of these huts. The other was furnished as two classrooms, one for painters and the other for ceramicists. Caya had only one city employee to help him. Even with these sparse beginnings his program was too rich for some councilmen, who complained, "We don't need that kind of activity around here." They were careful not to say it within Ruth Howard's hearing.

The University of California Extension Service offered to come out and conduct classes if the city would provide the space. With much prodding, the city did have a modular building constructed beside the quonset hut. The next year Ronald Reagan became California's governor and he cut the university budget. The extension service, in turn, dropped its aid for the community's painting and dancing classes.

In 1965 the fledgling arts program began using the walnut growers' warehouse on an off-season basis. Old-timers in Walnut Creek will remember the walnut growers' processing plant on the north side of Civic Drive (since torn down and the site now vacant) with an overhead conveyor belt connecting it to the warehouse on the south side of the street, commonly called the Nut House.

As has been demonstrated, in a number of cases, citizens with ideas have given of their time and money to bring to Walnut Creek the benefits of their knowledge. The enthusiasm volunteers keep pumping into the community is the essence of accomplishment. Among the many small groups of citizens who have made lasting contributions is one which began with recollections of college days at a dinner party.

Late in 1959, Ilene and Hal Zuckerman were having dinner with Grete and Clifford Egan, reminiscing about the two men's Glee Club days at the University of California, Berkeley. With happy memories of their days in Berkeley, the foursome decided to invite a group of their friends to join them in forming a light opera company. As a result, the Diablo Light Opera Company gave its first performance in January 1960 of Gilbert and Sullivan's operetta, "Pirates of Penzance," on the Las Lomas High School stage. Since 1960 the company has staged two large musicals every year. Until 1967, each production was also produced in the same auditorium.

After viewing the first production of the Diablo Light Opera Company, the inspired Ron Caya asserted to the Egans and their friends, "We need a theater around here." Little did he know his spark of an idea would set off an explosion and culminate in solving the problem he recognized.

The city's art program was making minimal use of the Nut House at the time, and the barn-like structure was little more than just that—a barn. The light opera enthusiasts knew an opportunity when Caya pointed it out. One of them recalled that San Francisco's Fox Theater was about to be razed. By quick negotiations, and no little perspiration, the group secured the seats they needed from the Fox, trucked them to Walnut Creek, and actually screwed them to the floor of the Civic Arts Theater. The same people hung the main curtain over the stage which the arts department had built. With no heating and no restrooms, the Diablo Light Opera Company advertised the first play in the new facility, "The Sound of Music." Portable toilet facilities were brought in and ticket buyers were advised to dress appropriately, "Black tie and Blanket."

For the first eighteen months the Light Opera Company was the principle user of the structure, but after the city bought the building for $50,000, volunteers among the many groups who wanted to use the building rehabilitated it. To encourage community involvement, and to raise funds to supplement the city's limited art budget, the Civic Arts Association was set up in 1968. Ruth Howard played a major role in the association's success. The Arts Commission, encouraged by all the assistance given the presentations, recommended the city enlarge its program. As a result, in the same year the city hired two people: Betty Bernstein to lead and Daniel Steward to help.

With the warehouse transformed into a theater, group after group came forward asking to use it. In 1968 the Civic Arts Theater Ensemble, Jay Hornbacher, director, put on its first play, Thornton Wilder's "Skin of Our Teeth." Since then, this group, now called the Civic Arts Repertory, has staged more than seventy productions. Among other groups using the "Nut House" are the Diablo Symphony Association and the Contra Costa Musical Theater.

Ron Caya left the program in 1974 and is employed in much the same capacity by the city of Scottsdale, Arizona. Gary F. Schaub moved here from Michigan to head up the local program in 1974. Since then the Civic Arts Program has grown in size and scope. Over 100 different arts classes are now available, along with a professional art gallery that draws viewers from throughout the region.

The earlier Civic Arts Association began to sponsor the popular "Brown Bag" series of free lunch-time concerts once a month in 1974. A variety of musical and theatrical groups perform at these events with their expenses underwritten by local business contributions.

By 1979 the demand for a place to perform outstripped the capacity of the Nut House. In 1980 the city made use on a temporary basis of Helen Means' Onstage Theater, on East Street. The use of this facility did alleviate the pressure, but Mrs. Means lost her lease two years later and moved to the old Pleasant Hill School. This meant that the city lost use of the second theater. Fortunately, the adjoining Walnut Creek Brake Shop relocated at the same time and the city advanced the money to turn the shop into a playhouse. The renovation and reconstruction of the 1535 East Street building cost $125,000, and money received from contributions returned most of that sum to the municipal treasury within two years. In 1984 six theater companies in Contra Costa County stand by ready to use it. The Civic Arts Repertory Company opened Stage II on March 24, 1982 with the play, "Indians."

Another cultural pillar in Walnut Creek is the Alexander Lindsay Junior Museum at 1901 First Avenue, in Larkey Park. Its genesis is best described by Mrs. Joan Howard. "Mr. and Mrs. Alexander Lindsay lived down the street from us [Walnut Boulevard] at the Seven Hills Ranch. Alexander, or Sandy as we all knew him, was still a relatively young man though he was already retired. He and his wife, Barbara, had four children. Sandy delighted in showing his children and their friends many wonders of nature. Neighborhood youngsters made a veritable Pied Piper of Sandy, as he intrigued them with facts of nature on the excursions he led. Many of the youngsters started collections then which still keep their interests in the natural sciences alive.

"About 1955 Barbara and Sandy Lindsay, Bobbie and Bill (Dr. Owen) Williams, Elsa and Matt Connelly, Ruth and Phil Bancroft, Jr., and a small group of us formed the Diablo Junior Museum. Our purpose was to acquaint as many of the children of the area as we could with the wonders of nature.

"We successfully asked for funds from the Junior League of Oakland and the National Association of Junior Museums. Drummond McCunn, president of the community college district, loaned us two professors, Ferd Ruth and Gene Goselin, to conduct classes. The Walnut Creek School District gave us the use of a classroom for a summer program. With that kind of help the program really took off.

"Alexander Lindsay died in 1962 and we renamed the museum to honor him. After being organized for about ten years, our association found the EBMUD was vacating its old water treatment plant in Larkey Park. Through the utility's cooperation the city rented it for one dollar a year and turned it over to the museum association.

"Of course the program has grown far beyond our dreams. We've raised funds every year to modify the interior, to build new exhibits and buy more equipment. We sponsor the youth group which acts as aides, curators, and interpretive guides. They also keep the cages clean, sweep the floors, work in the pet library, care for the display animals and lead guided tours of organized youth groups.

"The museum houses a miniature zoo with unreleasable birds and mammals, fishes, amphibians, and reptiles. The museum also offers classes, brings exhibits to schools and sponsors special programs and events. Its pet library contains animals children may 'check out' for a week."

Joan Howard has been a board member of the museum association for thirty years.

The museum is staffed by a full time director employed by the City of Walnut Creek, Mr. Sam Smoker, and one additional city employee. The museum association pays for one more full time employee. Five part time workers are on the city payroll and ten more are employed by the association. Additionally, between two and three hundred trained volunteers work on regular schedules.

Sam Smoker, director since 1967, speaks with pride. "The museum is a place where young people become aware of their natural heritage by means of our living, hands-on, and static exhibits. We vary our programs by trying to blend the need with the supply." He speaks of another aspect of the work done at the museum. "Many people know us, for the last ten to twelve years, as a wildlife care and rehabilitation center. They often bring us young injured animals, and we do our best to bring them back to good health. We then release them if they are naturally wild animals."

Palmer School's Adrian Mendes recalls Barbara and Sandy Lindsay with affection. "When they brought their children to our school and we met them for the first time, they were very friendly and warm. He said, 'We are Barbara and Sandy,' and they were just like that from then on. They always had animals around their house. Once they had a pet raccoon which came to their swimming pool whenever any children were around. If a youngster dove into the pool the raccoon would follow."

In 1983 the museum board of directors recognized the need to expand beyond the limited EBMUD pumping plant and initiated plans to relocate to a site in Heather Farm Park. This location is only shouting distance from Sandy Lindsay's old home at Seven Hills Ranch.

The Alexander Lindsay Junior Museum is a springboard to understanding for the area's young people.

During the 1940s when her husband was assigned to the Pacific Fleet and they made their home on Oahu, Mrs. Joseph (Marge) Bronson became absorbed in the native dances of the islands. She enrolled in classes and became a serious student.

Even though she had the responsibilities of a homemaker, including raising the first of her five children, Mrs. Bronson's zealous attention to the fine points of the various movements brought her an affinity from her native teachers. So pronounced was her dedication that one Hawaiian teacher, following custom in admiration of her student, bestowed on her her own first name, Kekuahooulu.

At the conclusion of her husband's assignment in Hawaii the Bronsons moved to Walnut Creek. However, within a few years Mrs. Bronson made numerous trips around the Pacific islands, watching native dancers wherever she could find them, and each time she returned to Walnut Creek with pent-up enthusiasm for what she had seen.

In 1958, Mrs. Bronson founded the Dances of the Pacific, introducing two classes in Hawaiian dance to Walnut Creek. The response was immediate. With the inspiration of Ruth Wallis, then director of the Walnut Creek Recreation Department, and team work amongst the teachers, the program steadily advanced and expanded to include not only dances of Hawaii but also of Tahiti, Japan, Samoa, Korea, New Zealand, Tonga and the Philippines. The couples class, organized in 1961, is still the most unique. It is a family affair with teens to grandparents learning techniques and skills in all Pacific dances suitable for mixed groups. In their desire for perfection, the teachers— several from the original staff and others coming up from the ranks— have traveled to various islands in the Pacific, studying first hand the

217

native dances, music and costumes to offer authentic material to their students and their annual productions.

In the spring of each year since 1961, it has been traditional for the teaching program to stage an annual pageant for the public at Las Lomas High School. This undertaking necessitated the formation of the Dances of the Pacific Association in 1962. It was incorporated as a non-profit group in 1969 and is now sponsored by Walnut Creek's Leisure Services Department. Each year the association donates all the profits from the annual production to worthy local charities. The dancers are non-professional, but their ability to create skilled and colorful entertainment with true ethnic flavor is widely recognized both on the mainland and in the Pacific islands.

In 1976, under the guidance of Dances of the Pacific, a satellite group of young dancers was formed to enter competition among other local dancing units. In July 1979, this group traveled to Tahiti, living native style in Tahitian family homes. They astounded their hosts with their skills in not only Tahitian dancing, but also in Maori, Hawaiian and Samoan. They appeared as guest artists at the traditional Tahiti Fete celebration. Transporting the myriads of costumes and musical instruments was expensive, but by dancing locally throughout the year, the group earned most of the necessary funds. The dancers make or buy their own costumes.

Friends who worked with her say Kekuahooulu Bronson was completely selfless in her attitude. They also say she captivated so many people at home with her fascination for what she saw, that her Dancers of the Pacific immediately created a happy troupe. Her helpful nature engendered dedicated cooperation from them which is still the spirit of the group.

Back in the 1940s, Mrs. Bronson not only raised her five children but also actively aided her husband in his drive to establish Acalanes High School. Her efforts to reveal an aspect of the cultures around the Pacific Rim continue to enrich the cultural lives of thousands of Walnut Creek area residents.

It is said by some that symphony performances in Central Contra Costa County before 1968 were very rare. However, sounds of symphonic music were heard evenings in the halls of Acalanes High School before that year. There, interested musicians and some students gathered to play in chamber groups and in an orchestra. Initially Jud Digard led them and even helped raise the money needed to put on concerts. Digard was transferred out of the area in 1968.

William Donaldson, a retired DuPont executive, helped to incorporate the Diablo Symphony Association in 1968 and became the group's first president. From that early beginning of a few musicians, the association has grown to a membership of 465, each of whom contributes to the orchestra's $25,000 budget. They finance the group; no admission fee is charged to any concert.

June Reeder, president in 1978-80, who helped form the program, is still very active in the association. She reports, "We give twelve concerts a year, thanks to many, many volunteers. Since the passage of Proposition 13, our funds are tight—where the City of Walnut Creek used to give us $5,000 a year and allow us to use the concert hall free, now they don't and we pay them to use the Civic Arts Theater."

The Diablo Symphony gives three sets of concerts a year, each set consisting of three performances. The first of each set is always played at Rossmoor's Gateway Clubhouse, the second in the St. Mary's Chapel and the third in the Civic Arts Theater. The orchestra also puts on two "family concerts" which parents are encouraged to attend with children. Another presentation each year is the "thank you" performance for association members. Finally the Diablo Symphony plays one concert a year in the Concord Pavilion, usually around the end of June or near the Fourth of July.

The association hires a conductor, an assistant conductor, soloists and a stage crew.

For the last three consecutive years, William Shreve has been the association president.

Once a year a Young Artists Audition is a feature of the Diablo Symphony. The winners receive a $300 cash prize, but more important to most of the contestants is the opportunity to perform with a symphony orchestra. One year's winner, Peter Shelton, now is the second chair cellist with the San Francisco Symphony. The 1983 winner, Robin Hanson, is an outstanding young violinist. A couple of the Young Artists Audition winners have made their Carnegie Hall debuts.

For a volunteer orchestra, the Diablo Symphony sets very high standards and its accomplishments are fitting attributes of any professional symphonic organization.

In 1973 three school teachers discussed the absence in Walnut Creek of any encouragement for youngsters ages six to nine interested in playing string instruments. In 1974 the trio of Joyce Anderson and her two friends, Muriel Strong and Mary Ann Marinak, set out to remedy that absence.

They found the Mt. Diablo School District agreeable and supportive and obtained the use of the Foothill Intermediate School assembly room for their practice sessions. The school district also supplied music stands and even sheet music for the group.

Fifty-five to sixty young people annually give three concerts, one in fall, winter and spring. They give two concerts, one for soloists and another in ensemble.

In 1982 Walnut Creek made the movement a part of its Civic Arts education program, thus picking up part of the group's expenses. However, the Young People's String Orchestra needs a budget of from $2,000 to $3,000 to operate, and a parents' group assumes the responsibility of raising the money. Joyce Anderson is still the sparkplug of the orchestra, and parents free her of all other duties so that she may devote her time to conducting the orchestra.

Anderson finds there are two levels (beginners and intermediate) of ability among the six- to nine-year-olds. She says that some years they have a third level (advanced) of accomplishment, and special attention must be given all three.

In 1980, the young people ten and older who had outgrown and left the initial program found that no place existed for them to continue their musical experience. Again, Joyce Anderson acted. She formed the Diablo Youth Orchestra to provide a place for the graduates of the Young Performers to continue performing. She called together the heads of the music programs in local schools, as well as the parents of the children in need of leadership. As a result she recruited Jonathan Khuner as conductor and Karla Lemon as assistant conductor. Both are paid for their services.

Many of the sixty musicians are recruits from the Young Peoples String Orchestra. They perform in March, May and November in the Civic Arts Theater. One requisite for membership is that each player must continue in his or her school's music program so that the demands of the Youth Orchestra does nothing to weaken any school's orchestra.

The performers go on retreats occasionally. They went on a three-day trip to La Honda in 1982 and also went to Yosemite Valley for a weekend. The Ahwahnee Hotel admired their performance so much they have invited them back to play again. On the way to Yosemite the Walnut Creek orchestra stayed overnight in Modesto, where they performed with the Modesto Youth Orchestra.

Asked if she had many problems with the group, Anderson responded, "Not really. About the worst that ever happened to us was the night we all met at the Civic Arts Theater only to find a scheduling mistake had reserved the stage for another group. That night we held our practice outside, in the parking lot."

Joyce Anderson takes well-earned pride in the orchestra. "They go out and play for any group whenever invited—the sun shines on us all the time—everyone wants the kids to succeed—everything is going so well—we're all very proud of what our players are accomplishing."

Particularly in the last thirty years, groups of citizens in this area have come together and planned and worked toward accomplishing a goal they saw as worthwhile. Most have succeeded and for no other reason than the willingness and commitment of their volunteers.

One such group is now at a pinnacle of accomplishment after only a dozen years. It is known as the Heather Farm Garden Center Association. It is not a garden club by itself but an association of clubs from all over Contra Costa County and other East Bay communities, as well

221

as individual members. The concept may be unique to California. The association stages flower and plant shows at its headquarters in Heather Farm Park. It provides a place for classes and demonstrations of horticultural specimens. Attracting enough groups to foster high quality programs, and paying for a building which cost $860,000, are accomplishments its organizers may be very proud of.

The history of the HFGCA goes back to 1967, when John Chamberlain suggested the idea of a small association to the then Walnut Creek city park director, Ruth Wallis. Recognizing the potential in the idea, Mrs. Wallis called a meeting of the presidents of three local garden clubs on May 31, 1967. They waxed enthusiastic over the suggestion and made a request of the city for use of 5.4 acres of Heather Farm Park. At the time they envisioned only their gardens; no building was even in their minds. The city insisted, for security reasons, some kind of a building be put up to house their equipment. As a result, what might have been only garden plots or a utility shed is now a two-story, completely equipped horticultural educational display center.

Robert Cowden was elected the first president of the group in 1968, and the following year Alice Radocay assumed the lead. Ruth Howard became president in April 1970 and served in that capacity for two terms. During 1971 the HFGCA incorporated.

The enthusiasm of horticulturists, botanists and flower and plant lovers for a central location, where they could share their ideas, has resulted in the expansion of the corporation from its original three clubs to include thirty-eight separate societies now. Over 4,000 individuals are in these thirty-eight organizations.

In order to finance the building of a headquarters on city property in Heather Farm Park, the HFGCA started holding plant sales. Their first in 1971 netted about $300. The next year they raised $1,500, and in 1973 they retained $3,000 in profit. The association consulted an architect in 1978, who told them they could expect to spend $100,000 to build a headquarters building.

Finally, when construction started in the fall of 1980, inflation had pushed the estimated cost up to $300,000. Virginia Johnson, president at the time, watched the association funds run out in the fall of 1981,

(Top) John Marchbanks' Heather Farm, 1924. End of race track right edge of picture. City Park, 1984 (below).

Claudia Halderman collection
Courtesy Henry Kalman

with the shell of the building complete, but no roof over it. The City of Walnut Creek loaned the group $100,000 to put on the roof, and then work stopped for a year. By their flower and plant sales and other fund raising activities, volunteers had brought in a total of about $600,000 by this time, but another couple of hundred thousand dollars would be needed to complete the interior.

To complete the project when they were very short of funds, the city on behalf of the association requested a grant of $250,000 from the California Department of Motor Vehicles "Special License Plate Fund" in 1982. Assemblyman William Baker of Danville made this funding possible when he authored a bill just for this purpose. Senator Boatwright ran it through the senate. It was a unique bit of funding.

The state deemed the HFGCA an educational organization (a prerequisite for a grant) and made the bequest as requested in time for work to start again on the interior of the center that fall. The building was completed in the spring of 1983 as was the entrance to the facility—the Ruth Howard Memorial Garden.

The focal point of the center is the 9,000-square-foot Pavilion. The main level houses a reference library, complete kitchen facilities and expansive outdoor decking. Lectures, demonstrations, flower and plant shows are staged on this level.

The lower level has a spacious work room and classroom area for demonstrations of different gardening techniques and practices.

Outside, member plant societies are developing gardens featuring their own specialities such as roses, camellias, iris, chrysanthemums, palms, fuchsias and native plants. The principal gardens are the Demonstration Garden, Stream Garden, Native Plant Garden, and Children's Adventure Garden. A water garden demonstrates methods used in micro-climate control by using rocks, pools and fountains.

A sensory garden of raised beds provides for blind and wheelchair visitors. A wide ramp extends around two sides of the building, giving wheelchair access from one level to the other.

HFGCA members can't praise their fund raising chairman enough. They all point to Jeanette Howard as the one person most responsible for the fund raising success. The largest single donor, who insists on remaining anonymous, gave over $50,000. The association's library received a $25,000 grant from Lawton Shurtleff as a memorial to his wife, Barbara. Chevron Chemical Company donated $25,000, and $10,000 came from the Stanley Smith Trust of Edinburgh, Scotland. The Walnut Creek Lion's Club is helping finance the Pavilion Room. The work room is being furnished by the Walnut Creek Rotary Club and the classroom is being completed by the Walnut Creek Soroptimists.

There have been many more members who put their shoulders to the wheel and made the HFGCA project a success—too many to list. Ruth Bancroft is one who, according to all reports, was always available to help in whatever capacity she could serve. Her husband, Philip Bancroft, Jr., was the first to petition the city council to create a city park at the former John Marchbanks horse farm. After Bancroft offered the city five acres of his adjoining land, the council seriously entertained his idea. As a result, the City of Walnut Creek now has one of the finest municipal parks in California.

The dedication of the Heather Farm Garden Center building took place on September 24, 1983 and was followed by an open house on September 24 and 25. The first show and sale in the new facility took place on December 3, 1983.

The total cost of the project has exceeded $860,000 excluding landscaping. Ultimately, native plants from the wide area that is this county—with its variety of growing conditions—will be planted around the headquarters building. Maintenance will be done by volunteers from all over Contra Costa County. Flower and plant shows involving all the specialties will be encouraged at this central display area in Walnut Creek. The members can take considerable pride in their accomplishment; it will raise the cultural awareness of every citizen who visits their periodic displays or attends their educational lectures in the handsome center.

RECREATION

As late as 1925 no recreational facility for youths existed in Walnut Creek. It is true that a skating rink operated on the ground floor of the old forty- by seventy-five-foot town hall—from the turn of the century into the 1920s—and adults skated there just as often as children. The baseball diamond at North Main and Lacassie streets (Gemco's gas station) was built for the town team games.

The earliest swimming pool was the one at the Charles Howard home on Walnut Boulevard. Peter Howard remembers coming home from Central School in the 1920s. "It seemed to me the entire school used to follow me home, particularly on hot days."

The first money spent for youthful recreation paid for the improvements to the town swimming hole. There, where the bridge on Duncan Avenue crossed the creek, youngsters swam in the wide pool and sunned themselves on the narrow sandy beach. Trees lined the west bank and shaded the community barbecue grounds. The Women's Club came up with money enough to buy the lumber, sand and cement for the bulkhead at the edge of the pool. Volunteer labor built the wall and spread the sand.

The swimming hole gave a large number of children their first chance to learn to swim, but unfortunately the pool was never supervised. One day in the 1930s a youngster drowned when he swam there alone. Swimming there stopped at once and never did resume.

The first tennis court in the community open to the public was built on the east side of Locust Street not far from the corner of Olympic by Ted Newell and pharmacist Ted Wiget. It was behind the small EBMUD building near that same corner today. They had the court paved and enclosed it with fencing.

Neither the city nor the school board included money for playground equipment in their budgets before 1950. So when the first school to take students from the old Central School opened its doors in 1949 there was no playground equipment. Volunteer mothers at the Walnut Festival that year kept a cake booth busy and raised enough money to pay for all the equipment used at that school for many years.

To their cake booth came an army of ants who found the cakes about the time the festival opened. The mothers kept their wares clean, brushing the ants away, but late in the day they searched for a safe place to store the cakes for the night. Fortunately, the Walnut Festival that year covered the city park, within sight of Lommel's Creamery. One enterprising and frantic mother approached Dick Lommel, asking for his help. "Bring them over—my refrigerator boxes have plenty of room for your cakes!" And so the cakes that would pay for the Parkmead School's playground equipment were kept safe and fresh in Dick's cold boxes until they were needed.

The mothers knew money would be needed a year before the school was completed and held a PTA dinner on October 28, 1948. For the benefit dinner they served beans, beans and beans! Sheldon Rankin was the master of ceremonies at this affair and introduced the first lady member of a school board in this area: Mrs. Reuben C. (Alice) McBride. Later, in 1955, Mrs. McBride became president of the Acalanes Union High School District.

Walnut Creek's attention to recreation encompasses youth, adult and senior citizen programs under Public Services/Leisure Services Director Darrell Mortensen. Leisure Services operates with two city employees.

A Recreation Commission of seven members (initially five) appointed by the city council advises the council, which sets the policy. Mortensen takes his directives from the council and implements them.

The council appointed the first Recreation Commission in February 1950. The five members named were: Elmer Hansen, chairman; Jack Wendt, vice-chairman; Donna Puckle, secretary; Russell Miller, treaasurer; Mrs. Darrell Jensen, publicity chairman; Gene Saalwaechter, city superintendent of recreation.

One of the first activities the commission recommended that year was a novel event, held on August 26 in the city park: a "Bicycle Rodeo" for boys ages ten to sixteen.

The sports program is guided by volunteers who offer the competitors the chance to run it themselves. They schedule use of city-owned fields and courts, get their own umpires or referees and run their own programs. They operate under two general classifications: Youth Athletic League and the Adult Softball League.

The senior citizen program was initially guided by a twenty-year city employee, Louise Gillette. She made herself available to the program at any hour of the day or night. The Senior Citizen Center, in the Civic Park, is where sewing programs, cards and dominoes, exercise and dance activities take place. The two city employees spend most of their time with the seniors, usually in a guidance role. One aspect of the local plan has worked to Walnut Creek's advantage, in the aftermath of Proposition 13. Where neighboring cities hired bus drivers and then had to let them go, thus eliminating this citizen aid, Walnut Creek took qualified drivers from its seniors to drive the two buses the Rotary Club donated. Hence, any reduction which might have been caused by the budget tightening didn't affect the Walnut Creek Senior Citizen Program. Bus availability is extremely important to the many older persons without private or public transportation available. Also, there are those with a mobility problem who can participate in activities with their contemporaries, because a driver will assist them from their door to the vehicle.

Mortensen reports, "Seniors contributed 53,000 volunteer hours to their own program last year [1982]."

SCOUTING

The story of scouting in Walnut Creek begins with adult men donating their leisure time so boys may learn to make decisions for themselves, so that they could learn what it takes to achieve and finally find out that working together they may enjoy life more.

Scouting commenced in England and came to the United States in February 1910. Undoubtedly the movement came to Walnut Creek before 1922, but the earliest record shows that Albert Sturger, of Troop 2, advanced to the rank of Eagle Scout in 1922.

Adult leadership made the difference between a successful or poor and sporadic program, wherever scouting began. The records of those who gave hours, days and even weeks of their time is very incomplete. It is regrettable credit cannot be given to the many who gave years of their time.

J. A. Mauzy, Walnut Creek businessman, headed the Boy Scout fund drive effort in 1922.

In 1925 two sponsors, the Walnut Creek Lions Club and Post 115, American Legion, provided support for Troop 201 and Troop 202. Seventy-five scouts attended the short-term Easter vacation scout camp that year.

The following year, 1926, George P. Jackson made Eagle Scout in May and Billie Avise achieved the same rank in July.

The movement faltered in 1926, '27 and '28, when only one troop remained active.

In 1929 the second troop returned to life and the community raised $250 for the Walnut Creek Boy Scouts in 1930. The active committee chairmen that year were: Rueben Freitas, and the teacher, county superintendent of schools and ex-Walnut Creek mayor, E. B. Anderson.

Recognizing "he has worked unceasingly in acquiring Camp Contra Costa" (near Long Barn, Tuolumne County), the Berkeley-Contra Costa Council awarded Shadeland's Ranch manager, E. B. Moyer, a five-year veteran pin, in January 1931.

That same year Charles P. Howard served as a member of the executive board of the council.

In the years 1934 and 1935 the Lions Club sponsored Troop 201, and scouts built themselves a campground in the center of Walnut Creek. Johnson A. Thomas and his son, Skid Thomas, were scoutmaster and assistant at the time.

Mt. Diablo Boulevard ended in a "T" at Main Street, and a Shell service station and the Bungalow Barbecue occupied the east side of the intersection. With permission granted by the Shell Oil Company, the scouts cleared a level area behind the service station and constructed their campground, spending numerous nights there. Troop 201's activity may be said to be an early "Jamboree."

In those years, 1934-35, Troop 202, also sponsored by the American Legion, met in the Veterans' Hall on Locust. Al Schroyer was scoutmaster at the time.

Bert Wiget became district commissioner in 1935.

The scoutmasters of the two troops in 1939 were J. W. Wendt and Lee Larabee. The next year J. W. Wendt and H. Pittman led the troops.

Apparently the first Cub Scout Pack was Pack 10, which was organized in 1940, M. E. Gibson, cubmaster. The Walnut Creek Rotary Club was the sponsor.

With 500 in attendance at a dinner in the Claremont Hotel in 1944, the council honored J. W. Wendt with his Veteran Award.

The story of Pack 10, Den 6, in Walnut Creek, goes back to 1944. Real estate broker Westland was cubmaster and paper box manufacturer Jo Shockey his assistant. Every Friday night the assistant drove his five Ygnacio Valley cubs to their Walnut Creek pack meeting. By 1946 he had ten youngsters participating. They regularly went on "cook-outs" up Mt. Diablo. In 1947, with many of his boys now twelve years old, Shockey organized Boy Scout Troop 408, with eight scouts. The troop grew and the scoutmaster advanced with it. He served on the Berkeley-Contra Costa Council for fourteen years and on the national council for four more.

In the history of scouting much of the success or lack thereof is traceable to the degree of dedication each scoutmaster is able to maintain. The job has always required the leader to give of himself regularly and in large amounts. He must inspire his boys to raise their levels of achievement. He needs to maintain enthusiasm at all times, for apathy is contagious.

Almost every scoutmaster starts out as an optimist, and thankfully, many do remain faithful to their inspiration. Among the many men who served with dedication in Walnut Creek was Darrell Jensen. He took over Troop 214 in February 1952 (formed in 1950) with William Sweetland as his assistant. The following year they traded positions. In 1952 Jensen and Sweetland led their scouts to Camp Bray, near Pinecrest, for winter sports.

In 1953 the two men started the boys on a paper drive which netted $116. The scouts contributed that amount to the Las Lomas High School Swimming Pool Fund. Later that year the two leaders took their troop to the Mt. Diablo Council's summer camp at Wolfboro. The Walnut Creek Elks sponsored Troop 214. When Darrell Jensen stepped down from his post, Jim Worthman replaced him.

Troop 227, Earl Allen, scoutmaster, has had the good fortune to have as its sponsor for thirty years the Native Sons of the Golden West. That troop, with twenty-seven boys in its 1983 program, has seven active adults.

The total number of involved boys and adults in the cub and scout program in Walnut Creek in 1983 is: 416 Cub Scouts with 128 adults; 336 Boy Scouts with 99 adults.

The Girl Scout program had its beginning during the Great Depression, grew only slowly during the second World War and then blossomed into a very active organization shortly after.

The Walnut Creek Parent Teacher Association sponsored the first troop of thirty girls in 1934. It took ten years for the organization to grow large enough for the national headquarters to establish the Walnut Creek Council. Mrs. Reginald Biggs was appointed the first Girl Scout commissioner. From that beginning of a single troop, the movement has increased to fifty-five and is still growing.

Cookie and calendar sales finance slightly more than half the annual budget. Camping and event fees, together with parent contributions, bring in a quarter of the funds needed, while the United Fund assists with a slightly smaller amount.

Back in 1949 Mrs. Ruth Howard led the Walnut Creek Council. Her interest in the girls having their own campground took her to the state capitol where she eventually, in 1949, consummated a rental agreement with the state for a site near Sierra City. The girls' selling activities financed the initial improvements and to this day they raise the money to maintain the camp. Each year, just before opening the camping season, Peter Howard, Ruth's husband, drove a truck loaded with supplies to the camp where he stayed to help open Camp Sierra Woodlands. The camp remained the responsibility of the Walnut Creek scouts until they were consolidated into the greater San Francisco Bay Girl Scout Council in 1963. At that time the local group changed its name to the Walnut Creek Association of the SFBGSC.

The year 1954 was important for the local scouts. Camp Sierra Woodlands served very well in summer but the girls lacked a place they could call their own the year round within the Walnut Creek area. The girls had been using Marsh Creek Park, a public picnic and recreation area, for a summer day camp. Their mothers not only had to drive the many miles to and from the park but also had to clean the restrooms each Monday morning. Mrs. Leonard (Helen) Ford of Walnut Creek was council president at the time. She resented the extra demands on the mothers and tried to find a way to reduce them.

To solve the problem, as she saw it, Helen Ford, assisted by her staff of Merry Kyle, vice-president, and Jeanne Christy, secretary, located sixty-five acres at the end of Springhill Road in Lafayette. Only a dirt road led to the site, and the property was without a water supply. The purchase price was $6,000, far more than the council could afford. At Mrs. Ford's request, the San Francisco Foundation agreed to match half the amount needed if the council would raise the first $3,000. A fund raising drive successfully met the goal, and with the matching funds the council bought the acreage. Water was a necessity and the East Bay Municipal District service was a half mile away. Mrs. Ford went to the local management of the utility for a solution. The manager told her if each household along Springhill Road would subscribe to EBMUD service, he could extend the line to the camp. She went from house to house, and although each household already had its well, she succeeded in signing up every property owner. Mrs. Ford so successfully led the Girl Scout program that she was elected council president for three terms.

By 1954 more than 3,000 girls were enrolled and used the day camp, "Twin Canyons," as a nucleus for their activities. Still, an office was needed for the staff. Three years later, while Merry Kyle was president of the council, after a search and another fund drive, a headquarters building was bought at 3570 Terrace Way, Lafayette.

Jean Christy became the first executive director. Later, Mary Bunecke succeeded her. By 1960 the enrollment in the Diablo Valley Council totalled 4,084 girls, assisted by 1,567 adults.

In August 1983, the Walnut Creek membership of the council totalled 682 girls. They are still committed to community service, which has a history dating back to 1952. In that year, Marjorie Banwell (Mrs. Richard Banwell) and Sally Wharton (Mrs. Dean Wharton) led a troop at the Walnut Heights School. These girls were among the first volunteers at Kaiser Hospital, who later became known as the "candy-stripers." They helped principally in the pediatric ward. Some of the girls later became nurses. For children at the County Children's Shelter, these same girls made toys, scrapbooks, and a doll house complete with furnishings. They made holiday decorations for all the convalescent hospitals in Walnut Creek.

During 1967 to 1970, years of more than usual racial strife, senior scouts ran a day camp for inner-city children at Twin Canyons, where the girls enjoyed all the activities offered there. Each morning for two weeks, two school buses filled with girls from Oakland arrived at the day camp. Through bake sales, cookie and calendar sales, and a Reader's Digest grant, the scouts earned enough money to pay for the bus transportation for their guests.

"Cadette" Scouts, seventh-, eighth- and ninth-grade girls, worked as aides for the local Well Baby Clinic and maintained trails at Twin Canyons. A troop of girls who owned their own horses used Twin Canyons as the base for their activities. A mariner troop owned several boats which the girls maintained themselves. One senior troop decorated Christmas trees at Letterman Hospital. In 1970, scouts brought joy to patients at the Veterans' Hospital in Martinez by baking and delivering cookies. A junior troop under the leadership of Mimi Knox (Mrs. Barnwell Knox) made "hero" badges for use in the emergency room at John Muir Memorial Hospital. There were cadettes that were junior grey ladies for the Red Cross and cadettes that gave style shows for senior citizens, wearing garments they had made themselves. In 1971, scouts filled sixty stockings for children at the Juvenile Hall Children's Shelter. At the same time the girls were starting a long association with Shadelands Ranch Historical Museum, where they committed themselves to a docent program. One early spring all the Girl Scouts in Walnut Creek met at Shadelands to plant the pathways with daffodils. Each spring these flowers still bloom. In 1972, Troop 970, under the leadership of Joanne Green, Sue Betts and Betty Stovall, put on the operetta "Hansel and Gretel" for the Valle Verde School. That year, scouts made twenty-five dozen cookies for the Heather Farm Garden Sale. They made dish gardens then and today continue to help at the garden center. Girls helped the Junior Chamber of Commerce at the pancake breakfast on Huck Finn Day (July 4). Under the leadership of Pat Terry (Mrs. Fred Terry), scouts began making tray favors for Meals on Wheels, a project they still carry on. These same girls put on a day-out party for the residents of various convalescent hospitals at St. Paul's Episcopal Church Parish Hall. They bake and serve the food and entertain their guests.

There is a continuing saga of community service through all levels of girl scouting. Girls have been active in the Salvation Army's Good Turn Day each year. They have also supported the Walnut Creek

Open Space program. They worked on a large clean-up project at the Sugar Loaf area of Open Space in 1982. They have put on demonstrations of ice cream making, butter making, and cooking with a Dutch oven at the Western Days held at the Borges Ranch. They have whitewashed an outbuilding at Borges Ranch and worked in the ranch garden there.

In spite of a decline in the number of school age girls in Walnut Creek in the past several years, the Girl Scout program here continues to grow.

WALNUT CREEK'S DOODLEBUG CLUB

*O*n 1954, two Walnut Creek teenagers received motor scooters, known as doodlebugs, as presents from their parents. From that beginning sprang the twenty-four-member drill team known as the Walnut Creek Doodlebug Club.

Within one year, newsreels of the team's activities were shown in movie houses all over the world. King Features News Syndicate, Universal, Pathe, and MGM all made October 29, a Saturday, the day to record the group's intricate maneuvers at Buchanan Field.

Darrel Jensen, father of Peter Jensen, taught his son and Peter's pal, Curtis Crook, how to care for their machines. He also taught some of the basic maneuvers in his back yard. A little later three more friends received similar vehicles from their parents. Jensen admitted he knew too little about drill teams when the enthusiastic boys put the question to him, "Will you teach us?"

Jensen went to Officer Phil Warner, drillmaster for the Oakland Police Department's national championship motorcycle drill team. "Would it be possible for some member of the Oakland team to . . . ?" Jensen asked.

"I'll do it myself," broke in Warner.

The boys, now grown in numbers, received permission to practice evenings on Capwell's parking lot. Officer Warner taught them the five basic maneuvers used by the Oakland police team. They practiced faithfully, but when the group grew to its ultimate twenty-four-boy members, Buchanan Field's larger paved area became the team's practice field.

Money for maintenance and repairs was always a problem, but Jensen found a sponsor in a local automobile agency, the Rett-White

Highway patrolmen show confidence in Peter Jensen.

Motor Sales Company of Lafayette and Walnut Creek. The boys' financial problems were solved by this new sponsor. A shop where they could all work on their doodlebugs together was a need Jensen solved by gaining the consent of the Las Lomas High School principal to use the shop there three afternoons a week.

The boys performed for the Walnut Festival. After Jensen took up a collection from local supporters, he bought a used bus Greyhound Lines put up for sale, and drove them to celebrations up and down the Sacramento and San Joaquin valleys. The boys showed their abilities at the Angel's Camp Jumping Frog Jubilee, a Fresno County Fair and a celebration in Santa Cruz.

The first twenty-three members were Peter Jensen, Curtis Crook, Ron Bledso, Darrell Sweetland, Byron Foreman, Ron Mangini, Gary Perata, Charles Wright, Ted Randall, Fred Danner, Charles Sommers, Garth Smith, Terry Hackett, Wally Turner, Dave Pringle, Steve White, Charles Cleveland, Jim Howe, Jim Husbands, Dale Sweetland, Norm Sutherland, Dennis Lockwood and Jerry Simone.

The intricate and occasionally hair-raising maneuvers the boys performed made them a big drawing card at parades and local celebrations all over Northern California. They rode in various formations, criss-crossed through a moving circle and passed in review. When the more proficient jumped their doodlebugs over four highway patrolmen, as they lay side by side on the pavement, the crowds cheered and applauded in appreciation.

In June 1955 the *American Weekly*, a Hearst publication with a circulation of eleven million copies, carried the story of Walnut Creek's Doodlebug Club.

ROSSMOOR

Any horseman riding up the valley in the spring of 1845 might have thought to himself, "How quiet, only birds speak above the rustling leaves." He would look for but not find Indian paths; years of rain and spring growth erased them long ago. He would see cattle munching green grass; the only fence in sight was the one he saw as he came into sight of Innocencio Romero's adobe.

The valley, later named "Tice," had only one family living in it, Romero and his wife Incarnación. They built their adobe by a large spring, near the entrance of today's Rossmoor. The horseman would be welcomed by the couple, asked to dismount and allow Romero to lead his mount to the corral. Meanwhile, Incarnación would motion the rider to the bench in the shade of their earthen porch and disappear inside to heat the beans and tortillas and to pour their visitor a cup of wine.

The rider, a stranger to the area, after complimenting Romero on his rancho, would politely give him the opportunity to reveal the vast area he owned and tell him how he came to own it.

"Only last year (1844) my brother, José, and I petitioned Governor Micheltoreña for the land, unclaimed by Welch," as he pointed to the north, "and Teodora Soto," as he waved to the hills to the west, and shrugging, to the south, "and some down by Rafael Soto's rancho."

The visitor would nod, and thoughtfully judge Romero a wise man to make such a claim.

The surplus land, in the claimant's mind, "Rancho El Sobrante (surplus) de San Ramon," encompassed five square leagues, 22,166 acres, from San Ramon Creek to Moraga.

Their claim of non-occupancy notwithstanding, Romero and his brother received no confirmation from their governor, yet in 1847 "sold" half the property to Francisco and José Garcia.

In 1853 they sold 100 acres to the first Anglo settler, squatter William Slusher.

In the same year, Innocencio deeded away almost all the remaining rancho to D. Punjal and S. Sanjuni.

These latter two held their purchase only a couple of years, then in 1855 sold out to another Anglo, James M. Tice.

A son, Andrew Jackson Tice, also took title to property in the valley, adjacent to James'.

But the James M. Tice residency lasted only until 1868 and after three owners in the next eight years, Joseph Naphtaly bought the 353 acres, in 1876. This new buyer was to own the land longer than anyone before or after him.

He bought out some squatters on adjoining plots and in 1899 also bought the 112-acre home ranch of Andrew J. Tice's widow.

Joseph Naphtaly increased his holdings in Tice Valley to a maximum of 1,436 acres. He planted a pear and apple orchard and a wine grape vineyard. He built a winery and distillery on the bench that is now the Del Valle High School.

If he had continued to concentrate on farming, the Joseph Naphtaly family would probably still own Tice Valley. But such was not to be.

In 1909 talk of an electric railway running from Oakland, thirty-one miles to Port Chicago, along today's Olympic Boulevard and running past the entrance to his property, may have interested Joseph Naphtaly. After all, such a line would allow him a shorter haul from his fields to ship his apples, pears and grapes. Whatever motivation did exist, the fact remains that S. L. Naphtaly and J. Naphtaly were two of the eight incorporators of the $2 million corporation, the Oakland and Antioch Railway Company.

Then three years later, the Danville Branch incorporated under the name San Ramon Valley Railroad, with S. L Naphtaly, president.

This branch commenced at the corner of Olympic and Tice Valley Road at the station called "Saranap." The branch ran up Tice

Rossmoor.

Valley Road and at the intersection of the entrance to the Naphtalys' home place, Rossmoor Parkway today, a spur ran up to the fruit packing shed.

The money the Naphtalys put into the railroad came from Mrs. Naphtaly and her side of the family. In assisting with the financing, a relative, B. J. Feigenbaum, took a substantial interest in the Naphtaly Ranch, according to county records.

The family planned a subdivision of small farm estates and named it "Wickham Haven." However, subsequent developments prevented this plan from materializing.

Unfortunately for the Naphtalys, competition from autos reduced passenger traffic, and only ten years after it started running, the company filed for permission to abandon. The last train ran on March 1, 1924.

Though strapped for cash, the Naphtalys held on to their ranch for another six years. In 1930 they were forced to sell. They formed the Tice Valley Land Company, taking shares which represented their individual interests, B. J. Feigenbaum included, and before the month was over they sold the company to R. Stanley Dollar, son of the shipping magnate, Robert Dollar.

Dollar's first move to improve his property was to tear down Naphtaly's decaying buildings, some of them fifty years old. He removed old corrals and bulldozed out the dead trees, what was left of the fruit packing shed, and traces of the spur near the entrance.

Not until 1935 did he build his summer home at the end of a winding road through the acreage. He had over an acre of grass planted by his house and had over one hundred varieties of trees shipped to his estate from all over the world. He had plaques put in place identifying many of the species.

When he expanded the house, making it his full time residence, he installed a large-faced clock over the front entry and planted ivy which grew to the top of the gable. A weather vane topped the house, a replica of the head of one of his prize Herefords.

He placed marble benches and marble statues around the ground. Near the front door, huge glazed Chinese bowls filled with camellias, picked up the color of the forget-me-nots bordering the walk.

Dollar built his son, R. Stanley Dollar, Jr., a single-story green board and batten house a quarter-mile downhill from his own. A white picket fence surrounded the brick walls, patio, and informal garden.

The Dollars bred purebred Herefords and raised show horses. Over the years they expanded the estate of 1,436 acres to 2,200.

The two homes became the scene for many social, charitable and political events. In 1955 Oakland's Junior League held its annual charity with about fifty-five hundred women walking through the homes and eating lunch on the grounds focusing on the swimming pool.

Contra Costa County Republicans staged a barbecue on August 19, 1956 which attracted notables from all over the United States. Governors and senators rubbed elbows with those who had elected them.

Even royalty and dignitaries from abroad enjoyed the hospitality of the Dollar families.

R. Stanley Dollar, Jr. lived on the ranch until June 30, 1960, the day he sold the estate to Ross Cortese.

Cortese, forty-three years old when he bought out the Dollars, came from Glendale. His early years belied the successful land developer he became. His parents were so poor he had to leave school when he was in the seventh grade. He helped support them by selling produce from a truck for several years, and only after World War II did he start on the path to success.

Cortese was short, well-groomed, and a conservative dresser. He wore a toupee well and was of medium height. He had the capacity to choose able men for his executive staff. His first administrator was an ex-mayor of Walnut Creek, Robert A. Nelson, 1952-63. Nelson finished his term as the city's chief elected officer in April 1963 and came to Rossmoor as administrator in December.

Cortese dreamed of bringing the best of his former retirement developments to Walnut Creek. Under the name Leisure World he had successfully built private communities in Maryland, Long Beach, Seal Beach and Laguna Hills. He called his company the Rossmoor Corporation. His opportunity to obtain enough money to build so large a community as the 10,000 dwelling units he proposed, came when Congress enacted legislation guaranteeing long-term low-cost financing if a developer first sold 90 percent of his community.

So, in 1963 Cortese started building and on February 27, 1964 he opened Walnut Creek Rossmoor Leisure World. Eunice Mignola was the second woman employee hired by Golden Rain Foundation of Walnut Creek, the managing agent for the housing projects, and is now in charge of manor records. She first worked for United California Bank Escrow Department, which was also located in the Gateway Clubhouse complex, and she recalls those first few weeks.

> At first prospects came to the sales office which was in a trailer located outside the grounds. Then when the Gateway Clubhouse Complex was completed, the sales counselors and the escrow department moved there. The first week, so many people came, we had to give them numbers, ask them to go out to lunch and come back to open their escrows. These people were not just lookers, they were buyers. Someone might get a number in the morning and we were so busy writing up contracts we wouldn't get back to them until the afternoon.
>
> At first, the housing projects were cooperatives, and the buyers purchased a share of stock in a mutual, which gave them the right of occupancy to a dwelling unit. The mutual corporation retained title to the land and to the improvements. In 1969, the last cooperative project was built and condominium projects were started. Also, each buyer purchased, and still does, a membership in the Golden Rain Foundation of Walnut Creek, which represents each individual's interest in the community facilities. The foundation takes title to the community facilities as trustee and continues to hold them in trust for the members of the mutuals.
>
> Each mutual, and at the present time there are thirteen of them, is a California corporation with its own board of directors and officers. Each board of directors adopts various policies and approves a budget. An association called Joint Mutual Boards was formed so that the directors of each mutual could meet to discuss matters which affect the whole community and to reach decisions for the benefit of all residents in the community. The foundation is the managing agent for all the mutuals.

244

Those first days the security gate was on Golden Rain; Rossmoor Parkway didn't go beyond Golden Rain.

The day we opened we sold 111 manors of the 542 in Mutual One. The rest of the week we sold 118 more. All told we wrote contracts for $1 million worth of manors that first week. People came from everywhere to buy.

Some of the most expensive two-bedroom, 1½-bath, corner units facing the golf course sold for $18,195, with $1,934 down, including the escrow charges. Buyers of those models committed themselves to $206 monthly payments which included principal and interest, taxes, maintenance, 80 percent medical coverage, free green fees, horse stable use, RV parking space and free lawn bowling.

Less expensive manors sold for $13,595, the all-inclusive monthly payment $171. Mutual One sold out in April that first year and Mutual Two, of 468 units, selling from $13,800 to $18,095 was gone before the end of the year.

Cortese sold only to persons age fifty-two or older; neither partner of a marriage could be younger. In 1968 that proviso was changed to age forty-five.

Initially the clinic occupied the Stanley Dollar, Jr. home. The Golden Rain Foundation operated it and still does, in another location. In his original concept Cortese contemplated building a 128-bed hospital which he would own and the Golden Rain Foundation would operate. His prospect for government funding disappeared in 1962 when John Muir Memorial Hospital received its commitment for federal funding.

In 1966, when Medicare became effective, the original 80 percent coverage for residents over sixty-five, with Blue Cross as the underwriter, was dropped. The monthly payments were lowered and residents over sixty-five were free to contract for any coverage they chose.

Disagreements developed between the Golden Rain Foundation and Cortese as he discontinued some of the maintenance services. He was in a financial bind. He could no longer maintain the eighteen-hole golf course, the stables, and lawn bowling greens as agreed. Fees were initiated for these facilities for the first time.

Cortese's Rossmoor Corporation sold the undeveloped land to Terra California in May 1967. Some community facilities to which the Rossmoor Corporation held title were included in this transfer.

For a time Gordon Sherwood became the administrator on behalf of the management firm operating Rossmoor, but in January 1968, his company, Gordon Sherwood and Associates, took over. Eighteen months later, on July 1, 1969, John Jerman came to manage Rossmoor, staying four and a half years.

On March 1, 1974, L. Wayne Davis, who had been the director of business operations since 1969, was hired as administrator to replace Jerman.

The disagreement between the Golden Rain Foundation and Ross Cortese, smoldering since 1966, ended in an expensive out-of-court settlement in 1973. That year, by virtue of a significant loan from the United California Bank, Terra California transferred to the Golden Rain Foundation titles to the eighteen-hole golf course, the maintenance building and the Stanley Dollar, Jr. Clubhouse. The Golden Rain Foundation already held title to all the other completed community facilities.

On July 23, 1979, Cecil Riley, former Oakland city manager, was hired by the Golden Rain Foundation to manage Rossmoor.

Terra California, the present developer, remains the owner of the undeveloped land within Rossmoor, and is free to build on it subject to approval of the City of Walnut Creek.

Cortese's 1963 plan to construct 10,000 units has been scaled down by the City of Walnut Creek to 7,350 manors which would accommodate about 11,000 people.

From the beginning, a portion of the total sales price of a unit was deposited, with the Golden Rain Foundation as trustee, for the purchase of the community facilities. Under the 1973 settlement, this portion of the proceeds, known as the community facilities fee, goes to the United California Bank (now First Interstate Bank), and the Rossmoor Corporation to pay off the debt.

The proprietorship of the dwellings rested in the name of the different mutuals (projects) as they were completed. For instance,

Walnut Creek Mutual Number One took title to all 542 manors in the project. The buyers each purchased a stock/membership and signed a separate occupancy agreement assuming their proportionate share, based on the price of their unit, of the mutual's expenses. Included in the monthly payment are the principal and interest payments for the unit. None may accelerate their share to pay for the unit outright. Each note covers all dwellings in the cooperative mutual (project) and is for a forty-year period. The mutual collects the money from the members in monthly payments and remits to the lending institution.

Walnut Creek Mutual Number Two made the same arrangement with its 468 members and so did each of the succeeding cooperative mutuals. But the number of mutuals increased over the years. Number Forty-nine is completed now, and the need for officers of each corporation, at least three to each mutual, has outstripped the supply. So as to reduce the number of corporations, unification began when First Walnut Creek Mutual assembled six of the earlier smaller cooperative ones into assuming ownership of 1,878 manors on August 31, 1967. Second Walnut Creek Mutual did the same five years later by incorporating nine of the smaller cooperative mutuals and assumed ownership of 1,387 manors on January 2, 1973.

Terra California began building condominium manors exclusively in 1969. In that plan of ownership, each householder makes his own financing agreement. The condominium-only Third Walnut Creek Mutual consists of 1,570 manors (December 1983). There are nine smaller condominium mutual corporations with a total of 512 manors.

In the case of the condos, the mutual organization's function is one primarily of overseeing the maintenance and making such contracts with the Golden Rain Foundation as are found necessary.

The average age of Rossmoor residents dropped from 75.8 years in 1964 to 74.1 in 1982. On December 27, 1982, 5,249 residents were female and 2,698 were male.

Mrs. Mignola chuckles over one resident now gone. "This 101-year-old lady surprised us by applying for a membership and qualifying for a forty-year payment loan and having it approved . . . and she lived for four or five years after too."

Mrs. Mignola reflects on the kind of people she has seen buy at Rossmoor. "I maintain it takes a special kind of person . . . the people who come out here to live. Some in their late seventies and eighties, many with no family nearby, even those who move out from the east . . . they like the valley, a high percentage get involved in the community, most are successful, well-educated . . . they seem to have a special interest in life."

Fires are uncommon in Rossmoor though they have occurred. The Fire Protection District responds most frequently to calls to resuscitate heart arrest victims.

Four units did burn in 1965. The fire badly damaged one-half of an eight-manor building. In 1974 fire took two lives at the same time, destroying all eight manors in one building. When a television set blew up in a manor on Rossmoor Parkway in 1978, three units burned completely and a fourth suffered major damage.

Residents have pride in the performance of their security force. The organization consists of a chief, three captains, fifteen uniformed officers, a clerk and a dispatcher. Their primary function is to admit only authorized persons to Rossmoor, but they do respond quickly to varying kinds of emergency calls. They are the first to arrive at the scene of an alert or a medial problem. They activate buttons at their guard house which call out a clinic nurse or a fire department crew. The staff also responds to request less urgent. They open doors for those who have locked themselves out, they activate breaker-switches when an occupant can't do it, and shut off smoke detectors when an owner isn't able. They serve manor owners in routine, functional ways when no other assistance is available.

Mrs. Mignola likes to remember the elderly widow and widower who met at Rossmoor. "Actually, when they were going to college they became engaged but didn't marry. They went separate ways, married and raised families. Only after a lifetime, when they each lost a mate, did they meet again, here. There was a happy ending, of course. Sweethearts once more, they married here."

Prior to the oil shortage of 1973-74, residents in Rossmoor decorated their homes at Christmas more profusely than ever seen before in this county. One resident who took the lead, next to the first entry on Tice Creek, was Joe Ghirardelli who, with his neighbors, erected arches of flowers and lights across the entry, from one building to the other.

So many strings of outdoor lights hung from manor after manor that airline pilots deliberately flew over the community, banking their planes so that the beauty below was visible to their passengers.

One notable guest came to speak in the Court of Flags and his visit is marked by a brass plaque on the ladies' room door in the Golden Rain Foundation offices. The brass plate reads:

President Gerald Ford
sat here
May 25, 1976

The visit took place when the president came here to speak in favor of Governor Reagan's candidacy. For two weeks in advance, for security reasons, secret service agents stayed in the administration office, and one hour before the president arrived, cleared the Golden Rain Foundation of its employees, leaving cabinet doors open, lifting cushions from chairs, etc., and reserved the ladies' room in case the chief executive needed it.

The visible Rossmoor is so pleasing, so secure, and so active that little thought is given to how many persons make it function so well. The Golden Rain Foundation employs 387 persons on a permanent basis in 1983 and hires sixty-eight seasonal workers, mostly gardeners, when needed.

Generally, a satisfaction with life permeates Rossmoor gatherings. There are those who busy themselves with one activity or another and others who wish to remain aloof from all group functions. Both succeed. For the more active, rooms are set aside for such hobbies as sewing, ceramics, art, photography, wood-working, working with semi-precious stones or making jewelry, dancing, exercising, playing billiards or ping pong, or attending the several different classes which are scheduled by the Community Relations Department.

Weekly luncheons are held by the Rotary, Lions, Kiwanis and Sirs clubs. Lawn bowlers have two courts for their competitions. Six tennis courts are used by the net enthusiasts. Recreational vehicle owners have two paved lots for vehicle storage, with water and electric hook-ups. Horse owners have an excellent roomy barn for their animals. Clubhouses are available when members wish larger accommodations for a private party. Two swimming pools, one heated, allow for year-round swimming. Even picnic grounds may be reserved. Golfers may use either a nine- or eighteen-hole golf course.

Life at Rossmoor means different things for different people, but just about everyone has something to increase life's pleasures.

THE WALNUT CREEK
HISTORICAL SOCIETY

To say the Walnut Creek Historical Society came into being because of the enthusiasm of one woman is correct, but it is only half the story. The other half is the record of the lady herself.

As a youngster, Isabelle Schuler was unable to walk. However, her father determined that his daughter would one day have a normal life. He coaxed, threatened, and increased her confidence so that in 1902, at age nine, she rose from her wheelchair and, with the aid of braces, learned how to walk.

The young lady never did go to public school but studied at home with tutors. She passed the entrance examination of the University of Nevada and three years later graduated with a degree in chemistry. She went on to Columbia University in New York, where she earned her master's degree in the same subject.

At age twenty, four feet eleven inches tall, and weighing only eighty-five pounds, Isabelle was recruited to manage the Ritter Hagermann Research Laboratory at East River and East Fourteenth Street in New York City. There the young lady directed the activities of 100 male chemists, all older than she.

Meantime, Isabelle Schuler had met a Californian at the University of Nevada, who also entered Columbia in the same class. He was Raymond Spencer, an Oakland native, who was after his master's degree *and* Isabelle Schuler.

After three years (1911-1913) of running the laboratory, which was investigating the various qualities of synthetic drugs versus natural substances, Isabelle gave in and accepted Raymond's marriage proposal. She agreed to give up her job and move west with him.

251

They went to Santa Barbara and were married there in 1914. They came to Walnut Creek in 1915 and bought the local lumber yard. Raymond was ill much of the time that they lived in Walnut Creek and turned over the day-to-day running of the business to his young wife. He died in 1935, and Isabelle continued to run the business until 1945.

In 1940 Isabelle Spencer married John Henry (Jack) Brubaker, local garage owner and Oldsmobile dealer. He was an excellent salesman, and his new wife, after she sold the lumber yard, became his office manager.

Always active in Walnut Creek's Women's Club, she became intrigued with the stories of local history she heard at club meetings. Finally, in the mid-1960s, Isabelle suggested that her fellow members take the lead in sponsoring a local historical society. The idea was solely hers and was only slowly accepted. At one meeting of the Walnut Creek Women's Club, with about fifty members present, she proposed an organizational forum for those interested in local history. In November 1967, with Mrs. Helen Jory president, they called a meeting for members and non-members interested in organizing the Walnut Creek Historical Society. Thirty-seven persons attended.

At that first meeting, on November 6, 1967, Adrian Mendes was chosen president; Russell Wiley, vice-president; Mrs. Ray L. Rosel, secretary-treasurer. Isabelle Brubaker was honored by being elected president emeritus. A total of 115 members attended a Charter Night banquet on February 14, 1968.

At an early society meeting that year, when someone asked, "What happened to the old school bell when they tore down the grammar school?" no one could answer. As a consequence, President Mendes made the society's first project one of finding the bell that he and his contemporaries heard ring all through their grammar school days.

The search began. Many weeks later the brass bell clanged as searchers carried it down from the attic of the Walnut Creek Elementary School District warehouse.

The Women's Club gave the fledgling society funds for a brass plaque and material for a concrete monument. Simon Hardware gave permission to erect a five-foot concrete base adjacent to its store, the former school site.

Architect Floyd Comstock gave the design and the general building contractor, Kirkham, Chaon and Kirkham, Inc. contributed the necessary labor. As a result, the bell and plaque remain on view as a reminder of Walnut Creek's only source of education for half a century.

In November 1970, the Gospel Foundation of California gave the City of Walnut Creek one and a half acres of land and the old home on it. The home was the headquarters of the Hiram Penniman farm on Ygnacio Valley Road in that valley. It had been built in 1904 and not lived in since 1950.

The director of the Gospel Foundation, Miss Mary Liddecoat, had expressed a desire that the home be used as a historical museum, and when the Walnut Creek Historical Society asked for permission to use it for that purpose, the city officials agreed. The society still operates the museum on land owned by the city.

Girl Scouts of Walnut Creek cleaned the house, decorated the interior with blooms, installed a few pieces of furniture, and assisted holding an open house in April 1972. This event triggered the opening of the museum by the historical society later in the year.

Meanwhile Miss Liddicoat gave the society boxes, crates, and trunks full of furniture and household goods which had been some of the house's original furnishings. Beds, bedding, and even several Persian rugs came to the museum-to-be.

Volunteers worked hard and long to prepare for the opening. Buzzie Palmer served as hostess chairman; Adele Laine, Kay Moran, and Bev Clemson were a steering committee. Pharmacist Marshall Maguire took care of the carpentry, hardware and security needs, with Steve Nybank assisting him.

On November 18 and 19, 1972 the museum opened with two receptions. Mayor John Clemson and Mrs. Isabelle Brubaker each gave short speeches commemorating the event, the opening of Shadelands Ranch Historical Museum.

An auxiliary of volunteers came together in May 1973. They named themselves Shady Ladies. They meet now, as they have for ten years, once a month, to maintain the home, keeping it clean and freshly decorated.

Funds to operate the museum come to the historical society in two ways. One is the membership dues from approximately 375 family memberships. The other is the income from a series of plays labeled Shadeland's Follies, which are given annually at the Civic Arts Theater in Walnut Creek. Beginning in 1971 a group of interested people, with Frances Schroder as chief coordinator, have earned money to help finance the operation.

In February 1973 Beverly Clemson accepted the appointment of museum director, and for eleven years has solicited artifacts and documents for the museum. She has identified, labeled and card-indexed them all. She directs volunteer activities, organizes docent training sessions, and answers mail inquiries from other museums and the public. Beverly Clemson is a volunteer who gives many hours a week to the historical society.

The museum is open to the public on Sunday and Wednesday afternoons and to groups any time by appointment.

Girl Scouts and Boy Scouts earn credits toward their scouting achievement awards by working at the museum.

A history room has been established on the second floor of the house where abundant source material has been organized for use by serious students of Walnut Creek history. A file of old photographs and negatives is kept in meticulous order by the director. Old maps and copies of 100-year-old newspapers may be seen upon request. Exhibit rooms, both upstairs and down, are filled with artifacts in common use a century ago.

It is the hope of the history society directors to develop the garden area around the old Penniman home into an attractive setting for lawn parties, ceremonies, and receptions.

In 1975, as enthusiastic about local history as ever, Isabelle Brubaker published a Walnut Creek history: *1850-1950: 150 Years of Growth*. This 1,000-copy edition sold out, in part due to the unique find of glass-plate negatives she made some years earlier. When an ancient barn was scheduled for demolition to make way for construction of the Firestone Store at Mt. Diablo Boulevard and Locust Street, the author rummaged through accumulated debris searching for anything resembling an antique. She found a treasure chest. In an old open box, hidden under clutter, she found glass-plate negatives, some a century old, all broken. Pictured were scenes dating back to 1871. Isabelle Brubaker searched for someone who could put them back together and finally found such a person in Crescent City, California. She paid several thousand dollars for their repair and used them in the history of Walnut Creek she published at age eighty-five. Nine years later she is as vitally interested in preserving Walnut Creek history as she was when promoting her idea of a Walnut Creek Historical Society.

EPILOGUE

No matter on what continent people have lived, or in which century, B.C. or A.D., stories abound about their search for a better land in which to settle and make a new home for themselves.

The accounts of those who came to California before the gold discovery show that same yearning. No matter the dangers; regardless of the physical hardships; they endured the scorching heat and the freezing cold, so they might start life in a different place, one where their hopes and dreams could come true.

Once here, in Contra Costa County, within a short walk of Arroyo de las Nueces, they faced work. They labored to build a shelter, a cabin, dig a well, and plant a crop.

A few who arrived at The Corners were tradesmen, some mechanics, and a smaller number merchants. A few of the latter came with money enough to set themselves up, in a small way, in their former trade.

By and large most of the men who stopped near The Corners had lived on farms. A few had sold out what they had back east and reached Walnut Creek with enough money to buy some acreage from a Mexican family for the going price of five to ten dollars an acre.

Most new arrivals had worked on a farm, a father's or older brother's, and came with little more knowledge than that experience. It was these arrivals who expected to work hard, to be deprived of some of their usual comforts, who hoped luck would come their way. And it did for many. Certainly those who worked the hardest had the most luck.

Within a three- to four-mile radius of Walnut Creek men broke virgin soil. In spring they were up with the sun milking a cow or two, and feeding a horse, pig or sheep. How did they get the animals if they arrived here with little more than hope? Often they worked for someone else during the plowing, sowing or harvest season, and received animals, seed or loan of implements for their labors. Hard money was scarce. Labor, as a medium of exchange, was not.

If the farmer had a son or two, ten years old or older, he hired them out too, no matter what time of year. Schools didn't "take up" during plowing, sowing and harvest months. Time was too precious. A crop was necessary for survival—a part time grade school education not that vital for a farmer.

Walnut Creek grew very slowly in population. But willing hands filled the farm lands around it very soon after statehood. And those hands, to repeat, whether young and inexperienced or mature and accustomed to callouses, worked early and late, and were satisfied so long as their efforts made a satisfactory crop.

Twenty years after the first settler came, in 1870, lots on Main Street, in the very center of what became the business district, sold for as little as thirty-five dollars. Even at that price, so small was the demand, it took ten years to complete the sale of all the lots between Mt. Diablo Boulevard and Cypress Street.

So much for the farmers and the few merchants on Main Street. What about their wives they brought with them? Some, newly married, would be teen-age, yet with children. What was their day-to-day life like?

Her husband would have lit the wood fire in their kitchen range before he went out to feed the animals. After the housewife dressed her youngsters, she cooked breakfast for her family and the hired man, if they had one.

When her husband carried in the pails of warm, fresh milk, she poured it into shallow pans to cool. Later she would skim off the cream, pour it into a churner, and then turn the handle until the butter stiffened.

She baked bread in winter and summer, usually twice a week. She

258

would first feed the stove with wood to heat the oven while she mixed the flour and yeast. Then after kneading the dough and filling her pans with it, she waited for the loaves to rise before she put them in the oven.

Once a week she heated water on the stove in her wash tub. When it steamed, she dumped in the dirty clothes and stirred them until the water darkened. When they were cool enough to handle, she ran the clothes up and down the corrugated washboard, occasionally rubbing skin from her knuckles. Finally, after rinsing in several pails of water and wringing each piece by hand, she hung the clothes out to dry in the sun.

When nature called all the family used the outdoor toilet. At night they sat on the chamber pot, keeping one under each bed. In the morning the pots would be emptied in the outhouse and rinsed out before going back to their places.

The housewife heated kettles and pans full of water for the once-a-week bath night. Her youngsters sat in the oblong tin tub while she bathed one after the other in the same water. Privacy for herself? For her husband? For adult children? They bathed in the kitchen where a door could shut them off from the rest of the family.

She cut the cloth and sewed clothes for herself and her daughters, and patched her sons' and husband's everyday working clothes.

In season, the housewife cooked berries and fruit, making jams and preserves.

Hopefully someone else would fill the coal oil lamps and trim their wicks, but if not, she did that too.

When did she sit down for a leisurely chat with a neighbor? Not often. She might visit on an occasional Sunday afternoon, but before the telephone appeared those opportunities were scarce.

Men, women and children labored at a wider range of tasks than outlined above. They expected to. Their lives were no harder, no more demanding, than those of their parents. The area around The Corners was safer than the frontier where many of them came from. During the last decade of the previous century, life in Walnut Creek started to change.

Lines of communication became available to every farmer at a mininum of cost. Weekly newspapers appeared. The twice-weekly paper printed at the county seat could be bought when the farmer visited the town. Rural Free Delivery (RFD) of mail and newspapers came after 1900. *Harper's* and *Century* magazines, and others, supplied news of the world.

Yet only one telephone existed in Walnut Creek from 1882 to 1894. Ten years later there were only six. At the turn of the century the telephone was unimportant to the average person around Walnut Creek.

Beginning in 1891 trains took passengers to and from San Francisco in a single day, although stage coaches still served sections of the county. Electric lights could be seen in the cities, and someday, ten or twenty years hence, maybe even Walnut Creek and the farms around might have them too.

Motor cars? One of the magazines, *Ballou's* or *Leslie's*, carried a piece about such a contraption, but no one in Walnut Creek or California for that matter had ever seen one.

Chances for more education were improving. Even the one-room school houses stayed open during the busy farm seasons. In the cities around San Francisco Bay, Berkeley, Oakland and Alameda, children were able to go to high schools. Maybe after 1900 the boys and girls of rural Contra Costa might have the same opportunity.

Yes, during the span of years from 1891 to 1911, life in our area changed, but only slightly. The number of people didn't increase at all.

Even the coming of the electric train in 1911 didn't have any immediate effect on the growth of the town. However, during the first few years after the train started running to Oakland and San Francisco, a few families did move to the country. The 1908 population was 400 persons and in 1920 Walnut Creek boasted 538.

Only after the end of the first World War in 1919 did the general public start buying automobiles. Service stations didn't exist until the early 1920s, and the growth of Walnut Creek between 1920 and 1940 is definitely traceable to the increased public ownership of automobiles. By 1930 the town claimed 1,014 people lived here.

Then, six years later, the Caldecott Tunnel brought two lanes of traffic, for the first time in each direction, between Alameda and Contra Costa County. Farmers and orchardists, slow to recover from the Great Depression, rid themselves of debt by selling off acreage to the motorists who now found themselves an easy drive from their work. The new tunnel unleashed a demand that had been held in check by the narrow, steep Fish Ranch Road. Walnut Creek's 1940 census showed 1,587 people lived in the town. Entrepreneurs followed, building stores and service shops along Main Street and even several along previously residential Locust Street.

The changes wrought during the late 1930s, as abrupt as they were, gave no clue to what was to happen ten years later. All growth stopped during World War II. Yet during the war years, 1942-1946, hundreds of thousands of military men and women rode through Walnut Creek on their way from Pittsburg's Camp Stoneman to Oakland and San Francisco. The comparison of life in Contra Costa County with life as they knew it so favored living here that, after the end of hostilities in the Pacific, thousands came back to make their homes here. Ever since, for almost forty years now, as fast as builders have been able to build homes and apartments, people have come to occupy them.

What disappeared while the growth accelerated? Farms and small acreage have vanished. At one time, until about 1970, a person could buy a two- or three-acre parcel, divide it into four lots, sell three of them, and retain a building site for himself which cost him nothing. That opportunity is gone. Until about 1970 it was practical for a handy, knowledgeable individual to buy a lot and build his own home, or at least contract for its construction himself. That opportunity is also gone.

The once common windmill and tankhouse are gone. Outhouses, walnut orchards and chicken houses are but memories of those fortunate enough to have once lived in that era. While it is important to remember the past, we must look ahead. When we do, we see another generation, who, some twenty years from now, are sure to ask the question, "How did my parents ever get by, living the way they did back in 1985?"

So it has gone for centuries, and will go on and . . .

261

If you have read this far, you are aware of how different our daily lives are from those of our grandparents, or their parents. And even in recent years we recognize the influences which are still changing our lives and those of our children: television and computers, rock music, and an auto for nearly every high school student. So much for today.

What will be the influences exerted on our families ten and twenty years from now? Do you have the urge to close your mind to the answer?

Let us appreciate the good and the enjoyable that has filtered down to us from those you have just read about. If we take a moment to say a quiet "thank you" to those who prepared so admirable a place to live as did the pioneers who lived in and around Walnut Creek, it will be almost enough. To fulfill any obligation to them, if you feel you have one, let us say to ourselves, "If I do my part as well as you did yours, Walnut Creek will remain as fine a place to live as any I can wish for."

Contra Costa County Historical Society

Looking east on Civic Drive from California Drive, ca. 1950. Today the Regional Center is on the property to the right. The Growers Square complex has replaced the building on the left.

1985–1991

$\mathcal{F}$rom the redwood forests of Del Norte County to the deserts of Southern California, nature's gifts are being torn down or paved over. The same is true in Contra Costa, from Martinez to San Ramon.

But here in Walnut Creek, while as many as 71,000 automobiles a day travel Ygnacio Valley Road, citizen's groups, the City Council, and the family of city employees are protecting and enhancing our natural setting, where 60,569 residents make their homes.

Walnut Creek's 2,835 acres of Open Space, laced with hiking trails, bring signs of the changing seasons to many neighborhoods.

The 6½ million square feet of retail and commercial space built between 1975 and 1985 initiated the formation of a grass roots organization calling itself "Citizens for a Better Walnut Creek". It prompted a height limitation initiative in March 1985. Measure A, which the voters approved, limited building heights to six stories all over Walnut Creek.

Eight months later, the same group sponsored another measure, one which would prevent all major commercial development. This, Measure H, the voters narrowly approved. It was challenged in court immediately and while it was overturned by the State Supreme Court in 1990, it did prevent additional commercial construction for five years.

Hundreds of volunteers staff the city's Recreation, Youth, Athletic, Seniors, Drug Abuse Resistance Education Program, as well as in operation of the City's thirteen landscaped parks, among them the 100 acre Heather Farm and the 14 acre Larkey Park with its Lindsay Museum. Eighty-one of the volunteers regularly assist the Police Department with clerical and record keeping duties.

In 1980 a group of dedicated citizens formed an organization called Regional Center for the Arts, Inc, committed to planning and raising

263

funds for a major arts complex for Contra Costa County. It raised $8 million from 2,500 contributors. The balance of the $20 million cost came from Walnut Creek citizens through their City government.

Walnut Creek's long commitment to the arts and the public-private partnership to build the Regional Center for the Arts, earned the City the 1989 *Most Livable City* award from the U. S. Conference of Mayors.

The Regional Center houses the 800-seat Hofmann and the 300-seat Dean Lesher theaters and the Bedford Gallery.

On October 4, 1990 Bob Hope, Vic Damone, Diahann Carroll, and Joel Grey headlined the gala opening night program.

In the Center's first six months of operation, 135,000 persons attended 150 programs.

The City Council does its best to accommodate its citizens' requests. Often, though, these are for neighborhood projects which benefit only a few households. But the Council must allocate funds where they will benefit most of their constituency. Through it all Walnut Creek has retired the last of its bonded indebtedness. At a time when the federal and state governments, counties and many cities are unable to find funds for basic services, Walnut Creek is free of debt.

In 1988, Donald A. Blubaugh succeeded City Manager Thomas G. Dunne, who retired in 1987. Blubaugh the former city manager of Hayward, California, directs the operations of 343 employees, who help make Walnut Creek a City with so distinctive a quality of life that it has been named, *The Most Livable City.*

The Regional Center for the Arts   City of Walnut Creek

264

APPENDIX

Homer S. Shuey sold lots in Walnut Creek's first subdivision to these buyers.

Grubelstein, Elizabeth	2-2-1871	Ah Lo	9-6-1877
do	8-11-1871	Jones, Jennie V.	9-15-1877
Hoag, William	do	Burpee, Winifred S.	9-24-1877
Stone, Delia	do	Williams, Arthur	10-30-1877
Huntington, Isaiah	do	Turner, Milo	1-8-1878
Howard, Susan	8-14-1871	Brutenbach, August	3-4-1878
Steele, Hewett	10-16-1871	Moreno, F. E.	6-1-1878
Kirsch, Michael	3-4-1872	Putnam, George A.	7-20-1878
Fales, Orris	9-18-1872	Dole, Eldridge	12-23-1878
do	3-15-1873	Fisher, P. E.	3-3-1878
Brutenbach, August	7-30-1873	Stone, Adelia	7-8-1879
Grubelstein, Elizabeth	7-13-1874	Dole, Eldridge	9-8-1879
Huston, Julia	1-21-1876	Foster, James	5-21-1881
M. E. Church	3-13-1876	Young, T. J.	7-22-1881
Shumway, Edward	4-26-1876	Presbyterian Church	1-9-1882
Brutenbach, August	5-19-1876	Seaman, E. A.	5-13-1882
Williams, Charlotte	6-7-1876	Sharp, Corodon	1-27-1883
Putnam, J. H.	7-12-1876	McCullough, J. M.	10-31-1883
Huston, Julia	11-13-1876	Ayres, Edward	11-7-1883

Mayors of the City of Walnut Creek

1914 to 1/7/1920	H. F. Spencer (Pres. Board of Trustees)
1/7/1920 to 3/3/1920	J. E. Lawrence (Pres. Board of Trustees)
3/3/1920 to 4/21/1922	H. F. Spencer (Pres. Board of Trustees)
4/21/1922 to 7/7/1926	J. E. Lawrence (Pres. Board of Trustees)
7/7/1926 to 5/2/1928	James F. Mauzy (assumed title of mayor in 1927)

5/2/1928	to	4/21/1930	E. B. Anderson	4/19/1971	to	4/18/1972	Newell B. Case
4/21/1930	to	4/16/1934	Norman F. Wilson	4/18/1972	to	4/16/1973	John W. Clemson
4/16/1934	to	4/18/1944	E. B. Bradley	4/16/1973	to	3/12/1974	James D. Hill
4/18/1944	to	4/20/1948	Lawson H. Weill	3/12/1974	to	3/17/1975	Sanford M. Skaggs
4/20/1948	to	8/13/1951	H. C. Cherrington	3/17/1975	to	3/15/1976	Margaret W. Kovar
8/13/1951	to	4/20/1954	Joseph Bell	3/15/1976	to	12/16/1976	Robert I. Schroder
4/20/1954	to	7/31/1954	Elmer Hansen	12/16/1976	to	3/15/1977	Sanford M. Skaggs
7/31/1954	to	4/10/1957	Edward P. Counter	3/15/1977	to	3/15/1978	James L. Hazard
4/10/1957	to	4/15/1958	John Connolly	3/15/1978	to	3/27/1979	Margaret W. Kovar
4/15/1958	to	4/8/1959	William E. Von Tagen	3/27/1979	to	4/15/1980	Richard D. Hildebrand
4/8/1959	to	4/19/1960	Farry Granzotto	4/15/1980	to	4/14/1981	William H. Armstrong
4/19/1960	to	4/5/1961	Frank A. Marshall	4/14/1981	to	4/20/1982	James L. Hazard
4/5/1961	to	4/17/1962	Fred A. Sanders	4/20/1982	to	4/12/1983	Margaret W. Kovar
4/17/1962	to	4/17/1963	Robert A. Nelson	4/12/1983	to	4/9/1984	Richard D. Hildebrand
4/17/1963	to	4/21/1964	Newell B. Case	4/9/1984	to	11/19/1985	Gail Murray
4/21/1964	to	4/21/1965	Fred A. Sanders	11/19/1985	to	11/10/1986	Mary Lou Lucas
4/21/1965	to	4/19/1966	Robert I. Schroder	11/10/1986	to	11/17/1987	Merle Hall
4/19/1966	to	1/17/1967	Newell B. Case	11/17/1987	to	11/1/1988	Ed Skoog
4/17/1967	to	4/16/1968	Douglas R. Page	11/1/1988	to	11/21/1989	Evelyn Munn
4/16/1968	to	4/11/1969	Peter Howard	11/21/1989	to	11/21/1990	Gail Murray
4/11/1969	to	4/21/1970	Benjamin H. Clarke	11/21/1990	to		Gwen Regalia
4/21/1970	to	4/19/1971	Robert I. Schroder				

Past Presidents—Walnut Festival

1947	Herb Perry, Jr.	1970	Earl Wightman
1948	Marshall Maguire	1971	Tom Henze
1949	Elmer Hansen	1972	Bennie Martinez
1950	Elmer Hansen	1973	William Francis
1951	R. W. Rinehart and Eldo Ewert	1974	Don Jones
1952	Terence Ring	1975	Kay Wightman
1953	Arch McKinley	1976	Syl Clark
1954	Barney Gilbert	1977	Bob Bailey
1955	John Osmundsen	1978	Joe Maranz
1956	Rowland Barrett	1979	Joe Maranz
1957	Harley King	1980	Jim Hazlett
1958	William R. Martin	1981	Jim Hazlett
1959	John T. Schroder	1982	Paul Freed
1960	Elliott Mauzy	1983	Ken Alexander
1961	Vance Perry	1984	Ken Alexander
1962	Robert Schroder	1985	Alice Applegate
1963	Ted Gurney	1986	Alice Applegate
1964	Jim Ring	1987	Charles Hazarian
1965	Bill Smikahl	1988	Charles Hazarian
1966	Ed Warrener	1989	Alice Hardy
1967	Emmett Hein	1990	Jeff Hazarian
1968	Dick Lieber	1991	Max King
1969	Earl Wightman		

Walnut Creek Postmasters

James R. McDonald	December 1, 1862
Hiram R. Penniman	March 16, 1866
William C. Pratt	November 21, 1867
John Slitz	September 20, 1869
James M. Stow	July 6, 1877
Allie Guyette	April 27, 1886
John C. Sherburne	August 21, 1889
Thomas J. Young	July 8, 1893
William C. Caldwell	July 13, 1896
Ellen Ford	September 6, 1900
Hiram A. Rudd	March 10, 1914
Edward B. Bradley	February 11, 1920
Thomas P. Walker	June 1, 1922
Hazel E. Avise	January 13, 1927
Laurence G. Barnholtz	July 2, 1947
Pierce Powers	February 1979
William O. Toteet	July 1979
York K. Henderson	April 1989

267

BIBLIOGRAPHY

Bartlett, John, *Bartlett's Familiar Quotations*, Little Brown, 1968.
Bird, Cricket, *Contra Costa Times*, Walnut Creek, February 1, 1981.
Blume, Dulcie, *From the Beginning, Rossmoor Walnut Creek*, an unpublished manuscript.
Bohakel, Chas. A., *The Indians of Contra Costa County*, Amarillo, TX., 1977.
Brubaker, Isabel, *1850-1950: 100 Years of Growth*, Walnut Creek, 1975.
Burgess, Robert N., *Memoirs*, Santa Barbara, CA, 1964.
Collier, George C., *Mexican Land Cases in Contra Costa County*, an unpublished manuscript.
Cowan, Robert G., *Ranchos of California*, Academy Library Guild, Fresno, CA, 1956.
Elder, Jeane Noble, *Walnut Creek Learns the Alphabet*, Alamo, CA, 1974.
Hulaniski, Frederick, *History of Contra Costa County*, Berkeley, CA, 1917.
Munro-Fraser, J. P., *History of Contra Costa County*, San Francisco, CA, 1882.
Sorrick, Muir, *History of Orinda*, Orinda, CA, 1970.
Vandor, Paul G., *History of Frenso County*, Los Angeles, CA, 1919.
Women's Club, *1941 Official Cook Book*, Walnut Creek, 1941.

Libraries

Bancroft Library, Berkeley, CA
City of Walnut Creek Archives, City Hall, Walnut Creek
Contra Costa County Library, Pleasant Hill, CA
Manor Records Department, Rossmoor, Walnut Creek
Pacific Telephone and Telegraph Company, San Francisco, CA
St. Mary's College, Moraga, CA
Shadelands Ranch Historical Museum, Walnut Creek

INDEX

269

270

271

272

274

275

Walnut Cree

Hew to the Line, Let

VOL. 1.   WALNUT CREEK, CONTRA COST

WALNUT CREEK INDEPENDENT

PUBLISHED EVERY FRIDAY MORNING

. . BY . . .

G. B. LEAVITT.

SUBSCRIPTION RATES :

One Year...................... ....$3 00

Six Months. 1 50

Three Months 75

ADVERTISING RATES :

One square of twelve lines, or less,
  first insertion $1 50

Each subsequent insertion up to four 1 00

Reading notices eight cents per line.

A liberal reduction made to regular advertisers.

☞ Office Main Street,

Religious Notice.

METHODIST EPISCOPAL CHURCH.—Rev. C. E. Rich, Pastor. Sunday services at 11 A. M. and 7 P. M. Sunday School at 12:30 P. M. Band of Hope at 3.30 P M. Prayer Meeting Thursday at 7 o'clock P. M. ☞ Parsonage rear of church.

LAFAYETTE.

Preaching at 2:30 o'clock Sunday. Sunday School at 1:30. Prayer Meeting Wednesday evening at 7 o'clock.

DOCTOR J. E. PEARSON,

PHYSICIAN and SURGEON.

Office at his Drug Store,

Walnut Creek.

J. S. MOORE,

DENTIST.   -   -   MARTINEZ.

All Work Warranted.

Barber Shop

—o—

MAIN STREET, - - - WALNUT CREEK

MICHAEL KIRSCH,

Blacksmith & Wheelwright

COR. MAIN AND DANVILLE ROAD.

—

Wagons repaired and new ones made to order.

New and second hand wagons always on hand.

Horseshoeing.

—MANUFACTURER OF—

Agricultural Machinery.

....

Farming Implements

BOUGHT, SOLD AND REPAIRED.
1 tf.

Oak Saloon.

COR. MAIN ST. AND OAKLAND ROAD.

C. W. ROGERS, Prop.

None but the finest brands of Wines, Liquors and cigars kept. I have also added a fine Billiard Table. The public will always be treated with the greatest courtesy.

JAMES FOSTER   J. M. STOW.

FOSTER & STOW,

Real Estate Agents,

NOTARIES PUBLIC,

AND CONVEYANCERS

LOANS NEGOTIATED.

P. O. BUILDING,   -   - MAIN STREET.

Walnut Creek,

Mr. Foster hopes to make his knowledge of the location, character, value and titles of property in all parts of the county, acquired by many years service as County Assessor, serviceable to the clients of the

---

Business Direc

CONTRA COSTA COU

Harness

MAIN STREET,

MARTINEZ, - - -

....

J. R. YOU

CARPENTER and BUIL

Walnut Creek, -

—

Contracts taken, also plans fications furnished at short not

POST-OFFIC